Waiting

NUMBER 127
Williams-Ford Texas A&M University
Military History Series

Waiting

One Wife's Year of the Vietnam War

LINDA MOORE-LANNING

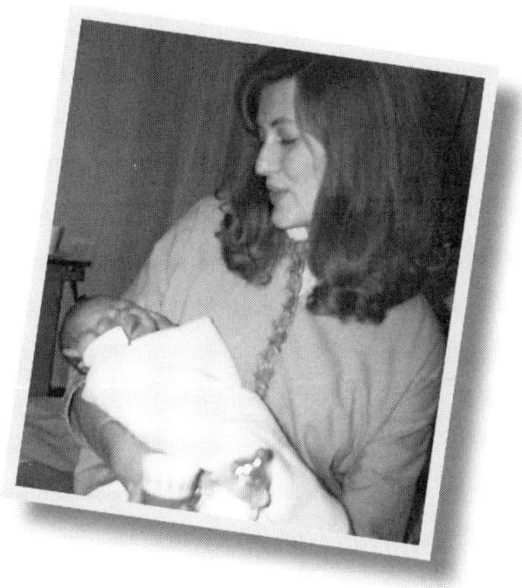

TEXAS A&M UNIVERSITY PRESS   COLLEGE STATION

First edition

This paper meets the requirements
of ANSI/NISO Z39.48-1992
(Permanence of Paper).
Binding materials have been
chosen for durability.

LIBRARY OF CONGRESS CATALOGING-IN-PUBLICATION DATA

Moore-Lanning, Linda, 1945–
Waiting : one wife's year of the Vietnam War / Linda Moore-Lanning. — 1st ed.
p. cm. — (Williams-Ford Texas A&M University military history series ; no. 127)
ISBN-13: 978-1-60344-139-1 (cloth : alk. paper)
ISBN-10: 1-60344-139-5 (cloth : alk. paper)
ISBN-13: 978-1-60344-162-9 (pbk. : alk. paper)
ISBN-10: 1-60344-162-X (pbk. : alk. paper)
1. Moore-Lanning, Linda, 1945– 2. Lanning, Michael Lee. 3. Military spouses—United States—Biography. 4. Vietnam War, 1961–1975—United States—Biography. 5. Vietnam War, 1961–1975—Moral and ethical aspects—United States—Biography. 6. Wives—Effect of husband's employment on—United States. I. Title. II. Series: Williams-Ford Texas A&M University military history series ; no. 127.
E840.8.M667A3 2009
959.704'38—dc22
2009010511

THIS BOOK IS DEDICATED TO

Susan Sheldon Hargrove,

my hero of the Vietnam War.

Table of Contents

PREFACE

I was twenty-three years old when my husband went to Vietnam in 1969. At the time, I considered myself a full-fledged adult who knew what she was doing and where she was going. I was, after all, as old as I had ever been and knew as much as I had ever known. Of course, anyone who has lived past that age knows exactly how much knowledge I had and what it was worth.

Nevertheless, I was undaunted by my own ignorance and inexperience as I threw myself passionately into life. My personality is such that I do almost nothing in half-measures, so it was not surprising that I approached love, marriage, and the role of a waiting wife in the same way.

When Lee was commissioned as a second lieutenant in the U.S. Army in 1968, we had been married five months. I took my vows quite seriously and applied the "whither thou goest" commitment without reservation. While I did not myself join the Army, I did wholeheartedly become part of the military family, totally relinquishing my standing as a civilian. Thus it was as a "family member" that I had my quarrels with the military, just as a member of any family might find faults and flaws within her clan. In other words, I could criticize the military system, but I would tolerate no outsider doing so. I was as fiercely protective of the Army as I was severely critical of it at times. One of those areas of criticism was over Vietnam—not the political aspects but the personal ones that affected me and mine.

Vietnam was a different kind of war from every perspective—from its stumbling undeclared beginning in the early 1960s to its inglorious helicopter rooftop lift-offs ending in the early 1970s. In previous conflicts this country had fought, American men—drafted from across the country—went to war as part of their military units and stayed for the duration. To Vietnam, the men went as individuals to join units once they arrived, and they returned on separate rotation schedules twelve months later. In effect, the war was a revolving door of warriors.

The good news part of that strategy for family members was that the men who remained unharmed had only a one-year tour of duty as opposed to being gone indefinitely. The bad news part was that those who waited did so as individuals without official or community support systems. This latter impact was especially important because, unlike other wars, Vietnam evolved into an extremely unpopular war in which the men who fought it became public villains to be scorned, shunned, and, in a few cases, spat upon. By association, waiting family members often became objects of the same ugly attitude and actions because in this war, unlike the preceding ones, many Americans were never affected or touched by the conflict except to have its news interfere with their evening television shows. America's treatment of its own uniformed service members during this time remains a deep scar upon the soul of the country's history.

Leading the charge and framing opinion against the war, the military, and the whole "Establishment" were groups of mostly male, mostly college-age protestors who themselves did not want to be drafted into the service, especially to serve in a war zone. While the vast majority of protestors participated for the camaraderie and the partying, supporting the organizers only so far as it was convenient to their lifestyles and plans, others made activism a way of life. Without a doubt, these professional protestors did parlay themselves into the limelight and did influence the outcome of the conflict.

Having had many years to contemplate the war, its outcome, and its aftermath, I have concluded that, while U.S. involvement in the war in Southeast Asia was problematic from the start, the reality is that Vietnam was simply the 1960s Gettysburg—a battleground upon which opposing forces fought for the direction of this country. The activists did not focus solely on the actual war but rather on the authorities who ordered it and the officials who executed it. In other words, the war was a flame to which the protestors could feed any and all kindling of complaints to ignite the fires of change. The protestors attacked the very system and fabric of the country as well as war policies—sometimes justified, sometimes not—creating a decade of unrest, questioning, and civil disobedience.

I was one of the many people caught in the middle of the national turmoil but without being consciously political myself. For the most part I was oblivious to being a player, however insignificant, in a larger drama. My interest in the war was strictly personal. My husband was a soldier—a proud soldier—and it never crossed my mind that he would not do his duty. His role was to fight; mine was to wait for him to come home.

Waiting

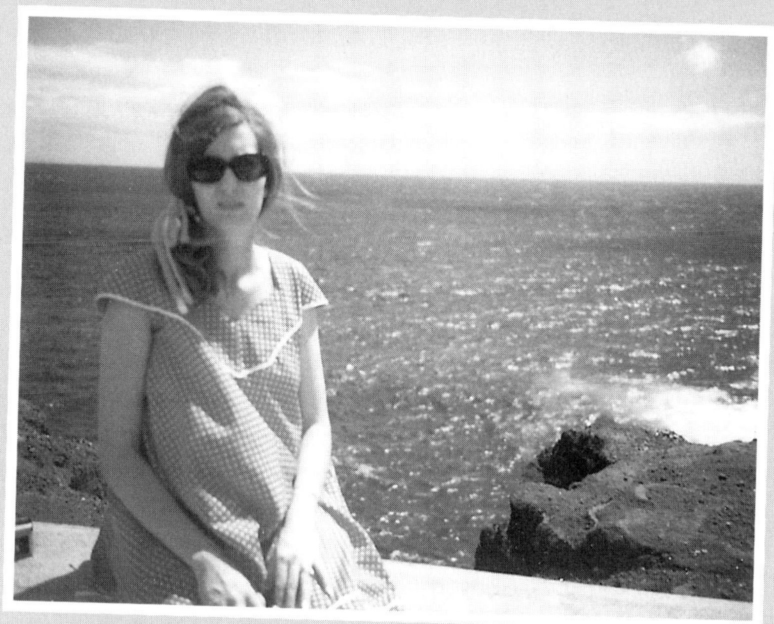

GREY
BUS
ONLY
BUS

SUTPHEN

April 1969

{Chapter 1}

"Nothing's going to happen to me," Lee said with complete military authority. I held tight, wanting desperately to believe him as we stood beside the Greyhound bus, all but deafened by huge planes lifting into the skies behind us at San Francisco International Airport. He then braced me at arm's length and added with a cocky, lopsided grin, "And if it does, I'll be the most surprised one there."

How could I not be madly in love with an idiot who said such things and thought going to war was a great adventure? He believed we were saying goodbye for a year's separation. I *knew* it was forever. He was never coming home. I had only just realized that this morning.

I needed to tell him, to beg him not to get on the bus. I couldn't say the words but neither could I swallow them. A lump of the unspoken lodged in my throat.

The minutes we had left together were ticking by. I wanted to just look at him a bit longer, to memorize every feature of his lean face that I already knew by heart—the ski-jump nose, bushy eyebrows, gray eyes. I wanted to sear every detail into my memory. He was so handsome in his khaki uniform. At six-foot-five inches and a head taller than me, he beamed with excitement. He was grinning; I was dying.

Another minute gone.

I struggled to retain my composure. After all, that's what an army wife does. Be composed. Be strong. Hold down the fort. That was the role.

I did not feel composed. Or strong. And I was in no mood to play a role of any kind. My husband was leaving me to go get himself killed in some jungle halfway around the world. I couldn't breathe.

Lee and I had a history that far exceeded his time in uniform. We weren't just military people, one-dimensional caricatures now so controversial. Lee and I had been in the second grade together in my hometown of Roby, and then we had dated through most of high school and all of college. The army was just our next phase of life—and it wasn't supposed to be our last.

Suddenly Lee pulled me to him, kissed me quickly, and jumped on the bus.

Gone.

Even though he was still in the parking lot, he was already gone.

I stood beside the bus, numbed by the pain. How could I not have known what this would be like? How could I be so surprised by how much it hurt?

• • •

Trudging my way up the incline from where the bus was parked to the terminal, I stifled my sobs and struggled to make sense of our complicated situation. We were at the airport, yes, but Lee was on a bus, not a plane, headed for Vietnam. I was the one who would be flying while Lee was riding the Greyhound to Travis Air Force Base in Vacaville. He would board his plane for Asia about the time I landed in Los Angeles on my way back to Texas. No wonder my head ached.

Inside the glass terminal, I ignored the mass of other travelers as I turned to watch the bus with its belches of black smoke waffling upward. My stomach contorted into yet another knot. *This is it*, I realized, *really it.* A year, I could do. If only I believed it was for only a year. The door to the bus was still open. If only. . . .

I turned frantically toward the crowd. Did these people not see that I was desperate here? Did they not see that I needed someone to stop that bus?

A man in a business suit, jacket flying open as he pulled a blue hanging bag in his wake, strode past me through the door. A hippie with a ponytail in a dark T-shirt shuffled off to my right. A woman with long red hair bent over her two small children. Then came another suit with a head riding above a bib of white. A blur of green and then smears of reds and grays, pink florals bleeding into tie-dye oranges—heads bobbing, circling in every direction. Colors and motions appeared as if on a carousel on fast spin.

I closed my eyes, dizzy from the whirl of weeks, overdosed on tales of knights in olive drab, possessed by a dreadful certainty that I would never see Lee again.

Inhaling deeply, I opened my eyes. All around me were normal people carrying normal luggage in a normal airport, greeting and chatting, waving and smiling. Untouched. Unaffected. Nobody cared that Lee had just gotten on that bus. They all thought it was a normal day, not the end of my world. Bare feet, backpacks. Well, this was San Francisco in 1969, so those, too, were normal.

I turned back to the bus. Relieved that it was still idling there on the asphalt, I felt another stream of tears on my cheeks. I watched a distant khaki figure toss his duffle bag into the luggage compartment of the bus and then peel the green envelope cap from his shaved head as he stepped up through the darkened narrow door.

Oh, God, please don't let this really happen. Never mind that we planned it for so long. We were wrong, so wrong. I wasn't a mature 23-year-old army wife heroically sending her man off to war. I was a frightened child. Lee was not a gallant soldier. He was my husband, the man I wanted to spend the rest of my life with—to have babies with, to grow old with. Fifteen months ago in the Chapel at Texas A&M University, the minister had asked about "for better or worse, in sickness and in health." He hadn't mentioned a pledge to send this man off to war.

Oh, God, we are so young and so stupid. This was not one of those poignant Hollywood movies with the romantic farewell scenes. This was real. There was no baby—now there never would be.

Panic, it's just panic. Somewhere in my head a recording clicked on and I heard Lee's deep voice say with conviction, "Honey, I've had the best training the Army has to offer." Panic took a firmer hold. The party line. He believed. I didn't. I had seen enough in the past year to know that "the best" was a relative term. I had watched his officer training programs get shortened by weeks, seen the rush to mold young lieutenants into passable form so they could be shipped faster and faster to Vietnam. And there was a reason they needed so many replacements so fast.

Training. I remembered how Lee had come home from Airborne School at Fort Benning, Georgia months ago so exhilarated about parachuting out of perfectly good aircraft. In our small brick duplex at Fort Bragg, North Carolina, he had demonstrated the proper jump techniques by shuffling, right foot in front, from the dining room side of the kitchen door jamb into the opening, where he extended his hands across the wooden frame to "stand in the door"—this being the correct approach from the back of the plane to the exit. Then he propelled himself through the doorway and out the "plane" into the narrow kitchen, landing almost at the back door atop the green and white marbled linoleum tiles. While I cooked dinner, he blasted over and over from the dining room into the kitchen, showing me how he checked to see that his chute opened, how he glided down with arms spread on the risers, and how he brought his knees and feet together for landing—all the while providing jet roar and whistling wind sound effects.

Now the Army was sending a man who jumped out of door jambs to fight a war. *Dear God.*

Still, the Army had been preparing him. I, however, had not been so instructed; no one, not even my friends, had told me what it would feel like to say goodbye—really, truly goodbye—to the man I loved. Lee was the first among his peer group to get orders so I hadn't even known anyone standing right where I was who had done this.

I hated self-pity. I squinched my eyes tight and tried to see Lee coming home a year from now. No vision came. I was more terrified than ever. I had known it was coming since the beginning of the year. I had thought I was ready.

• • •

"I'm on orders for Vietnam," Lee had announced triumphantly over the phone from Ranger School in January just four months before. "We finally got what we've been waiting for."

Of course, that was what *he* had been waiting for, what *he* had wanted—he had volunteered to go. In fact, he had been fearful for the past two years that the whole thing would be over before he could get there.

"When?" I asked with dread, feeling like a bad sport for not being happy for Lee, wondering at the same time what kind of wife would be excited about her husband getting himself blown to smithereens.

He couldn't tell me when he would leave; he didn't know himself. All he knew was that his name had appeared in the *Army Times* columns of agate print that published the newest list every week under the heading "Orders—Vietnam." That made it as good as official because that newspaper source was often more reliable than formal channels.

Now we knew for sure *when* in the most certain of terms. He was leaving on April 18, 1969, and he had been gone from me for five minutes according to my watch, even though the bus still sat in the lot.

Knowing that Vietnam would become a reality had made every minute since that January telephone call more precious, more elusive. In fact, the impending departure for Vietnam had created a maniacal intensity in our lives and those of all of our army friends. Second lieutenants came into the Army double-timing between duty stations and schools while we wives packed, unpacked, loaded, and reloaded so that we could go along when we were allowed.

We had come to measure life in sets of weeks and series of shuttle runs between posts. After he graduated from Texas A&M, Lee and I had spent four weeks at Fort Bragg before he left for three weeks of Airborne School at Fort Benning, Georgia. He returned to Bragg for five weeks before we packed the car and moved temporarily to Columbus, the town just outside of Benning, for the six-week Infantry Officer Basic Course. Because he had to wait for a slot in Ranger School, we returned to Bragg for four weeks until he could start the eight-week Ranger training, which included a one-week Christmas break. When his Ranger Tab was secure, we returned to Bragg for eight weeks prior to his four-week leave before heading for Vietnam. It had all been breathtaking and crazy-making.

It was a whirlwind of induction and training that pitted the Army against the wives—and my friends and I used every available strategy to outwit and undercut the military's claim on our husbands. The system begrudgingly tolerated us. In most cases we were *unauthorized*. Had the Army wanted lieutenants to have wives, so the saying went, the Army would have issued them. We represented distractions where the Army wanted concentration; we evoked emotions where the Army demanded cool calculation; we offered tenderness where the Army ordered tough.

The system staunchly protected its new crop of officers, corralling and prodding them like young, pawing bulls. We wives saw them as lambs—cute, adorable, lovable, and, in unguarded moments, as innocents being prepared for slaughter.

Snatching our small victories when we could, we were no match for the military machine. Still, we surrendered not a moment uncontested nor failed to seize any chance for another memory.

I stayed with my parents in West Texas while Lee endured a winter cycle of Ranger School's rigorous physical training at Harmony Church; freezing nights atop mountains in Dahlonega, Georgia; and icy swamp marches in Northern Florida. Two days before he was to graduate, I drove through East Texas and across the South to arrive in Benning before Lee was to return there with his coveted black and gold Ranger Tab.

I went straight to see my friend Cheryl Hightower, whose husband Steve was in Lee's Ranger class. We hugged like long-lost companions since we hadn't seen each other in three months, the Hightowers having remained at Benning the last time we returned to Bragg. I planned to stay with Cheryl until our husbands arrived.

Cheryl and I had a lot in common, not the least of which was that, as slender young women standing five-eleven, we towered together over the other wives and many of their husbands. While I had shoulder-length brown hair and angular features, Cheryl wore her black hair short as a frame around her angelic, always smiling face. We had developed an immediate rapport when we met, for Cheryl had married an Aggie and commuted between quarters at Bragg and an apartment at Benning during the summer and fall of 1968, just as I had.

Before we had even completed our reunion greetings that frosty January evening, Cheryl excitedly told me that six of us wives had been invited to the graduation ceremonies the next day at the Ranger Camp at Eglin Air Force Base in Florida. I couldn't imagine how that was possible until Cheryl explained. One of the wives, a friend of hers, was married to the son of a general who had intervened to get permission for his daughter-in-law to see his son get his tab. The invitation had been extended to include me because I was staying with Cheryl. I was thrilled, as this was definitely one of those otherwise unauthorized times to see our husbands.

Long before sunrise the next morning, Cheryl was shaking me awake. "I've made coffee," she said cheerfully.

I dragged my exhausted body off of the sleeper sofa and into the tiny kitchen of the guesthouse Cheryl and Steve rented behind "the big house," needing the brew to help me open my eyes. Cheryl poured me a cup, and after dousing it with cream and sugar, I sipped it expectantly. *Ugh!* I grimaced at the soured, bitter taste before I could stop myself. Cheryl saw my face and sighed with disappointment, "You don't like it either."

"What is it?"

"Oh, it's coffee," she said, reaching into the cabinet for a jar of instant. "I just re-use the grounds. Steve hates it, too."

I had never thought of recycling coffee grounds, and my surprise must have been obvious because Cheryl said with a shrug, "Coffee's expensive and I just can't see throwing out all those grounds after only one time. Besides, we can't afford new grounds every day."

I understood. Another commonality we shared, along with everyone else we knew, was very little money. But that did not dampen our spirits.

In fact, collectively the six of us who piled into my Oldsmobile Cutlass that morning had less than $50 among us. But south to the Panhandle of Florida we raced to see our husbands get Ranger Tabs pinned on their left shoulders. With Vietnam looming before us, money—and the lack of it—was not important. Extra stolen moments with our husbands were.

As we made the round trip to Florida, the six of us matched experiences and traded impressions about who had been where during which set of weeks. Sometimes the dates and names differed, but the stories were the same. It was fun to compare tales and to laugh about our oh-so-similar recent pasts. We just didn't mention the future because we all had husbands in the pipeline for Vietnam. We drove eight hours to spend less than thirty minutes with them that day of Ranger School graduation.

Now all those weeks of flurry had brought us to this day in San Francisco. I had come as far west with Lee as I could. Beyond the Golden Gate loomed Vietnam and a world I could not enter, the terrifying black hole into which Lee was about to disappear forever.

On our way to California, we stopped in El Paso to see Lee's brother Jim and Jim's wife Judy where they were stationed at Fort Bliss. The visit had been filled with artificial cheerfulness and constant activity. We went to the dog races in Juarez and the horse races at Sunland Park. We celebrated the recent announcement that Judy was pregnant with their first baby, due in September. The infantry brothers swapped stories about the Army.

But the time had also been riddled with awkward pauses when Jim, who had spent eighteen months in Vietnam as a rifle platoon leader and company commander, had things he wanted his little brother to know, saying "Well, I'll tell you, Lee. . . ." But he never told him. He only managed to say repeatedly, "You've got to be careful over there."

Then Jim wanted Lee to see a firepower demonstration. Judy suggested that we not go, but I was unwilling to miss any time I had left with Lee. That afternoon at MacGregor Firing Range, as we sat in the bleachers with the mixed military and civilian crowd waiting for the show to begin, Lee held my hand, an unusual public display of affection for him. I was all set to enjoy the beautiful desert scenery while the Army demonstrated its latest lethal gadgets on the range in front of us.

A senior officer read a scripted monotone introduction, and then suddenly explosions blasted through the air, ripping fire from the ground where the whistling projectiles landed down range. Faster and faster they came, rocking the stands with their violence, throwing geysers of dirt into the air. The deafening noises jolted me to the sound of war. Next week these sounds would be trying to kill Lee. I closed my eyes and covered my ears, hoping to escape the images flashing in my mind. Terrified, I looked over at Lee, only to see that he was watching with cool military detachment, leaning over occasionally to shout something in Jim's ear.

I rushed blindly from the stands. Judy understood and followed me to the car. We sat, imitating a normal conversation, while I pretended not to cringe at every boom and she pretended not to notice that my tears that kept brimming over. Judy was empathetic with my situation, having married Jim when he was home on leave after his first year in Vietnam. She endured his voluntary extension for another six months from her home in Coleman where she was working. She had only just "joined the Army" herself since his return home. She had been where I was, yet she hadn't. Her way of helping me was to distract me from the topic as much as possible.

{Chapter 2}

I found myself sitting in a chair near a boarding gate with an opened paperback in my hands, though I had no idea how I had gotten there or what the blurred pages said. As I looked up, a man's face appeared in my green-tinged line of sight. I jumped.

"I didn't mean to startle you," he said, stepping back. "But are you all right?"

I opened my mouth but no words came. I simply nodded.

"You look upset," the man continued with concern.

I shook my head, grateful that I still had on my sunglasses. He turned away and then back, saying, "Look, I don't want to bother you, but I can see that you're crying. Is there anything I can do to help?"

Only then did I realize my shades were not the disguise I had believed them to be.

"It can't be all that bad," the man said, seating himself one chair away.

I looked at him sharply to see why he was so interested, but all I found was a middle-aged, balding man in a sports jacket looking truly sympathetic. I didn't want to talk, yet being rude seemed wrong. I tried out the words for me as much as for him when I hoarsely said, "My husband just left for Vietnam."

"Oh, I see," he said softly.

More tears I could not stop.

"Here," he said quickly, reaching into his back pocket, "use this."

I shook out the white cloth and wiped each eye underneath my glasses. I blew my nose and then in despair realized that I had no way to return his handkerchief clean. More tears flowed.

Growing distressed himself, the man said, "Don't cry. He'll be home before you know it. A year's not so long." *If it were only a year and not forever.*

He kept gently extolling well-meaning platitudes while I choked and struggled to breathe. The harder he tried, the tighter my chest constricted.

"Oh, I know," he said suddenly, reaching into his other back pocket and pulling out his billfold. "See, I do understand how hard this is. See? I'm in the Reserves." He handed me his military identification card, different from Lee's only in color.

I looked at the small laminated ID, wondering how the hell it was supposed to make me feel better while mentally begging, *Please don't be nice to me. Don't take away my last defenses. Ignore me. Bombard me with anti-war slogans, but please don't be nice because I will fall apart.* Nodding my head was the best I could do.

"They've called my flight," he announced as he stood and replaced his card in his wallet. I looked at the wadded handkerchief and then up at him. "Keep it," he said smiling, "and remember, your husband will be back." He waved over his shoulder as he fled. We were both relieved at his departure.

I spoke to no one else until I landed in Los Angeles, communicating with the flight attendants with nods and shakes. I closed my eyes and wondered if I could sleep for twelve months. But after take-off, my eyes popped open and I was facing a gorgeous blue sky and a few puffy white clouds.

I instantly found the idea of being up in the sky, up in the heavens, calming. I felt physically closer to God, and I realized that while I had no control over what happened to Lee, He did. In His infinite wisdom, He would watch over Lee.

I prayed. *Please, dear God, please take care of Lee and bring him back to me.* It was a prayer I had been repeating frequently, asked of the God I'd worshipped all my life. *Amen.* Immediately a heavy burden lifted from my chest. I breathed deeply, knowing I would offer my prayer hundreds of time during the coming year.

I checked my watch. Where would Lee be now? Surely at Travis. Maybe already airborne.

Without warning, the adage leaped to mind: *God works in mysterious ways.* Preachers had always emphasized that, and now the saying was reverberating in my head. I remembered the warning that we should always be careful what we prayed for, for God just might deliver.

P.S., God. When I asked you to take care of Lee, what I meant was, please don't let him get hurt or killed and when I said please bring him back to me, I meant alive and not in a silver box. Amen again.

I was feeling better. I would just turn all this over to God. But then from nowhere came the flash, *God takes care of those who take care of themselves.* I went back a third time. *Okay, God, I get it. I just don't know how much soldiers can actually do to take care of themselves so please have some extra mercy and patience with Lee and keep him safe.*

Having covered all my bases, I hoped, I was too tired to concentrate on anything, even Los Angeles, which had seemed like such a good idea a couple of months ago when I planned the visit with my life-long friend Connie. I had known there would be a let-down after Lee left, and with L.A. so close to San Francisco, how could I not take advantage of the proximity as a way to divert my attention from his departure and catch up on Connie's life? What had seemed like a grand plan before today now seemed like a monumental effort. I would drag myself through the motions. I had nothing else to do anyway. But wait.

Wait for a year. I closed my eyes again. I sat bolt upright when I realized that I could no longer see Lee's face in my mind's eye. I could have touched it four hours ago; now I couldn't even remember it clearly.

I looked out the window to find God again. Instead, I saw below the splashes of buildings beginning to thicken along thin blue ribbons and the growing spread of rooftops. We were approaching Los Angeles. Still distressed, I nevertheless felt a twinge of excitement. I would absorb all the details so that I could share them with Lee in my first letter to him.

Had the plane held to the flight path, my impressions of our approach would have provided no more than a sentence or two when I wrote to Lee. Had we touched down on schedule, the landing wouldn't have merited a footnote in my memories. But this day was not yet over. While I had known for a long time that when Lee left for Vietnam my life would change forever, I had naively assumed his departure would be the only cause.

Intent on my observations, I watched Los Angeles expand. The horizon rolled more of the city toward us and soon the floor of the earth was filled with buildings in every direction.

This place is huge. So many people. How many people? How many people, each with their own individual lives, their individual needs, their individual prayers? I focused on a dot of a passing roof. *How many people live in that house? If I multiply that by the number of houses . . . God, how many people can You listen to at once? How many prayers can You answer?* Still the city kept spreading.

"Ladies and gentlemen." I jumped. It was the PA system, not God striking me for my growing doubts. The pilot's voice said there was a delay. We were in a holding pattern.

For the next hour, we circled Los Angeles, stacked up with other planes. Millions of people down there, hundreds up here riding in winged tubes that I could see over us and under us.

I felt a sense of physically shrinking as the enormity of the universe dawned on my distressed mind. I saw irreversibly that God couldn't possibly oversee the whole world with the individual attention I was counting on. No one god or God could handle the demands. This was only one city in one state in one country. Alarms went off in my head. My Old Testament, West Texas God was out of His league here. It had seemed reasonable to me as a child that He could send or withhold the rains on which our farms and lives depended and send the Light to the local sinners who caused gossip in our small towns. As a teenager, I could be persuaded that we needed to heed God's will. In college, I had questioned the professor who espoused that religion changed to meet people's needs but not the Baptist tenets that were literal and unchallengeable. In the last year I had not examined my beliefs even when they differed drastically from others. I'd simply said my prayers and gone to bed.

But now, as I looked down over the magnitude of this one metropolis, I felt my faith giving way, peeling back like layers on a papier-mâché mask. I couldn't stop the disintegration. Each rotation of our circling pattern stripped away more of the façade. I sat helplessly watching what had been, to me, a real and tangible Heavenly Father, like the black smoke from the bus, disappear before my eyes. I knew with certainty that I could never paste the tenets back together again.

I don't remember the touch down, only the lonely realization that I was back on the ground not only without Lee but also without a god.

{Chapter 3}

Connie embraced me briefly when I stepped into the terminal and guided me toward the baggage claim. I concentrated to catch her welcoming chatter, but I couldn't seem to tune into her words. Some autopilot part of me must have been responding because she marched us through the corridors as if nothing were amiss. From another dimension, I looked at Connie beside me: five-foot-six, strangely much shorter than I remembered. Her shiny brown hair with its reddish highlights curled around her face in a neckline frame. Her green eyes darted with energy and impatience toward the luggage chute as she talked. Then, looking up at me with her arms crossed, she said something and threw back her head in laughter.

Connie grabbed my bag as quickly as it bounced into sight and led the way across the parking lot. Within minutes, traffic and acres of suburbs were whizzing past at a nauseating speed. Connie played tour guide from behind the wheel while I acknowledged to myself the mistake I had made in coming here. Her efforts to be especially amusing were wasted, for I could think of nothing except Lee in a plane over the Pacific.

When we walked into Connie's apartment, a greater sense of disorientation hit. It was not the apartment itself with its rented modern Danish furniture that affected me; it was the fact that it was her home, albeit temporary, that brought me to an abrupt realization. All I wanted was to go home, only I no longer had a home. How could I not have thought of that until now? I had no place of my own to go. Mother and Daddy's house was no longer *my* home, and the quarters at Bragg had long since been issued to someone else. I didn't belong anywhere.

Connie ignored my periodic gasps for breath, keeping the one-sided conversation fast-paced and cheerful. Her only direct question about Lee came when she stopped mid-sentence and asked, "Well, did you see him off?" I nodded, and she continued talking.

Part of me was thankful that she kept up the monologue that relieved me of the responsibility of participating. The other part of me wanted to shake her by the shoulders and shout, "Who gives a damn about that? I've just sent my husband off to die and I've lost my faith in God!" But instead I swallowed and nodded at the story about her nephews.

I knew what she was doing, of course. I caught her several times stealing worried looks at me as she spoke and then introduced me to her two roommates as they arrived home from work. When they sat down, Connie announced dinner plans. The thought of food added to my nausea. But she had arranged for her date and Allan Goforth, one of our high school classmates also living in Los Angeles, to take us all out for pizza.

Any other time I would have been delighted to see Allan and would be inquisitive about his job at Lockheed. Shorter even than Connie, Allan had ears scaled for an infinitely larger head than his, much like the *Mad Magazine* role models with which he had entertained us for years. But he belonged in another compartment of my life; seeing him here was as bizarre as watching a Western movie in which a police car pursues a speeding stagecoach.

"Connie, I'm really not hungry," I said, wishing they would all just go away.

"Of course you are," she insisted as she pushed me toward the door. Resisting would have taken more energy than climbing into the car. As the six of us rode down the lighted streets, I wondered if I was the only one who thought it strange that I was on my way to a pizza parlor while Lee was on his way to war.

Fortunately, the sing-song clamor of Shakey's Pizza made conversation difficult. Even between banjo-driven songs, the other five had to shout to hear each other. They spoke English but their words were foreign to me. It wasn't what they said about jobs, bosses, or traffic that sounded alien. It was what they didn't say. No one mentioned temporary duty, DD Form 1049s, field exercises, or booby traps. And certainly no one mentioned Vietnam.

I turned to face the busy dining room. A man yelled for another pitcher of beer, a child shrieked, whole groups roared with laughter, and everybody talked at once. The din of voices drummed against my head. What did I expect? Draped doorways and mourning dirges of a country at war?

I was relieved when the pizzas arrived because everyone focused on dividing the slices. I took a bite of mine, rolling the rubbery cheese back and forth across my tongue, feeling my throat tighten as I debated what to do with this disintegrating gummy glob in my mouth.

". . . Lee in Vietnam." I gulped. Someone had said the "V" word. I saw Allan looking directly at me. "Maybe you can tell me," he said. "Exactly why are we in Vietnam?"

Did he think I had inside information? Did he think that I had special insight into the Domino Theory, the Gulf of Tonkin, and Ho Chi Minh because I was an army wife? I had no view of the forest or the trees of war; I was struggling to comprehend the leaves.

With startling clarity, I saw that the five people around me had no realization of what the war was to the military. For us, it wasn't an abstract struggle over political power or communist aggression. It was individual soldiers trying to stay alive: soldiers who were simply men in uniform, who had sweethearts or wives, children, and parents; men who had dreams and plans and unique personalities just like everyone else; men who liked beer and pizza and who would rather have been sitting here with us than fighting in muddy paddies or tangled jungles.

"The war is about staying alive," I said. Their blank faces told me my simplistic answer was not what they expected. So I added, "War is just very personal."

"You mean Lee went because he personally believes in the war?"

Did I tell them that the military did little to explain to soldiers why they were fighting? Soldiers were trained to perform their jobs and leave the decision-making to the chain of command. The president, as commander-in-chief, said fighting in Vietnam was their job. For soldiers it was no more complicated than that.

"No," I corrected him. "Lee went because he felt an obligation to go. It's his job. And besides, he wanted to."

How could I explain to them that Lee saw war as the greatest adventure of our generation? They wouldn't be able to comprehend it. I barely did, myself.

To forestall useless discussion about philosophies and politics, I said, "For me, this war is all about Lee coming home alive. It doesn't get any more personal than that."

No one spoke. I had just made the war personal for them, too, if only for an instant. They suffered the discomfort of not knowing what to say.

My alienation was complete, for I now realized that I lived in a world apart—apart from them, apart from Lee, apart from Vietnam, apart from everything and every home I'd ever known. The only thing I had to hold onto was my sanity, and my tenuous grasp on it seemed tethered by a thin and fragile thread, indeed.

• • •

I awoke with a jerk. Sunlight streaming into my eyes, I blinked and looked around the strange bedroom. With a devastating crush, I remembered where I was and why.

In the quiet, I lay there remembering the relief of finally being alone last night. How long had I cried? Only exhaustion had finally put me to sleep. I sat up slowly, feeling bruised and sore.

I found Connie on the couch, stretching herself awake. She looked at me and then she leaped up, planting her hands on her hips.

"I don't know what to do with you," she said, "but I'm not letting you sit around here all day and cry. Get dressed."

Like a scolded child, I retreated to the bedroom where I guiltily realized that I, too, was exasperated with myself and my morbid sense of doom. I could not survive a year of yesterday's emotional intensity. I had to get hold of myself.

I sat on the bed and looked at the clock. What time was it in Vietnam? Six, eight hours earlier—tomorrow already? Lee and I no longer lived in the same date zone. Even so, I could calculate that with his having just arrived there, he would not be in any real danger for a couple of days. It was okay for me to enjoy the day.

"We're going to Hollywood," Connie announced as she directed me to the passenger seat while the roommates climbed into the back of the car. I chuckled. The idea that Connie—serious, studious Connie—would spend a day touring Tinsel Town struck me as so absurd that I could not help but be amused.

Away we went to Hollywood and Vine, a trash-ridden intersection that proves that anything can be glamorized. We saw the stars' footprints and the famous landmarks. "Don't expect to see any celebrities," Connie warned. "They will be disguised as regular people." Elvis could have joined us and I wouldn't have noticed.

Next on the itinerary was Universal Studios. Connie herded us aboard the trolley that bounced through the back lots and past dimly familiar street facades. The other three seemed excited to see how the tricks of illusion were created. To me it was déjà vu: I had been behind the movie scenes yesterday. Now I was simply seeing where they filmed those silly romantic farewell farces. My companions saw one-dimensional scenery; I saw the bus leave the terminal in a cloud of smoke.

But Connie kept the distractions coming. After we left the studio, she stopped at a street corner and approached a man waving some kind of paper in his hand.

"What is she doing?" I asked the roommates. They shrugged.

Connie returned to the car and held up her prize: a folded single sheet of paper that posed as a map to the stars' homes. The poorly reproduced black lines wandered over the page with handwritten labels. Periodic boxes framed names along the lines.

"Are you kidding?" I asked as we all peered at the paper.

"No," she said, starting the car. "I just paid five dollars for this map. Where to first? Bob Hope or Tony Curtis?"

We spent the rest of the afternoon driving through Beverly and other Hills, stopping frequently to study the "map." We found ourselves on one-lane paths that wound into the far canyons and at dead ends where we expected major intersections. Everyone had a turn at navigation before we hysterically concluded that the black lines did not even vaguely match the street layouts. Challenged, we bought two more maps and cross-plotted locations.

I was surprised at the seclusion the terrain offered despite the invasive tactics of tourists like us. Besides the ever-present roll of the land and the thick stands of trees, we found dense high-rise hedges blocking our views of what we were sure were famous mansions. In the coming months, I would learn about the other side of the privacy coin—the isolation—but today it was just fun to take turns guessing who lived where.

The frivolity of following bogus maps to movie stars' homes was as perfect an antidote for my depression as Connie could have found. Participating in such an activity at first seemed stupid, then silly and ridiculous, and finally hilarious. It felt so much better to laugh than to cry.

Even so, the irony of spending a day searching for other people's homes when I didn't have one myself did not escape me. I didn't covet their palatial dwellings, only envied that they belonged somewhere. I felt as much an outsider to my own life as I did as a tourist standing behind the hedges that separated us from the stars' property.

I borrowed stationery from Connie that night to write Lee my first letter. So much had happened since yesterday. Was it only yesterday? I stared at the paper. If I made the letter light-hearted by exaggerating the entertaining aspects of the day, would he think his leaving had not affected me? I had made him promise to tell me the truth about what was happening to him so my imagination would not try to read between the lines of his letters. Yet I found I could not do likewise. I couldn't burden him with how devastated his leaving had really left me. I searched for the fine line between upbeat and honest, between love and loneliness. I settled for a factual compromise and tucked the letter in my suitcase to be mailed when I had an address for him.

• • •

I realized that Los Angeles had not been a mistake after all. Connie had helped me through the difficult first day and a half of the next twelve months. She did not understand what was happening to me, but she had not allowed me to go crazy. I would always treasure her efforts then as I would those she would exert in support later in the summer.

Mother and Daddy met me at the Midland-Odessa airport. Daddy had donned his best Stetson for the occasion and stood tall above the others at the gate, his blue eyes smiling, his lean face creased into a grin as he impatiently shifted from foot to foot. At six-foot-four, he was the epitome of the authentic cowboy he had always been—rugged, confident, ready.

Mother, quiet and unassuming, was beside him grinning, too, as she managed a timid wave. Her graying brown hair was teased into a bouffant that suggested she had been to the beauty shop the day before.

My spirits lifted momentarily, but by the time we pulled onto the interstate heading east, I was again fighting waves of grief.

Daddy asked, "Well, did you see him off?"

The trick was not seeing him off but getting him back, I thought. But Daddy's question was not a question; it was a way to open the conversation. I gave them the highlights of the trip, becoming aware that they were being particularly careful with their questions and comments. Daddy had been a soldier in World War II, so he knew a lot about the Army and something about military life. However, he had been chosen to stay stateside in California as a drill sergeant at Camp Roberts when his fellow trainees had been shipped overseas. Mother had been with him there, so while they shared some of my wartime experience, theirs had taken a different path.

We rode past the sand dunes pretending that as long as I was dry-eyed there was nothing to cry about. It wasn't that Mother and Daddy didn't care. Had I openly wept, they would have joined me. But we didn't do things that way in our family. We remained stoic and unemotional. Yet what had seemed normal just a few days ago no longer seemed familiar. With a deepening exhaustion, I felt stranger than ever and dealt with the strain by escaping into sleep.

{Chapter 4}

The next morning, I awoke in my old bedroom groggy and spent. Even with little reason to get up, I crawled out of bed, wishing I had someone to talk to who understood. Lee would have been my first choice, but he was now the perpetrator of my misery rather than my consolation. In trying to imagine what he was doing at that moment, I tried to superimpose his image on news film clips I watched on television. My absurd vision only made him seem farther away.

Because Lee had been the first among his year-group to go to Southeast Asia, all my military friends still had their husbands at home. They wouldn't understand yet. And even then, they probably wouldn't allow themselves to wallow in the emotional pit I had made for myself. Judy? I could call Judy, but, no, I couldn't talk to her about my dreadful fear that her husband's brother was going to get killed. Mother? She herself had been stateside through wartime, but with her tender sensitivities and retiring manner, she would never have indulged herself in the full throes of the emotional upheaval I had felt for the past two days.

Lee's parents? Maybe they could help me shake this oppressive dread that had taken up residence in my soul. I fantasized about the three of us consoling each other through Lee's absence and drawing strength from one another. The image was yet another movie scene superimposed on life—and just as much fantasy as my others.

As I drove east out of Roby and then south on the farm-to-market road, I prepared myself for the arrival ritual at the Lannings. I had learned it years ago when Lee first took me to his house, and the routine varied little except to be more intense when they had a son in Vietnam.

Lee's parents lived twelve miles from the small collection of houses that remained at the otherwise deserted cross-roads of Sylvester. The last five miles to their house was a lane-and-a half dirt road that wound past a cemetery. The car kicked up a cloud of red dust in my wake, and I braced myself. The Lannings neither had nor wanted a telephone; therefore, every arrival of company came as a surprise, which Mrs. Lanning assumed was bad news. Mr. Lanning usually stepped out of the front door at the first sound of a car, squinting suspiciously to see who was invading his private domain. Mrs. Lanning always came rushing onto the porch behind him, clutching her chest with one hand, clinging to the screen door with the other, and calling, "What's wrong? What's happened? Is everyone okay?"

As teenage drivers, Lee and Jim had added to the ceremony by honking the horn to reassure them that everything was fine and that the arriving party was friendly. It was a useless gesture, for it in no way affected the scenario except to add more noise to the confusion of shouts as everyone choked on the fog of dust from the road.

Now I turned into their front yard, hit the horn in quick successions, turned off the ignition, and jumped from the car, waving and yelling, "Everything's fine. Nothing's happened." They, of course, couldn't see my gestures through the fogging dirt or hear me over their own shouts.

Once inside the house, it inevitably took several minutes for everyone's adrenaline levels to drop back to normal and for conversation to fall into rhythm. Mrs. Lanning's face was engraved with fear, the same look I'd seen throughout the year and a half Jim was in Vietnam. Her wall-sized map of Southeast Asia was back in its place in the living room. Mr. Lanning, wearing his khakis and brown high-top boots, sat down in his recliner to smoke a cigar as Mrs. Lanning showed me the colored pins on the map—Long Binh, where Lee was to have landed, and Pleiku, where Jim had been based during his tour.

I watched Mrs. Lanning—make-up on and every black hair in place—as she carefully peered at the map and reverently touched the locations with the tip of her index finger. Her deep brown eyes looked puppy-dog wounded as she turned from the chart with its blue expanses inlaid with irregular shapes of soft pink, yellow, and green—pastels incongruent with what they represented for us.

"God A'mighty," Mrs. Lanning said as she wiped her hands on her apron, "I don't know if I can do this again, Linda. You just can't know what it's like to have a child in Vietnam."

No, I thought, but I'm learning what it's like to have a husband there. I followed her into the kitchen, noting the drinking water pail and dipper on the small stand inside the door and the cracked linoleum on the floor. The Lannings had been planning to build a new house since I had known them, but they postponed the commitment time after time although they could have afforded practically any house they wanted. When Jim was in Vietnam, they had lost all interest and withdrew into the security of the house where they had lived for more than thirty years. The place was now in a state of disrepair and their plans were again on hold with a second son in the combat zone.

"Did you see Lee off okay?" Mrs. Lanning asked as I sat down at the Formica table. There was that question again. I started to tell her about San Francisco, but she cut in, "You know, Lee was such an easy child to raise."

I bristled as she continued to talk about Lee in the past tense. She took a metal ice tray from the freezer and put it on the gas burner as she always did, letting the flames thaw the edges of the cubes. While she was making me a glass of tea, she reminisced about Lee, repeating stories I'd heard dozens of times. I felt a knot of familiar hostility taking shape in my stomach. Every time I'd visited the Lannings without Lee, I'd heard the same word-for-word renditions. The portraits she verbally painted cast Lee as the perfect son, the perfect man. My usual reaction after hearing Lee's praise for a couple of solid hours was to begin to disdain this character she described. The more she proclaimed his saintliness, the more I found his flaws.

Today Mrs. Lanning's monologue unnerved me more than usual as she banged pots around the kitchen and recounted the sleepless nights she had spent while Jim was in Vietnam. She said over and over that no one who had not had a child in such danger could understand. One part of me wrenched at her pain, another part grew quarrelsome. Lee might not be my child, but I loved him desperately. Did she think fear was reserved for parents only?

With every sentence in which my mother-in-law implied that I was still an outsider who couldn't share her concern, I realized how foolish I had been to think I'd find any comfort here. I remained polite but curtailed my visit. Lee would expect me to see his parents frequently even though the only serious arguments he and I ever had revolved around them—their unaccepting attitude toward me and his refusal to acknowledge it. There was no reason for him to know how distressing it was now.

Shortly after I got back to Roby, Judy called. "How are you, really?" she asked.

Tired of pretense, I blurted, "Exhausted. All I do is sleep."

"Me, too," she laughed, referring to her pregnancy.

"Maybe my test was wrong," I joked in return. There was an awkward silence. I could all but hear Judy trying to decide how to handle my apparent refusal to accept reality.

"It's probably just nerves," she said.

I was chagrined at my foolish comment and hung up depressed.

Lee had been gone three days. How would I endure 362 more?

• • •

Mother shook me awake the next morning, saying, "You've got mail."

I sat up, shocked to hear from Lee so soon, and quickly grabbed the two pieces she held. The first was an envelope postmarked in California. My heart fluttered—Lee had written me even before he left. I unfolded the two pages and read that he was writing from a motel in Vacaville because his plane had been delayed for a day. All the time I had been crying my eyes out he had been just up the road, still safely on American soil!

I was crushed. Then I was furious. Emotions tore me one way and then another. I grabbed the postcard, reading the revised itinerary he had jotted on the back. "Am in air somewhere between Hawaii and Okinawa—Had 30 minutes in Hawaii airport—Love, Lee." It was like having him leave all over again.

• • •

Slowly, painfully, the days began to blur into each other. Daddy went early each morning to the post office with the understanding that if I received mail, he would bring it to me before going to the coffee shop. Otherwise, I slept until noon almost every day, knowing instantly when I awoke of my own accord that I had nothing from Lee. That realization flattened me to the bed for several more minutes before I could exert the energy to face another day.

I reverted to an adolescent stage of no responsibilities. I helped Mother with meals, but even though she was my mother, it was another woman's kitchen. I moved listlessly about the house, thinking I would start some project yet never summoning the enthusiasm to follow through.

Even though I slept late, I often took afternoon naps and then stayed up late writing Lee long letters filled with boring details. I tried to keep them cheerful and funny, but mostly I aimed for volume to give him lots of pages. Jim emphasized that letters were extremely important to soldiers so far from home. As the letters were often delivered in bunches, I carefully numbered each envelope so Lee could read them in order.

The only incident that penetrated my consciousness that first week was another call from Judy, this time telling me that she had just learned that she had been exposed to German measles during the second month of her pregnancy. I could hear fatalism in her voice as she told me the doctors didn't know if or how it would affect the baby. "We'll just have to wait and see if it's deformed," she said with a calm that left me reeling. "We're not telling the Lannings until we know more. Jim's afraid this will send his mother right off her rocker." I selfishly wondered if it was an omen of things to come.

On Sunday, I went to church with Mother and Daddy. Years of indoctrination were not easily cast off. In the hard pew, I vividly recalled my experience over Los Angeles and wondered if God would punish me for not believing by letting something happen to Lee, which made no sense at all if I really no longer believed. I was in a moral dilemma: I didn't believe but I couldn't stop thinking in terms I'd been taught about believing.

• • •

Lee left on April 18. His first letter from Vietnam, dated April 22, arrived in Roby on April 29. After the eleven-day wait, I was both relieved and excited when Daddy woke me with a thick legal-sized red-and-blue-striped airmail envelope. Carefully peeling back the self-adhering flap, I peered inside to find military documents and then lined pages with handwriting, which I pulled out, leaving the other papers inside.

Lee wrote that he had been at Long Binh about thirty hours and had been assigned to the 2nd Battalion, 3rd Infantry Regiment of the 199th Light Infantry Brigade, which meant nothing to me. He wrote:

> The 199th base camp is here at Long Binh—near Binh Hoa—our area of operations is SW of Saigon—I understand things have been pretty quiet
> Should be about 10 days before I go to field—

I quickly calculated. Ten days from the twenty-second would be the second of May. But that was Vietnam time. In Roby time, it would be the first, or two days from that morning. I felt panic and turned back to the letter for more details. But the remainder of the three pages was an explanation of the enclosed pay vouchers and finance papers about which he wrote, "These are correct so don't worry about them." He also confirmed that I would receive a check for $691.00 for travel, dislocation, and May pay—all of which I would gladly have traded for another page of the letter reassuring me he missed me as much as I missed him. Instead, I read that he had allotted $200 for me, $50 for himself, and the rest of each month's pay to the guaranteed 10 percent government savings account for which he was eligible because he was in a combat zone. This was the disbursement we'd discussed, figuring I wouldn't need much money while in Roby and that I would find a job as soon as I returned to San Francisco to live with Susan Hargrove when Tom left for Vietnam in two months.

Now that I had his address, I wrote Lee a quick letter confirming my receipt of his and rushed the stack of ten envelopes to the post office. I read and re-read his first in-country letter, studying the handwriting, laughing at Lee's use of dashes instead of periods, and feeling thrilled each time I saw "I already miss you—" at the bottom of the page.

The next day another letter arrived. This one, hardly thicker than the envelope, was a single page dated April 24:

> Dearest Linda—
> I now have my company assignment—C Co as a platoon leader. What I've heard it is a good co—only problems being in practically

no experienced NCOs—Plt ldrs really have to work—Co has had several Lts wounded lately—none seriously—

I will probably finish orientations on Sat and will be going to the field on Sunday—Lts in the Battalion usually spend at least 6 months in field.

2nd of 3rd is part of the Old Guard—Estab. 1774—oldest Infantry outfit on active duty—Other part of 3rd is at Wash D.C.—They guard Unknown Soldier, etc.—Outfit has been in every US war—Really has an outstanding history—

199th has the mission to protect Saigon—Base camp here at Long Binh but after Sunday will seldom ever be back here.

Companies in a Light Inf Brigade are a little smaller than a regular Inf Co—Only difference is fewer people for weapons plts and drivers. Run about 120+ field strength. Co runs mostly search & destroy & ambushes—Little airmobile operations.

Did you get Letter # 3??

I love you very much,

Lee

My emotions scrambled to sort themselves out as I decoded the cryptic writing, reeling from learning that most of the company's lieutenants had been wounded and that Lee had gone to the field far sooner than his last letter had indicated. And why had he spent half the letter giving me a unit history lesson I didn't care about? I didn't want him in an outfit with *fewer* people. Terror gripped my stomach. I ran to the bathroom and threw up.

After I washed my face, I re-read the letter, trying to convince myself that it made no difference that Lee had been in danger for four or five days longer than I knew. This letter made it plain that I would rarely have any idea exactly where he was at any given time. My only option was to assume he was in imminent danger at all times. At least I knew he had still been alive six days ago.

I thought I was getting a grip on what my life would be like for the next year until I threw up again the next morning.

May 1969

{Chapter 5}

The house was quiet when I awoke on the first day of May, 1969, but something was wrong. I rushed to the bathroom and stood gagging over the sink. Two days in a row. *Do not think what you are thinking*, I told myself. But I was shaking with a hope spreading like flames on dried kindling, racing ahead of my ability to contain it.

I ate a cracker and felt better. Another good sign. Now I was trembling with excitement. Fantasies of being pregnant. What if. . . .

I made a doctor's appointment in Hamlin and after lunch drove the thirty miles feeling progressively more foolish. Dr. Hawkins had been my doctor on the few occasions I'd needed one, and I decided I would feel more comfortable—and maybe less idiotic—in front of him than the physicians in Roby. Besides, if I went to the local hospital, everyone in town would know I'd been there.

I sat tight-lipped on the examining table, finally hearing Dr. Hawkins whistle his way down the hall before throwing open the door and greeting me with a big smile. He ambled in as if he had neither a care in the world nor a lobby full of waiting patients.

"So what can I do for you today?" he asked as he dropped into his chair. It was impossible not to be charmed by his casual good humor.

"I just need a check-up," I answered tersely.

After receiving multiple lab punctures, I was once more atop the exam table where I endured pokes, probes, and stirrups. As I continued to lie on the table, Dr. Hawkins whistled his way in and out of the room. I tried to identify the tune but finally decided there wasn't one, just cheery noises coming from a man who had probably cured as many patients with his bedside manner as with his medical techniques.

I was surprised when Dr. Hawkins re-entered the room without my hearing his approach. He wore the most sober expression I'd ever seen on his face as he stood above me.

"The test results aren't conclusive," he said in a forthright manner, patting my shoulder, "but I think you've got the Egyptian flu."

I closed my eyes and felt hot tears welling up. The flu.

"The twenty-four hour kind?" I asked.

"Oh, no," he shook his head. "It lasts for months."

I looked helplessly at Dr. Hawkins.

"You do know about the Egyptian flu, don't you?"

I shook my head without taking my eyes from his.

"The Egyptian flu," he said somberly, "means I think you're going to be a mummy." Then his face broke into a big grin, displaying how pleased he was with his joke.

I wanted to hug him and run shouting down the halls. Lee and I were going to have a baby!

I'd never wanted so desperately to talk to Lee, and I decided I would tell no one before I knew he knew. I struggled through supper to appear calm. Mother and Daddy noticed a change but said nothing. I could feel a building need to burst forth with the news.

After supper I rode with Daddy to check on the cattle at my grandparents' farm, northeast of town, that he now leased from them. Always having enjoyed the stillness that settles on the wide open spaces at dusk, I found the quiet, broken only by the distant lowing of cows, matched my expansive mood. I loved the red dirt, the softening sun, the gentle animals, the smell of fresh hay, the crooked fence posts, the trickling creek, the wobbly wooden bridge, the sunflowers in the borrow ditch, the cooling breeze.

As we started back, Daddy talked about planting, insects, and rain, pointing to the neighboring fields as we drove past. I pretended to pay attention, but my mind was half a world away. If I mailed Lee a letter tomorrow and he received it within, say, a week to ten days, and if he wrote back immediately, I would get his letter a week to ten days later. That would be two or, more likely, three weeks until I knew he was aware we were having a baby. I began to wonder if Lee would really care if our parents found out before he did. Damn it, if he wanted a say in things like this, he should have stayed here where he belonged! He'd told me to do whatever I thought best while he was gone, but that was before he knew he was going to be a father.

The idea that Lee was going to be a father struck me as hilarious and I laughed out loud in the middle of Daddy's discourse on farming. As he shot me a surprised look, I realized that Lee and I weren't the only ones affected by this baby. Mother and Daddy would be grandparents.

"I went to see Dr. Hawkins today," I said, watching Daddy's profile as he leaned forward with one arm over the wheel.

"Elmer John?" he asked as he jerked his head up.

Trying to imitate the doctor's pose, I said, "He thinks I have the Egyptian flu."

Daddy pushed himself upright in alarm.

"I'm going to be a mummy." I added quickly, "Lee and I are having a baby."

My father pushed his Western straw work hat back on his head, a sign he had something to think over, allowing a few strands of black hair to escape onto the white skin above the farmer's tan line that horizontally halved his forehead.

This was not what I had expected. He was supposed to be happy. He was supposed to be excited about being a grandfather, for goodness sake.

Daddy reset his hat and asked, "What's Lee going to say about this?"

My mouth dropped open. Did he think I did this alone? And besides, whatever Lee would say could hardly make a difference now. I couldn't understand Daddy's reaction, because he had always been my biggest supporter in whatever I wanted.

"Have you told your mother yet?"

"No," I answered, feeling as though I were a high school sophomore whose illegitimate pregnancy was about to disgrace the family. I was crushed and then defiant. Well, let them think what they wanted. If Lee didn't come home, this baby would be all I had. I felt ferociously protective.

When I told Mother after we arrived at the house, she had an identical reaction to Daddy's. "I thought you'd both be happy," I said and went to my room.

Hurt and perplexed, I pulled out a new box of stationery, propping myself up in bed and writing "1 May—#13" on the inside of the box lid so I could keep an accurate count. That sounded like a lucky letter in which to make the announcement.

I crawled back into my euphoria and gave my melodramatic flair full rein, knowing I would either add an update to the letter the next day or never send it.

> Dearest Lee,
>
> Lee, this is letter number 13. And it is a very important letter, and I hope, special letter. Lee, we are going to have a baby. At least I think so and Dr. Hawkins thinks so. We'll know tomorrow for sure.
>
> Finding out like this is not quite like the movies, is it? I tried to think of some clever way of telling you, but somehow the simplest and most direct way seemed best.

I wrote five more pages giving him the play-by-play of the visit to the doctor, but no matter how many exclamation points I used or how I drew out the most minute details, I didn't feel the marks on the paper fully connoted my joy. I tried to imagine what he would say in response to each line, wondering whether the particulars would be of interest or not.

I was up early the next morning. At breakfast, Daddy was distracted and cool. When he left, I asked Mother what was wrong with him.

"He's just worried about you."

"Why? I thought you would both be happy for me."

She hesitated. "Well, you might end up raising this child alone."

In West Texas, "raising a child alone" for a woman was synonymous with hardship. I shook my head in disgust. With a college degree I'd earned in three years, I would not be destitute. Surely my own parents could see that I could take care of myself and a baby. After all, I was twenty-three and knew what I was doing.

I paced the floor until Dr. Hawkins called to confirm what I already knew. I added a note to my letter to Lee and dashed off to the post office. I was deliriously pregnant.

The next morning I drove to the Lannings with every intention of being pleasant and patient. I had written Lee that I was not going to tell them about the baby until I had his reaction to relay to them. Even before I reached their porch, I knew something was wrong. In that instant before rational thought could catch up with my imagination, I was paralyzed with fear. Had something happened to Lee?

Mr. Lanning must have seen my face because he said to his wife, "Tell her before you scare her to death."

In the living room, Mrs. Lanning wiped her eyes and turned away.

"Judy's had the German measles," Mr. Lanning said heavily.

Relief washed over me. Now that I could think again I knew I was listed as Lee's next of kin. It would be me, not the Lannings, the green army sedan would come to find.

"Jimmy wrote and asked us to call," Mr. Lanning continued. *No wonder Mrs. Lanning hates telephones.*

"Well, the doctors aren't sure," I emphasized and repeated what Judy said about being exposed. "If the effects were drastic, the tests would show that."

Hoping to lighten the mood, I told them about Lee's unit, omitting the reduced numbers a light brigade carried and embellishing on what a fine platoon he had. Mrs. Lanning sat stone-faced on the couch, staring straight ahead.

"God A'mighty," she said in a low, angry tone, "how much is a person supposed to bear? We've already sent one son to Vietnam. Now we've got to do it again. I don't believe I can stand it if anything happens to Lee."

Oh. Although I shouldn't have been, I was surprised to find that Mrs. Lanning's real concern was not for Jim and Judy's baby but for her own. I felt tempted to slip into their despair.

Instead, I made a decision. I firmly slapped the arm of the couch and said brightly, "What you need is some good news." Each in turn looked at me as though I were the court jester, and then they turned back to their private thoughts.

I ignored being ignored and announced, "Lee and I have some good news. We're going to have a baby, too."

Mr. Lanning jerked his head up, and when I nodded, his weathered face broke into a big smile. "Oh, boy," he said rubbing his hands together. "Did you hear that, Alice?"

Alice heard but Alice did not respond. She sat mute, staring at the floor.

Silence. I looked around the room, at the ceiling, the floor, the blank TV screen—wondering how I should react. I caught Mr. Lanning's eye and he shrugged slightly. We sat there.

Finally, I rose and said, as if nothing were unusual, "Well, I've got to be going."

Mr. Lanning held the door.

• • •

At lunch, I told Mother and Daddy how the Lannings had reacted, or rather, failed to react. Daddy pushed his chair from the table and leaned back. "Well, Hon," he started.

"Don't," I said firmly, jumping up. "Don't make excuses. Why isn't anyone happy for us?"

Neither could respond before I grabbed the car keys and slammed out of the house. I swung the car back toward the Lannings. Mrs. Lanning didn't have to like me or the fact that I was having Lee's baby. She never had to see this child as far as I was concerned. But she had damned well better not let Lee know how she felt until he was out of danger. Fury had gained momentum over devastation.

My in-laws were surprised to see me again so soon; Mrs. Lanning began hurling the "Who's dead now?" questions from the porch. I didn't bother to reassure her until I had climbed the steps.

"If Lee gets killed, you'll know all too soon," I snapped and walked into the house.

I sat down without waiting to be asked. The two of them exchanged shocked glances before they, too, sat expectantly. Lee would not approve of what I was about to do, but, I thought, I should be so lucky as to have to deal with him over this.

"I came back to get one thing straight," I said. My insides were churning but my voice was steady. "The only irreconcilable arguments Lee and I have ever had have been over the way you treat me."

Mrs. Lanning knew that I was talking to her. "We just didn't want Lee to get married before he graduated," she said to the wall. "We were just surprised, that's all."

I had heard that before. This time I did not let it pass. "We dated for six years and gave you four months' notice before the wedding. How could you possibly have been surprised? Don't you understand that I want what's best for him, too? And right now that is not to be bothered by petty family problems.

"Under no circumstances are you to write anything to Lee about this baby except that you are happy. I don't care if you have to lie. In your next letter you will give some appropriate, positive response, and not ignore it like you did with me this morning. And," I continued, looking Mrs. Lanning straight in the eye, "there had better not be any innuendos to the contrary."

The room was quiet. My implied threat hung in the air. I could have, if I chose, created a rift in their relationship with their son. I didn't want that, but neither did I want Lee involved in our dispute. One war at a time was enough.

"That's all I came to say." I got up and went to the door. Mr. Lanning stood, unsure whether to follow me or stand beside his wife. "When will you be back?" he asked.

"I don't know," I answered, letting myself out.

I returned to Roby with fury dissipating, feeling only drained. Lee had been gone for what already seemed forever, but the calendar showed only two weeks.

{Chapter 6}

Letters from Lee set my daily mood and carried over to my parents. On days when I got mail, the atmosphere was cheerful and the conversation light. That was Day One. Day Two was still pleasant because I did not expect another letter so soon. Day Three was more subdued but by no means glum. By Day Four, tension began to mount and a quiet pallor spread through the house. If the wait stretched to five days, no one talked above a whisper and spoke only when necessary. Mother and Daddy became just as susceptible to the ebb and flow of waiting as I was. Then, happily, a muddy envelope would appear to shatter the dreadful count, and we were back to Day One.

Lee was conscientious about writing whenever he had the chance. Although he wrote every three or four days, his letters frequently arrived in bunches, making the days between almost unbearable. At one point, we reached Day Nine before four envelopes arrived. There was never any explanation or rhythm to the unpredictable mail service. It just added to the suspense.

I studied the letters with an analytical attention to detail. The first thing I did when I opened each letter was to note the date and experience a relief that Lee had still been alive as recently as two weeks before, seven days before, ten days before—whenever. Intellectually, I knew that if he were killed, the green army sedan would drive into the yard within two or three days. Letters could have easily arrived after he had been dead for weeks. Emotionally, however, I needed the reassurance that only his letters could provide. I did not necessarily trust the Army.

In fact, when it came to notification of next of kin, I did not trust the Army at all. At Fort Bragg, Lee had served as a Survivor's Assistance Officer, which was the label the military hung on officers unlucky enough to have the extra duty assignment of notifying and taking care of surviving wives and families. Lee's case had only required him to handle the paperwork and arrangements for the widow of a sergeant killed in a stateside accident. Most of his friends, however, had drawn Vietnam widows. I heard them tell stories about having to chase women down streets and alleyways to notify them because the women seemed to believe that what they did not hear was not true. The Survivor's Assistance Officers also talked about embellishing heroic actions by the dead to comfort the families and about making arrangements for burial ceremonies. At the time, I agreed with Lee and his friends that it was irrational for wives to run out the back door to avoid hearing the truth that awaited them at the front. I had imagined then that I could stoically confront such an occasion with dignity. Now I realized I would run farther, faster, and forever.

I was also aware now that no matter what the Army told me, I would never know the truth about how Lee died. I had heard too many fabrications, too many well-intended stories. The facts were that the Army rarely knew exactly what really happened and even more rarely revealed the awful truth.

Two years earlier, when Jim was home on leave from Vietnam, I accompanied him on a visit to the fiancée of one of his men who had been killed. I would never forget the tragic anguish on the young woman's angelic face. She was so grateful to Jim for coming to see her, and she clung to his every word. She didn't cry, only asked question after question about what had happened, how well Jim had known her solider, and what he had said and done in the days before he died. Desperate for information, she listened intently as Jim answered her as consolingly as he could, repeating for her the official version of how the company had been moving through the jungle and her man had hit a booby trap and died instantly.

When we left, Jim was drenched with sweat. "Now tell me what really happened," I said as we walked to the car.

He hesitated and then shrugged. "Nobody knows for sure. It could have been a booby trap. But he probably caught the pin of one of his grenades on a limb or vine and blew himself up."

"And did he die instantly?"

"No," he said, shaking his head at the memory. "He was a bloody mess, yelling and screaming even after we gave him morphine. He probably lived five minutes."

I looked at him, questioning the differences in versions inside and outside the house. He stared at the ground before he finally looked up and said, "It's better for her this way."

That was how soldiers thought about families, I knew. I had been disgusted with all men who would valiantly charge a barrage of AK-47s but who didn't have the guts to tell women the truth.

The arrival of every envelope helped me suppress those kinds of thoughts, but during the periods of waiting, I expended a lot of energy to keep them out of my head.

I grew adept at judging a letter's contents by feeling the envelope. The really thick ones were disappointing, I learned quickly, because they either contained military documents or, more often, a copy of the brigade newspaper that Lee wanted me to save. What the Army was doing publishing full-fledged newspapers in a war zone I could not understand, and I was irritated every time I got one.

Very thin envelopes held one-page letters that rarely exceeded fifty words. Those were the hardest, especially if I'd been waiting four or five days for mail. The longer the wait between, the longer I needed the letters to be. My needs and the pages seldom matched, but I never stopped hoping.

The magic letters were those whose envelopes had just the right thickness to hold two or three pages. I savored every word and read as slowly as I could force myself to proceed. Lee still included too many military details for my liking, but at least in the long letters he told me more about what was happing to him, what he was thinking.

I cherished every letter—even those with only five sentences—because each had the potential to be the last one. I memorized every line and scrutinized every stroke of his pen, contemplating whether a long dash meant anything different from a short one. I looked for any kind of message between the lines.

The letter for which I waited most impatiently, of course, was the one responding to the baby news. In the meantime, I received the early letters he wrote from the rice paddies of the Mekong Delta. I felt obligated to share his news with the Lannings because he didn't always have time to write to them. As cross as I was with his parents, I would not withhold information.

So I made the trek back to their house only a few days after I had spoken my mind. I made my peace offering by honking the horn and enacting the arrival ritual. Mr. Lanning welcomed me with open arms. The first few minutes were uncomfortable; Mrs. Lanning was cool and formal until her husband threw her a dark look. She swallowed hard and then behaved as civilly as she could. The only reference to our previous encounter came when Mrs. Lanning said, like a throw-away line, "I wrote Lee how happy we were about the baby." We had struck an uneasy pact.

I stayed to watch the *CBS Evening News* with them. About the war, the commentator reported, "In Vietnam today, causalities were light."

As the screen filled with shots of U.S. troops carrying the wounded, Mrs. Lanning observed woefully, "There's no such thing as 'light causalities' when it's yours." I would never hear another newscast summary that did not remind me of her words.

I doggedly continued to look for someone who would share my happiness about the baby while I waited to hear from Lee. I called Susan Hargrove in Georgia, where she and Tom lived while he trained at Fort Gordon. Tom would be going to Vietnam in mid-June, at which time I would join Susan in San Francisco, where we would share an apartment.

After telling Susan about the baby, I asked if she wanted to back out of our deal. She hesitated and then said, "No, no. I'm really happy for you. Gayle, you remember Gayle from Fort Bragg? Well she's having a baby, too. I just want to get pregnant myself and I'm running out of time."

Susan then told me that her parents had leased a flat in San Francisco that she and I could sublet from them for $100 a month each while they were away on an overseas construction project. The only stipulation was that we allow her brother Miles and an Arab teenager, whom her parents were sponsoring, to use the apartment as a weekend getaway from their schools.

As pleased as I was to learn that Susan and I had a place to live, I still wanted someone to share my jubilation. I next turned to Grandmother Knox, Mother's lively mother of 76. When I told her the news, she clapped her small, aged hands and cried, "Oh, joy, joy!" There was no hesitation, no hidden agenda, only the spontaneous happy reaction I'd been seeking.

I didn't know if it was Grandmother's unique personality or her perspective at that stage of her life that made her response different, and I didn't care which. I would forever be grateful to her for not being distracted by the doubts and details that attached themselves to everyone else. Whenever I felt that waiting was taking too great a toll, I talked to Grandmother about the baby and got excited all over again.

Lee received his first mail from me on May 2; I learned that when his return letter arrived in Roby on May 12. He had also received mail from Mother and Grandmother, both of whom wrote him while I stood over them like a stern school master.

The lag time in turnaround correspondence was maddening. But I was becoming optimistic. Then President Nixon gave me more reason to believe that events in my life had taken a turn for the better. In mid-month, he announced his plan to de-escalate the war by bringing troops home. My spirits soared, hoping Lee's unit would be first. Maybe he wouldn't have to spend the whole year in Vietnam, and he might come home alive after all. Maybe there was a God and my view of Him had simply been obstructed by Los Angeles smog.

My soaring heart was blindsided by another thought. If Lee's unit was not one of the first to be withdrawn, he would be left there with even fewer reinforcements, fewer Americans for support. And if the enemy now knew that Americans were pulling out, wouldn't they bide their time to take full advantage of our smaller numbers? But surely Nixon knew what he was doing. Meanwhile I had the more immediate concerns of waiting for the mail.

Finally, on May 16, two weeks after I got the call from Dr. Hawkins, I received Lee's letter addressed to "My Dear Pregnant Wife."

> Well, I'll be damned, that was my first reaction. I got the letter about 1600 yesterday but it was about 1900 before I got to read it—I had just read the first page when I got a call for a special mission so it was several more hours before I got to finish the letter.
>
> I hadn't even thought about your being pregnant till the morning before your letter—then for some reason I thought about it.
>
> Honey, I am very happy about the idea—or the fact, I should say—I think it is fantastic.

I was ecstatic at his reaction, which I hadn't doubted at all until I had met with our parents' lack of enthusiasm. Now, certainly, no one else's opinion mattered at all.

Mother sighed with relief when I told her Lee was excited, too, and Daddy re-channeled his concern for me into impatience at having to wait so long to play with his grandbaby.

I went back to see Dr. Hawkins. He projected my due date as December 2. Writing Lee that night that he would have a personalized Christmas present, I was suddenly aware of how far away that season seemed from this May night. It was as if Lee and the baby were in cahoots. I could do nothing but wait for both of them.

{Chapter 7}

My spirits soared when I thought about the baby and plunged when I let myself dwell on the dangers Lee faced. I was riding on an emotional rollercoaster propelled by hormones as well as an overactive imagination, both of which were raging out of control. At least I never had to worry about bad dreams. There was no need for my subconscious to work through suppressed fears; I was experiencing them in living color during my waking hours.

Lee was keeping his promise to tell me in detail what was happening to him, which calmed part of me at the same time that it fueled my sense of dread. He wrote:

15 May 69

Dearest Linda,

We are still on operation—It is a rough one—You asked if I have been in combat—I have not been shot at—at least not real close—We have been hitting booby traps—Yesterday 7 of my men were hit by a mortar shell booby trap—3 real bad but I think they will live—My RTO was one of them—It got men in front and back of me—also man next to me—This was the second time the man next to me has been hit—I guess the Good Lord is looking after me.

It is wet out here—Everyone getting nervous—hoping to leave this area today—Hope I can get this letter out on resupply.

Am down to 20 men—only 15 in field—Some are sick or recovering from wounds.

When my men were hit yesterday we had been spread out good—Co CO told us to go into an area—I advised against it but

> he said go. We had to get close to get through—that's when we hit the booby trap—Worst thing I have seen here—My men did react well—I had a dust off (medi-vac) in in about 10 minutes—
>
> You said tell you everything—I have—Don't worry as these are only 2 contacts I had made—Booby traps seldom kill—They do wound quite a few.

I could not fathom what had actually happened when the booby trap exploded, nor did I want to be able to see too clearly. But I did not have to imagine how close the radio-telephone operator (RTO) had been to Lee. I knew the communications man was never more than an arm's reach from the platoon leader.

When my adrenalin rush subsided, I was drained and shaken, realizing that I had been playing a game with myself, a game in which I let my worries run wild so that I could reassure myself nothing was really as bad as these figments of my imagination. This technique had been my safety valve. The letter dispelled that notion, the pages stained from Lee's sweaty and dirty palm confirming not only that this was for real but also it was more frightening than I had ever conceived.

I did not understand war, never having been closer to it than the silver screen. Even in war movies that made me cry when the hero died, I knew the actors got up at the end of the scene and walked away, which certainly seemed saner than Vietnam.

Lee's reassurance that I should not worry was well-intended but ineffective. I was not in the mood to be thankful that booby traps seldom killed when I knew he was walking among them with every step he took.

His next letter said that the worst of the wounded had been transferred to Japan where they could receive more sophisticated medical treatment and recuperate. I applied for a passport. Never having heard of any family member traveling to Japan to visit the wounded did not deter me. If Lee were sent to Japan, I would be on the next flight whether the Army liked it or not.

Such contingencies reminded me of the old story about the kingdom with a dilemma. The grain crop from a bountiful year had become contaminated by a poison that caused insanity. If the king destroyed the harvest, most of his subjects would starve because not enough good grain from previous years remained to feed everyone. Yet, if he allowed the people to eat the poisoned grain, madness would prevail. Finally, the king decided to feed the people the contaminated grain to sustain their lives but selected a few subjects who would eat only the untainted food. His reasoning was that at least a few would be aware that the rest were insane.

I did not know which grain I had consumed. Certainly, I must have appeared crazy to those around me, with my jumpy nerves and distracted, short attention span. I was manic on mail days, depressed in between; obsessive about war news, compulsive about writing letters. Yet, given the insanity of my situation, wouldn't I have been crazy not to have been affected? By the end of the month, I had no answers for anything. The only thing I was sure about was that both kinds of grain had been served up and the "kingdom" was in turmoil.

Peace protests shared the headlines and lead stories with the war, often receiving more coverage and usually a more sympathetic presentation. The protestors, mostly my age, were as alien and as incomprehensible to me as the Viet Cong, and I felt about the same toward both groups. I didn't hate them; I blamed them both for prolonging my misery.

I couldn't clearly remember when the war and the flower children and peaceniks had crept into my consciousness. Surely during my early college days I was obliquely aware of the Vietnam "conflict," and I knew there were young people out in the streets wearing flowers in their hair and saying the war was wrong. I thought they looked ridiculous, and I had dismissed both sides of the entire event until the fall of 1965 when Lee's brother Jim was making noise about getting to the war before it was over. Knowing someone who was going to Vietnam made the war a little more concrete, but not by much. When Jim actually went in the spring of 1966, I felt sorry for his parents and wondered why Lee was so envious. Meanwhile, the protestors attracted more supporters, but the peace movement did not extend to small campuses like mine.

Now the protestors irritated me most when they attacked the military and really evoked my wrath when they pretended they were trying to protect soldiers from being sent to war. They didn't give a damn about the troops; most were just trying to protect their own cowardly hides—not that I blamed anyone for not wanting to fight; rather, I resented their dishonest tactics. Mostly I was surprised that the media and the politicians, supposedly mature adults, would pay so much attention to anything twenty-year-olds said. To me, student protests should have been ranked right in there with a two-year-old child's tantrums.

In Roby, I didn't have to deal with anti-military attitudes since most people were unquestioningly patriotic. The farmer friends I ran into when I was with Daddy would frequently pat me on the back and say, "Tell Lee to take care of himself. I remember how it was in World War II." Sometimes they would tell me stories of their experiences and I would be reminded of the reservist in the San Francisco airport, again wondering how these stories were supposed to help and yet amazed to find that many of these men whom I'd known all my life had shipped out from this little town to places all over the world: France, North Africa, China, Burma, and the Philippines.

Mother's friends, too, were sympathetic, but they rarely mentioned the waiting ordeal itself. They talked instead about rationing and victory gardens. They laughed at their shared stories, which stood in stark contract to my circumstances. At the time, I was the only person in town who had anyone in Vietnam.

My sense of alienation from everything familiar continued to haunt me even in the most familiar surroundings. Sometimes I did errands for Mother, going to the grocery store or stopping by the drug store. I approached these tasks leisurely to elongate the amount of time I could expend, but no matter how many times I walked around the close and crowded aisles, I could never take any sufficient quantity off the clock. An afternoon in Roby was longer than a month at Fort Bragg.

I dutifully continued to visit the Lannings three or four times a week during May, knowing I would be leaving the next month. Mr. Lanning had been right about his wife and the idea of the baby. She came as close to apologizing for her behavior as she was capable when she said, "I just needed time to be sure it didn't mean Lee wouldn't be coming back. It scared me, that's all."

Mr. Lanning seized the opportunity to say, "I hope it's a girl. We haven't had one born into this family for sixty-five years. It's about time."

I laughed but didn't tell him of my growing certainty that I was carrying a boy.

In one of the letters I received late in the month, Lee mentioned R&R for the first time. In October, he would be eligible for this rest and recuperation—or was it rest and recreation? I was never sure of the official wording because by 1969, the initials had taken on a special meaning of their own. But he suggested that because of my condition we should probably wait until January. My disappointment was momentary. Five more months or nine, it was an eternity either way.

Before May came to an excruciatingly tedious end, I received a letter Lee had written in mid-month saying his unit had moved to a more secure duty not far from Saigon at the Binh Dien Bridge where they should stay for about twenty days. Unlike Mrs. Lanning, I did not have a map at the ready, so the location told me little. "More secure" and "twenty days" gave me the slight reprieve I needed so I could concentrate on other things.

June 1969

{Chapter 8}

When Lee and I returned to Fort Bragg for the last time after Ranger School, we found Tom Hargrove, a long-time friend from Fisher County with whom Lee had gone to Texas A&M, living on post with his wife, Susan. As couples, we spent many evenings together, sharing our experiences and adjusting to military life. Inevitably, we talked about the pending orders for Vietnam for Lee and Tom. Susan said she planned to return to San Francisco for the year when the time came. I was still at a loss as to where I would spend my time. I had no reason to return to Houston, where I had worked before getting married, and the idea of spending twelve months in my hometown did not seem practical. Ultimately, Susan and I decided that if the timing of the orders worked out we would share an apartment in San Francisco while we waited.

When Susan and I talked on the phone again after Lee left, I could detect the symptoms of Tom's being within days of leaving by her inability to carry on an extended conversation and in her tone of voice. I did not envy her upcoming weeks, so I volunteered to arrive in San Francisco a couple of days after Tom's departure. Even though Susan's mother would still be there, I knew, if I had learned nothing else, the importance of nonstop activity during the transition stage, and I would do what I could to create diversions. At least I would understand as no one else around her would. Thinking that I might actually do something constructive lightened my step. Besides, I craved conversation with someone my own age who shared my circumstances.

As independent as I like to think I was, I found myself nervous about driving alone to San Francisco. I asked Daddy to go as far as Tucson, where he could see my sister Brenda, and then fly back home. I called

Connie to see if she would ride with me from Los Angeles and spend the weekend in the Bay Area. That left only the stretch from Tucson to L.A. to handle by myself.

Thinking that I could make it all the way to California while Lee was still safely guarding the bridge, I planned an extra day with my sister and sent Lee my itinerary so he could determine when to change the address on his letters to me.

The closer the time came for my departure, the more panicked I became about going four days without access to mail from Lee, and maybe longer if his letters had to be rerouted. I tried to calm myself. That effort lasted until I received a letter that reignited my worries:

> Have been having it fairly easy. Was op con-ed (borrowed by another unit) the other day. Just my plt. The company we were with hit several booby traps—We didn't hit any—We were in an area supposed to be the worst for booby traps. I feel fortunate—My people are getting good at spotting the traps.

So much for the comfort of bridge duty or counting on Lee to stay put. He also said that three more of his men had been hit—this time by "friendly fire" from artillery landing in the wrong place—and that his unit would soon be moving north into the jungle, which, he said, was supposed to be a "bad area." He finished by writing, "It will be hell up there—No more VC—Plenty NVA. I am confident in my plt however."

The last letter I received in Roby told me that Lee was on "a 6-day sweep of pineapple fields." A sweep of anything except the floor sounded dangerous to me. My anxiety was at an all-time high.

Even the good news Lee included in his letters did little to quell my apprehensions. He wrote that the battalion commander had come to the field to pin on his silver bar when he was promoted to first lieutenant. Nice, I thought, but the colonel really should have been paying more attention to military strategy and less to parade field pomp and circumstance. With the number of men in his command, he could spend his whole tour doing nothing but glad-handing promotions and presenting awards. Who was overseeing this war, anyway? I wanted everyone in Vietnam to concentrate all efforts on one thing: getting Lee home alive. I had no tolerance for activity that did not contribute directly to that end.

The fact that Lee made first lieutenant meant more pay but not more money for me. Knowing that the savings allotment would get the increase, I was growing more realistically concerned about my finances, already facing a monthly deficit before I even moved. My rent would be $100; the car payment was $80. That left me $20 each month for food, utilities, and miscellaneous. While a good manager, I was no magician, so I decided to make up the deficiency by withdrawing amounts from the $690 check I received after Lee left and the little I had been able to save while in Roby.

Lee asked in several letters if I needed more money, but every time I started to write him that I did, guilt would overcome me. Here I was with all the creature comforts while he slept on the ground. I couldn't ask a man who ate his meals out of C-ration cans to provide more money for my comparative life of luxury. I desperately wanted him to change the allotment, but I would not ask him to do so. If he figured out the expenses and decided to send me more, I would be grateful, both for the money and for his paying attention to my needs. If he did not, I would somehow manage.

I had to force myself not to renege on my travel commitments. On the scheduled Tuesday morning, Daddy and I left before sunrise. As Mother waved to us, her expression held an odd mixture of sadness and relief. She wasn't glad to see me go, I knew, yet there was a relaxation in her face I hadn't seen for weeks.

Daddy and I took turns driving. He napped when I was at the wheel, but when he drove I could not sleep, so we talked as we crossed the monotonous landscape to El Paso. Our conversations were mostly aimless, easy talk, strolls down memory lane through the years when I was little. I enjoyed being with Daddy. We laughed and then we were quiet, though I noticed he never let the silence go too long. As we finally neared Tucson, Daddy began clearing his throat and shifting uncomfortably behind the wheel, a sign he was about to broach a difficult subject. "Now, Babe," he said in all seriousness, "I hope living out there in San Francisco isn't gong to affect you too much."

"I'm sure it won't," I said lightly, in part because I was amused that the city seemed to him the equivalent of the proverbial den of iniquity, but mostly to indicate that I wasn't interested in having a heart-to-heart at the moment. I couldn't allow a crack in my armor—even with Daddy—or a flood of tears would overwhelm me.

"Well, I worry that if anything happens to Lee," he began, and then hesitated. He shifted in the seat again. "Well, I just wouldn't want you to end up bitter."

"It won't be San Francisco that makes me bitter," I said.

"Folks out there don't think the way we do," he countered, referring to the protestors and flower children who had made the city synonymous with the peace movement.

Accepting that he was insisting we have this conversation, I said, "I'm not bitter about Lee going to Vietnam. He volunteered. The only reason I would ever be bitter would be because our government didn't give him every bit of support it has to give. If this country uses all its resources and he still gets killed, then it's Fate or God or bad luck. But so long as we are not doing everything humanly possible to provide every troop with all the firepower and protection available, then the government is wrong. But I don't agree with the protestors. I think they are wrong, too."

My voice rose as I spoke, surprising me with how much anger I'd voiced. Daddy must have been unprepared too, because he backed off quickly, mumbling, "I just thought I should mention it."

I looked out at the growing darkness descending on the distant hills, feeling the sensation of displacement surfacing again. Lee had been gone almost two months, and I was still foundering.

"I'll bet Brenda is already watching for us," Daddy said, to change the subject.

I looked over to see him smiling at the thought of seeing his youngest child. I hoped he knew I wasn't mad at him, but I could think of no way to say so without risking another encounter neither of us wanted. "I hope she's got supper ready. I'm starving," I said. "How much farther?"

Brenda was, in fact, watching for us when we drove into the trailer park where she and her husband Danny lived near Monthan Air Force Base, where Danny was assigned. She greeted us with big hugs and her dazzling smile. I was always unprepared for her to be the taller of the two of us, at six-foot-one. With Daddy at six-foot-four, I was the shortest person around, which I hoped accounted for why I felt like a small child again.

When we called Mother to let her know we had arrived safely, she told me I had received a letter from Lee and that she had forwarded it to Brenda's. She stressed, "They promised it would be there tomorrow. The envelope was pretty beat up. It's got something round in it. I taped it up the best I could."

Brenda was glad to have company because Danny was away at a four-month training school in Texas. The three of us had a pleasant visit that night and over coffee the next morning as I adjusted to seeing Brenda, five years my junior, in her own home. When I thought of her, I kept remembering her in high school, not grown up and married.

Brenda and I took Daddy to the airport and then returned to wait for the mail. When the postman finally came, he offered up a tattered, bulging envelope held together by Mother's freezer tape. The poor thing had had a hard trip. Lee had addressed it upside down, ignoring the "Via Air Mail" wording and writing "free" in what he designated to be the upper right corner because no postage was required from the combat zone. Mother had reversed his mistake when she forwarded it and added a stamp in the corner she deemed correct. That it had arrived at all was a miracle.

The bulge was a roll of undeveloped film and most of the accompanying pages were shot-by-shot descriptions of pictures Lee had taken but which I could not see. According to the list, Lee was in some shots, so I was frustrated that I would have to wait until I got to San Francisco to get them developed. I consoled myself by remembering that I was lucky to have gotten the film at all.

Early the next morning, I departed Tucson with a map and directions to Connie's on the seat beside me. I was accompanied only by a lonely sense of missing Lee and the ever-nagging concern that the car—less than two years old—would break down. I had the car serviced and checked thoroughly before I left Roby, so I felt relatively confident. Even the battery cables, which tended to corrode over to block the connection, were behaving since Daddy gave them an authoritative whack with his trusty hammer.

I sped through Phoenix and spent the rest of the morning and most of the afternoon rolling west on Interstate 10. As I passed the exit for Palm

Springs, I enjoyed a momentary thrill of being near the glamorous place. But then shortly thereafter I found myself dumped into a torrent-like flash flood of traffic that swept me faster and faster down freeway lanes that multiplied in ever-widening rivers of asphalt. I gripped the wheel tight and found each lane I tried seemed more dangerous than the last.

The green exit signs flipped past in illegible blurs, and I wondered if I would be able to find a lane slow enough to allow me to read the markers without being run over. Cars and trucks in the four other lanes going my direction blew by on both sides in numbers and with a velocity I had never encountered. Trapped in the second lane from the inside, I held on for dear life.

That's when I heard the *pop! whap-whap-whap* and felt the car trembling. A blowout. I fought for control and put on the blinker, naively assuming the other drivers would let me cross to the shoulder. If they noticed, they ignored my wobbling car. The more I slowed, the more the traffic behind me moved to pass me on the right, blocking my way to the exits.

Around the next bend we went. *Whap-whap-whap.* I finally gained one lane. The car's shimmy was stronger. *Whap-whap.* It sounded as if I were driving a helicopter. *The baby!* I fought against panic. Another curve and a straightaway later I got to the right lane in time to connect with an off-ramp. By the time I got to the stop sign, I was shaking more violently than the car had been. A car behind me honked. I timidly eased across the intersection to a service station.

"Lucky," said the little man in coveralls as he looked at the culprit tire. "Yep, you're lucky all right that it only threw the rubber. Lucky, too, 'cause this is the last station for a good ways. Lucky lady."

I felt a lot of things—deserted, scared, helpless, stupid—but not "lucky." I should have just stayed in Roby. By the time the man finished putting on a new tire and tallying the bill, I added "broke" to my list.

Reentering the freeway was like climbing back on a horse after a fall, but I did it with determination because I was so angry with myself for feeling like such a coward and—mostly—because I had no other way to get to Connie's. Miraculously, I drove to the apartment complex without further mishap, amazed that it was actually possible to single out one location in the maze of so-called civilization with its crisscrossing streets, roads, freeways, avenues, drives, parkways, boulevards, and cul-de-sacs.

Where Connie's world had been so disorienting to me two months ago, it now seemed a familiar haven—her apartment comfortable, her roommates old friends. Connie first stared at my slightly bulging tummy and said, "Oh, my." Then she said after an undisguised assessment, "You're better."

When we left the next morning, Connie and I took the coastline highway for the journey north, appreciating the beauty of the panoramic Pacific Ocean views in our individual ways. Connie remarked on the magnificent force of the waves crashing against the rocky shore below us while I noted to myself that for all the good it did me, I was a thousand miles closer to Lee. We spotted the residue of the Santa Barbara oil slick that had been so much in the news, a spill that replaced Vietnam in the headlines and generated an outcry over the loss of wildlife. Americans seemed relieved to focus on environmental issues rather than human tragedies. I wished my biggest concern was for sea otters.

We stopped for lunch at a scenic outdoor restaurant overlooking the Pacific. The sky was crystal blue, the leaves and grass crisp green, the temperature pleasant, and the breeze gentle. It was an ideal spot for a leisurely meal. Connie, always the more intense of the two of us, seemed in no hurry as she ate and chatted over her seafood salad while I downed my meal and asked for the check. Finally, putting her napkin on the table and leaning back, she asked, "Don't you ever relax any more?"

I laughed self-consciously and said, "I thought I was." But her question made me aware of my taunt muscles and stiff posture.

"Are we on a schedule or something?" she asked.

"No, no," I answered. "I guess I was just hoping I might have a letter waiting for me. Days without mail make me nervous. I didn't mean to rush you."

"I see," she said as my explanation registered. Then snapping into action, she said, "I didn't realize. Let's go."

For the rest of the trip, Connie concentrated on getting us to San Francisco with all due speed, ordering gas station attendants to hurry when we stopped and pushing the speed limit when she drove. My anticipation became hers, and I found that having her share my objective allowed me to actually relax somewhat, like knowing that a trustworthy trooper was on duty so I could rest.

"I should prepare you for Susan," I told Connie as she urged the car northward. She shot me a quick look of apprehension, so I explained what I knew about Susan's background of growing up overseas as her father followed engineering and construction jobs around the world. She had lived in the Philippines and the Aleutians when she was small, spent several years in Tehran, gone to a French school in Lebanon, and visited her parents frequently in Kuwait while she was in a Swiss finishing school.

"Don't be surprised," I warned Connie, "when Susan talks about trips to Rome and London in the same way you and I talk about going to Sweetwater and Abilene."

"How did she end up married to Tom Hargrove from Rotan, Texas?" Connie asked with a laugh, for although she did not know Tom except by name, she did know Rotan, a town ten miles north of Roby.

I filled her in on the details of Susan's mother being from there and Susan visiting her grandmother during the summers.

"And, just so you know," I added tentatively, "Tom just left for Vietnam this week."

"Oh, gosh," Connie said with trepidation, "is this going to be a repeat?" For someone who wasn't herself sending a man off to Vietnam, Connie was certainly getting a lot of experience with the ordeal.

My answer was that I didn't know what Susan's state of mind would be, but I knew she would be in the throes of some big project, going helter-skelter in all directions. I didn't know Susan all that well, but this much I did know about her.

"Don't you feel strange about moving in with someone you hardly know?"

"Connie," I answered with a sigh, "I feel strange about everything all the time. This doesn't even faze me."

When we pulled up at the address Susan had given me, Connie jumped out of the car and said, "Now let's hope there's a letter."

{Chapter 9}

We parked facing downward on the side of a steep hill packed with two- and three-story houses whose descending red tile rooftops looked like a staircase for giants. Neatly landscaped with miniature front yards and low trimmed hedges, the stucco houses exuded an air of understated elegance and cautious aging.

Connie and I hurried up the flight of Mexican tile steps to the front door and rang the bell, all the while scrutinizing my new surroundings, which appeared to place me much farther from West Texas than what the mileage logged on my car's odometer indicated.

Susan answered the door in dungarees and a work shirt. She was barefoot and wore a red bandanna pulled tight over her hair. I could see from Connie's open mouth that Susan did not fit her image of a Swiss finishing school graduate. Well, there were certain things about Susan one could only learn first-hand.

Susan leaned against the opened door and looked us over for a moment before she laughed and said, "God, you are pregnant. Come on in. We're just trying to get stuff moved around. Everything's a mess. Mother said we should try to finish before you got here, but I said, 'Nah, we'll just put them to work, too.'"

After quick introductions, Connie and I entered the foyer, seeing the kitchen doorway straight ahead, the living room to the right, and a hallway to the left. Stepping over the vacuum cleaner and its snaked hose, we moved into a living room filled with unplaced furniture and moving boxes. Large windows let streams of sunlight into the spacious room and its adjoining dining area.

So this would be home, I thought, feeling good about the prospect. It was a lovely old place with high ceilings and a fireplace. Looking at the carved mantle from across the room, I spotted the corner of an air mail envelope jutting from behind a figurine. My heart skipped a beat.

"Susan," I said, eyes locked on the red and blue stripes.

"Oh," she said, grabbing the envelope, "this came for you today. Boy, was I disgusted when I saw your name instead of mine."

She handed me the letter and then continued talking, her words becoming brisk and busy. "Mother's getting cleaned up. She's just exhausted because we've been running around trying to deal with the movers and getting her stuff out of storage. We've got to get the place in order before it drives us crazy. You wouldn't believe how much trouble we've had getting–" Susan clicked on the vacuum cleaner and picked up the hose, the noise of the motor drowning out most of what she said as she continued talking to Connie, who threw a questioning look at me. I nodded, indicating that we now had the answer to our question about how Susan was coping. But first things first.

I sat on the sofa, fingering the thickness of the envelope and smiling as I guessed three pages. The letter was dated 16 June—only four days ago . . . well, five because of the International Date Line. Still, it was so current I felt just one step removed from hearing Lee say the words he wrote from the brigade main base where he was on stand-down for three days, meaning out of the field and out of danger, before heading north, where he would be now.

The second paragraph wiped the smile off my face when I read about Lee's last airmobile mission in "the pineapple": "Most contact I have seen—We were ducking bullets for 2 hours—We didn't lose anybody though the company next to us did." I calculated back to pinpoint what I had been doing about that time and remembered my sense of panic before leaving Roby. I dreaded a premonition almost as much as the green army sedan. Yet there was no concrete correlation, I knew in my heart, only a desperate grasping for a sense of immediate connection with Lee.

The letter was a magic one; Lee elaborated about loving and missing me. I felt terrific and reassured.

Susan turned off the vacuum, abandoning interest in the floor as quickly as she had taken it up. "How's Lee?"

"Fine," I said, "just as long as he keeps dodging bullets." Both of my friends looked at me with horror-stricken faces. "He is in a war, you know," I reminded them.

Connie found her voice first. "Does he write you about that?"

"Of course," I said with surprise and read to them the airmobile paragraph.

"How do you stand it?" Connie asked, stunned.

"Why do you think I'm such a mess all the time?" I laughed. They were taking the news harder than I was. Besides, this particular contact didn't bother me anymore. Lee had survived it.

"Well," Susan said, her face growing red, "Tom had damned well better never write me anything like that."

"I'm the one who made Lee promise to tell me what is going on," I said, defending him. "How else will I know what he's going through?"

"Well, I don't want to know," Susan said angrily and busied herself with collecting empty boxes.

"I guess I had no idea," Connie said as she sank to the sofa, "not really. No wonder you can't relax."

I was amazed that they thought this was bad. They didn't even know about the booby trap explosion. "I'm sure there's lots he leaves out. But I'd rather have facts than my imagination."

A door opened down the hallway and a petite woman in slacks and a sweater came toward us, a towel wrapped around her head. She was trailed by a miniature Dachshund and a Siamese I recognized as Susan's cat, Daphne. With her hand extended and eyes smiling, she introduced herself. "I'm Marjorie Sheldon and I'm sorry to be such a mess. You must be tired. Sus, did you offer them something to drink?"

Before heading for the kitchen, Susan picked up the dog and said, "And this is your new roommate, Oscar. He's mother shadow, but he'll be staying with us."

I liked Marjorie Sheldon instantly. "Please do forgive my turban," she said. "I just had to get out of those filthy clothes and take a shower. Susan is working me to death." She laughed, at once embarrassed, gracious, formal, and genuine. Warmth emanated from her face, which gathered into gentle laugh lines when she smiled. "What do you think of the place?"

Susan stepped into the role of tour guide and directed us first to the kitchen, a large room that suffered hangover decor from the fifties, with its gray, mottled linoleum blocks and L-shaped gray ceramic-tiled counters trimmed in black. A strip of incongruent turquoise blocks formed a thin line across the backsplash above the counters, and two large, unadorned windows over the sink revealed a small enclosed yard at the back of the flat. "I don't know, maybe some curtains will help," Susan said about the drabness as she led us past the room's eating area and down the hall to the two bedrooms. The two curious animals followed.

"We'll share this one as long as Mother is here," Susan said as we entered a surprisingly spacious bedroom that had an attached bath. "We got the twin beds out of storage so now we just have to decide how to arrange them. Of course, Daphne gets first choice." She pointed to the railings, bedsteads, and mattresses leaned against the walls, laughing as she scooped the cat into her arms. She knew I hated cats, and she had enjoyed watching her Siamese torture me with attention in their quarters at Bragg. Now I was going to be living with the damned thing.

Susan then showed us a smaller bedroom across the hall as well as the main bathroom before she took us downstairs. At the back of the garage, a doorway led to a yard that was a manicured miniature of the Japanese Gardens Lee and I had visited on our tour of San Francisco. The red and pink flowers bowed respectfully to the Oriental poses of the slender sculptured tree branches, while the soft golden and purple blossoms invited visitors into serenity that defied the noises of the surrounding city. It was an enclave of escape within a high stucco wall.

After touring the flat, the four of us fell into step and proceeded with settling in. Connie helped me unload the car to add my trappings to the clutter; Susan and Mrs. Sheldon assembled beds and located linens. On one of my trips up, Susan came running down to meet me, yanking the suitcase from my hand. "You shouldn't be carrying this," she scolded and then yelled, "Mother, Connie, don't let Linda lift anything heavy." She exaggerated over her shoulder as she headed up the stairs, "Jesus, I'd have to call ol' Lee up in Viet-n-a-m and tell him Linda had a miscarriage. I don't even have his phone number, so don't do that again." I followed her, feeling simultaneously pampered and useless. It hadn't occurred to me that I would have to alter my ways; I had just been getting accustomed to doing them a little more awkwardly.

Our combined efforts soon shaped the outlines of order from the tangled chaos. Because I was not allowed to participate in furniture arranging, I turned my attention to the tasks of hanging clothes and finding homes for all the ornamental accessories stacked on every ledge and sill. Enchanted with the collection of exotic treasures, I continually asked about the history of each. The figurine on the mantle that had all but obstructed my view of Lee's letter turned out to be a rearing stallion carved from a single slab of lapis lazuli, a gift from a close friend and member of the Kuwaiti royal family. Beside the horse sat two jewel-encrusted golden headdresses that Mrs. Sheldon explained were actually only papier-mâché and glass costume pieces worn in the film *The King and I*. A friend had given them to her. From the time she and I decided that they alone should adorn the mantle, they became favorites of mine as they sat poised, waiting for the return of their dancers.

I found myself surrounded by Chinese nests-of-tables and an intricately carved ebony standing bar, piles of Persian wool and camelhair carpets, Turkish copper pots and brass trays, a thousand-year-old pottery vase unearthed in the Arabian Desert, antique Japanese screens, Philippine mother-of-pearl dishes, jade figurines, and cloisonné bowls. Museums would have envied the cache. I delighted in running my fingers over each discovery and listening enraptured to the episodes Susan and her mother related about the procurement of these wonders, which, to them, were simply the accessories with which they lived.

I noticed that Connie, too, became mesmerized by the sagas that I continued to extract from Mrs. Sheldon. By the time we collapsed for a makeshift dinner, the three of us had imposed the role of storyteller on her, a function that she reluctantly accepted though she periodically pleaded, "Oh, you don't want to hear about how I got that old thing." Then Susan, who, of course, knew all the stories by heart, would eagerly prompt her, "Yes, Mother, but isn't that the time you took the boat to Adak?"

Mrs. Sheldon's life had been a series of adventures and misadventures of travel, foreign posting, and cultural adjustments. Hers might have been no more unusual than those of other expatriates, but her sense of humor and naiveté provided a fertile background for amusing escapades, which she recounted as oral cartoons and slapstick skits. She spoke with obvious affection for her friends, some whose names I recognized from the newspapers.

Had Mrs. Sheldon been at all pretentious, I might have been intimidated. But as she sat lotus-style with Oscar asleep on her legs, I detected that interwoven into all her tales was the perspective thread of a girl from Rotan. I intuitively recognized the viewpoint and values that West Texas indelibly instilled and appreciated the propensity those mindsets could provide for international calamities.

I realized that for the first time in months, I did not have a knot in my stomach. I felt a pinch of guilt to acknowledge that I had gone for hours without consciously worrying about Lee. Even though I was exhausted when I climbed into bed, I felt rested in a way that had nothing to do with sleep or tired muscles.

"Linda?" Connie asked hesitantly a few minutes after we turned out the lights, "does Susan love Tom?"

"Of course, she does. Very much, I think. Why?"

"She doesn't seem upset that he's gone."

"If you knew her better, you'd see the difference. When she's happy, she's not this high-strung and she's extremely methodical. Today she jumped from one thing to another and she talked fast and joked about everything. She's just going to deny it for awhile. Then she'll crash." I felt confident about how well I knew Susan but dreaded my own prediction. I had seen a look of wild panic flash in Susan's eyes more than once that day—just before she put down one thing and started another.

"You two are so dissimilar. I thought you were going to lose your mind the night Lee left," Connie groaned.

"Well, you know me," I laughed, "I throw my whole being into the emotional vat and wallow in it. I guess I hope that if I suffer enough everything will turn out okay. Besides, Tom's going to be an advisor, not a grunt in the field. It's dangerous for any American over there, but his job's a little safer, I think. Of course, that's a relative term."

"And Lee is really getting shot at?" Connie said, still disbelieving.

"Perhaps as we speak," I answered fatalistically.

"What will you do about this baby if he gets killed?"

The one thing I always appreciated about Connie was her directness. I laughed, "Have it, Connie. I'm sort of committed."

"No, no, I mean," she said, "you're young. You've got the rest of your life ahead of you."

As frightening as the topic was, the conversation became less scary as we talked. "I could never be sorry about having Lee's baby. Connie, he has been the center of my life since I was seventeen. I know that everybody thinks I'll go crazy if anything happens to him. And I will for a while, probably a long while. I doubt that I will ever completely recover. But I'm not fragile. I'll crack into a million pieces, but I won't come apart."

"I know you won't," she said, reclining back to the pillow. Then she laughed and added softly, "But you'll give a good rendition of it."

I laughed too. "Yeah, I probably will. But you'll be there to see to it that I hold together."

"Oh, my. I hope to hell Lee knows what he's doing." I could see Connie's dim profile staring at the ceiling. "Does Lee snore?"

"No," I answered, surprised at her unexpected question. I wondered if she was thinking the night noise might get him killed.

"Do you remember when we were in high school and I asked you what you would do if you married Lee and found out that he snored?"

I chuckled at the memory of this one among many inane conversations we had then. "Yes, I remember."

She continued, "And you said, 'I'd harmonize.' I'll never forget it." She paused and added, "That's what you're doing now. You're harmonizing. Goodnight."

The guy at the gas station had been right. I was lucky. I had a safety net—of my family, my oldest friend, and my newest friends—that felt comforting as I balanced on the tightrope across this abyss called Vietnam. I gently rubbed my swollen tummy and added, *and I've got this baby.*

The next morning, over coffee served in an assortment of whatever unpacked mugs and cups we could find, the four of us summoned our energy for another day of moving in. The plumber arrived to connect the washer, the electrician came to add outlets, the landlord—daughter of the city's mayor, no less—dropped in to check on our status, and the phone rang incessantly as friends called to see if it was true that Marjorie was back in town.

Amid the activity, the four of us studied the placement of furniture. Then we would reshuffle, try again, and finally determine that this was, indeed, the perfect place for the couch, the corner for this table—the kind of trial-and-error, let's-see-how-it-looks approach that fulfills women and drives men insane. Because there were no husbands around, we did this to our hearts' content and could have decorated four apartments with our efforts.

By early evening, I began to feel guilty about Connie. I had invited her to San Francisco, not a move-in fest. When I mentioned this after dinner, Susan suggested we see the sights at night.

Within minutes of taking off from the flat to "see the lights," the motion of the moving car lulled us into admitting our exhaustion. So that Connie could say she'd been there, Susan drove us through tourist-filled streets and across the Golden Gate Bridge before we headed back to the apartment. Once there, we got comfortable and again cast Mrs. Sheldon as storyteller, making a slumber party of the occasion.

Sunday morning was a repeat of Saturday without the handymen and callers. I went to see if Connie was ready to go to the airport and to apologize for her lack of sightseeing.

"Are you kidding?" she asked. "I wouldn't have missed this for the world. These are the most fascinating people I've ever met."

Susan went with me to drop Connie off at the airport, and when we returned, the apartment seemed quiet and still, and yet homey. The three of us puttered around with a few more of the unfinished tasks before declaring the working weekend done.

Over bitter coffee dregs, Mrs. Sheldon suddenly laughed playfully and said, "Do you know what I'd like for dinner? Breakfast."

The homemade waffles, bacon, eggs, and toast she described sounded delicious. Who cared that it was seven o'clock at night? As we pulled out the mixer, griddle, and ingredients, we giggled over the fact that none of our husbands would find this an appropriate evening meal, and we scurried around like naughty children left too long unattended. Mrs. Sheldon, who threw elaborate dinner parties for sheiks and ambassadors, could also whip up a mean waffle. I found it amusing to see what a treat she considered this to be and then agreed with her as I experienced the warm, cozy sensation the food brought. It was like snuggling down under a protective blanket on a cold night.

Susan grew progressively quieter as we ate. For two days, she had been one continuous motion of energy and dialogue, heaving boxes and furniture and running up and down the back steps, all the while taking Connie under her wing like a long-lost friend and learning that the plumber had two kids and a baby who looked just like his wife. She had plied us all with witty comments and lightly sarcastic observations.

Now with her napkin in both hands, Susan deliberately wiped her mouth in a downward motion, leaving harsh red marks, and stared at the floor. Suddenly she scooted back her chair and took her plate to the sink. "I'll clean up tomorrow," she said hoarsely and she ducked her head, swooped up Daphne, and left the room.

Mrs. Sheldon and I looked at each other helplessly. We both knew the crash had begun.

{Chapter 10}

On Monday morning, I awoke to Daphne's large eyes peering into my face with a mix of curiosity and impishness. Damned cat. I tried shooing her away, but she ignored me until I picked her up and put her on the floor. Then we both slipped quietly from the room to keep from waking Susan.

Mrs. Sheldon was having coffee and reading the paper at the kitchen table. "Good morning," she said brightly. "Is Susan up?"

I shook my head and saw her face fall and her eyes water.

"Oh, dear," she signed heavily. "I just wish she weren't so angry about Tom's going to Vietnam."

"I don't think it would matter," I said, setting my coffee on the table and pulling up a chair. "I'm not angry, and it's still awful. Let's let her sleep."

I asked directions to the Presidio because I was eager to take the film I had received in Tucson to the Post Exchange to be developed. I called Letterman Army Hospital to make an appointment at the prenatal clinic, pulling the foyer telephone as far as I could away from the bedroom.

Even after Susan got up, just before noon, Mrs. Sheldon and I continued to talk and walk quietly. Susan tried to make her morning greeting sound natural, but the lack of energy in her voice and body betrayed her. She took the paper and went to the living room with coffee and Daphne.

I dashed into the bedroom to get dressed. Shortly, Mrs. Sheldon tiptoed in and, looking furtively over her shoulder, handed me a letter. We didn't exchange a word, only a conspiring eye contact, before she slipped back out of the room.

Feeling excited and guilty at the same time, I quickly sat down with the thick envelope—too thick, meaning more military papers. To my surprise I found the only document was a pay chart that accompanied another three-page letter, which, to my disappointment, was devoted to our finances. The last page read:

My pay as of July pay raise:
440 Base pay
110 housing
48 Subsistence
65 Combat
30 Separation
$702
– $40 for chow
20 SS
400 savings
50 me
You will get about $200—is that enough?

No, I thought, it wasn't enough, but I knew I wouldn't tell Lee, not until I absolutely had to. I looked at the chart and wondered how the wife of a private E-1 survived on a base pay of $123.00. How strange that Uncle Sam paid a private who was fighting a war so little, and how bizarre to add $65 for getting shot at, or at least being in a combat zone. Who decided that the cost of being separated could be compensated by $30?

Caught up in my grappling over money, I didn't hear Susan come in until it was too late. I jumped when she said tersely, "You don't have to hide your letter. I heard Mother go downstairs for the mail." It was an odd sensation to feel both so good and so bad about hearing from Lee.

"Maybe you'll hear tomorrow," I offered lamely.

"It won't change a goddamn thing if I do," she snapped and then left the room.

I knew Susan wasn't angry with me, yet I was sorry she didn't blow up. A good, shrieking tantrum followed by convulsive sobs would have been easier to deal with than her silent withdrawal, but I'd seen no sign of tears. I wondered if I should goad her into an eruption, and then reminded myself that she was entitled to deal with this in her own way. A sense of inadequacy overwhelmed me. How foolish to think I could help someone else through this trauma. No wonder the military had no training program for wives—nothing could have prepared us.

I could not help but compare this experience with World War II—at least as related through the movies. In that era, men had shipped out in whole units, and there was no household in America unaffected. Those waiting wives must have had a place in the society of their country at war.

• • •

Following Mrs. Sheldon's directions, I cautiously headed toward the Presidio, and after topping a couple of breathtaking hills, I found myself at the back gate of the post, a miraculous five minutes from our flat. Being on a military reservation again felt like being home, even though I'd never before seen the two-lane road that curved through the thick trees and down to San Francisco Bay. I followed the signs to the post exchange (PX).

Instantly, though, I recognized the difference between this garrison and Fort Bragg. Besides its scenic location beneath the looming arch of the Golden Gate Bridge and its diminutive size, the most notable feature was the men. In their dress greens, they walked like civilians in uniform. Nowhere did I see fatigues and jump boots. No one swaggered with the cockiness of combat troops. Movements were conserved, voices muted. This was not the Army I knew, where soldiers were rambunctious when dismissed, talking loudly and punching shoulders in horseplay. No, this was a somber place with an elitist attitude.

The PX was familiar, however, with its displays of lead crystal and name brand items that I never had been able to afford. None of the merchandise compared in value to the roll of film I held tightly clutched in my hand. I was reluctant to entrust it to the processing envelope and then crushed to learn that developing would take almost a week. Commercial companies would have done it more quickly but also more expensively. I would have to wait.

At least the delay provided me with something to look forward to, I decided as I climbed back into the car and turned the key. Nothing happened. I tried again. Nothing. Damned battery cables. I popped the hood and got out.

I cursed the white and green acid barnacles growing atop the battery poles. They knew they were now safely out of reach from Daddy's hammer. I leaned awkwardly past the hump in my abdomen to try shaking the cables. They refused to budge, taunting me with their stubbornness. Furious, I reached down and yanked off my right shoe. I'd show those connectors. I struck a resounding blow at one with the heel. As I reared back to bring down my strike toward the second, I caught the sight of an Army jeep stopping behind the car. I froze. Two military policemen dismounted. While one momentarily disappeared around the vehicle to approach me from the left, the one on the right adjusted his holster against his leg and with the flick of his wrist loosened the cover. They both looked very young. I stood motionless, stooping over the engine with my shoe still poised above my head. The MPs moved in ever so slowly, crouching slightly, knees bent for action. Good god, did they think I was holding a gun? I was afraid to move except to raise my other hand in surrender.

Finally, when they had satisfied themselves that each was in position and that I was surrounded, the MP on the right asked officiously, "Trouble, ma'am?"

"Can I stand up now?"

"Slowly, please."

Were they kidding? How threatening could a pregnant woman beating on her car battery be? I slowly straightened my aching back into an arch, bringing my arms down cautiously and said, "Shoe. It's a shoe." I held it out for both to see.

Each eyed the pump and me with suspicion. "It's just a connection problem," I enunciated each word carefully.

The speaking MP adjusted his holster again and asked, "This your car, ma'am?"

I fought back a retort. *No, I always go around molesting other people's car batteries.*

"Yes," I answered politely and pointed to the corrosion. They inched forward to peer under the hood.

"You should tell your husband to get that fixed," the same MP instructed. Apparently the partner was a mute.

Regretting by now that my shoe was not a weapon that I could brandish in his face, I said, "I don't think he can do much about it. He's in Vietnam." This guy I would have gladly offered up to the enemy in Lee's place.

"Well, then," he said, "he should have had it fixed before he went."

The MPs retraced their cautious steps in rewind fashion, climbed aboard their jeep, and then drove out of the parking lot.

As I turned back to glare at the cables, I saw that a small crowd had gathered at a distance to watch the MPs' daring performance. Now a couple of the uniforms broke away and headed toward me, followed by more on-lookers, and soon I found myself edged to the side as several men elbowed in to examine the engine and speculate. I tried to interject, watching in horror as they tentatively pulled wires loose, unscrewed caps, and daintily tinkered, careful not to get their hands too dirty. What was it about men and raised hoods that made them think they could diagnosis trouble with motors they knew nothing about? It was obvious from their comments and unskilled fumbling that they were unschooled in auto mechanics, yet, as though expecting a testosterone boost to provide them with clairvoyance, they fiddled.

Fortunately, the novelty wore off quickly, and the men began wandering away. As soon as I could re-insert myself next to the car, I again took off my shoe, whacked the second cable, and tried the key. Thankfully, the car started and I drove away. Another five minutes and one of them might have done some serious damage.

The cables had rarely given me consecutive problems so I risked a stop at the commissary, a nondescript warehouse near the water, where I flashed my ID card and entered the long, narrow building. I filled one cart and then a second before joining the checkout line that stretched across the store and down the aisle to the rear. The wait to pay took almost two hours.

Relieved at being able to find my way back to the apartment, I pressed the opener and pulled up the incline into the garage. Susan was down the back steps before I could get out of the car. Alarm covered her face and I froze.

"Are you all right?" she asked.

"What's wrong?" I asked, unable to breathe.

"You were gone so long," she huffed and leaned against the car, "we were afraid you got lost or something."

My muscles went slack. God, I was becoming as bad as the Lannings, panicking at the slightest nuance and assuming a doomsday delivery was lurking behind every expression.

"No, I just went to the commissary. Here, grab a couple of sacks," I instructed, opening the trunk.

As I eased the last sack onto the counter, I explained about the overcrowded commissary and dramatized my episode with the MPs, which had become hysterically funny to me. I reenacted the scene of holding up my shoe and then the other hand while replicating my stooped stance of surrender. Mrs. Sheldon and I laughed so hard that we had tears in our eyes. Susan sat stone-faced.

"Do you mean to tell me that those MPs drove away without helping you?" she asked, tight-lipped.

"At least they didn't arrest me for assault and battery," I punned. Mrs. Sheldon and I went into another fit.

"Shit," Susan said, really angry now.

"Susan!"

"Oh, come off it, Mother. I cannot believe those fucking military bastards didn't help Linda."

Susan knocked her chair back as she jumped up. Scooping Daphne up, she headed down the hall, muttering, "Military bastards."

Mrs. Sheldon and I looked at each other. Obviously, my story had triggered an overreaction; the two young MPs were now being held accountable for all military sins, the biggest of which was sending Tom to Vietnam.

"Oh, my," Mrs. Sheldon sighed. "Her language."

"I'd never have enough nerve to say those kinds of things about the military," I admitted, surprised at my own timidity. "I know Susan's angry, but I just can't relate to it. I mean, sometimes, I hate the Army and the way it does things. But Lee wanted to go so I can't really blame the Army. Tom volunteered, too."

I felt a tinge of sympathy for Tom. It must have been difficult for him to leave with Susan so hostile. Lee had my support, such as it was. Then suddenly I wondered if that was noble or stupid on my part. Maybe Susan was right, and if all women reacted that way, and had the guts to voice it, maybe there would no longer be war because nobody would show up. The ancient Greek women had pulled off foiling a war in one of their dramas. Maybe we could have, too.

The next day Mrs. Sheldon and I thought relief had arrived when Susan and I both had letters. As an old pro, I noted the thickness of Tom's envelope and wondered if he, too, padded his letters with military paperwork. I hoped not, because I feared we would have a bonfire in the bedroom if Susan saw anything that looked official.

Susan's mood worsened, if anything, after she read the letter. I hoped Tom hadn't been dumb enough to sound excited about his trip and job, though I suspected he had done just that. After all, he was a West Texas boy, too, fulfilling his desire to travel and see the world. Writing Susan how thrilled he was about his adventure would be a dreadful mistake.

I, on the other hand, was on a roll, receiving mail three days in a row. Had I known this was possible I would have come to San Francisco sooner. Lee's letter, however, quickly dispelled any ideas I had about coming to expect daily deliveries. He wrote from Long Binh:

> We got extended for another day here—Will go north tomorrow.
>
> When we get there we will pull 5 days in Fire Base—guarding arty—then 15 days in field—1 hot meal every 3 days—resupply, mail in and out every 5 days and of course sometimes longer—So don't worry about no mail. All my records, Next of Kin, etc., are in order—If anything happens to me U. Sam will notify you immediately—No mail merely means no resupply.
>
> Lots of bad rumors about the north—Many NVA but no booby traps—those damn booby traps had everyone damn near crazy around here.
>
> Everyone having a good time here—they have band and entertainment for us at night plus free beer—good break.

Lee had confirmed in an earlier letter that in a war soldiers were bored 95 percent of the time and terrified the other 5 percent. I envied their knowing which was which because I lived in fear 100 percent of the time.

I knew only after the fact when I needn't have worried, which gave me no timeouts, no king's Xs. In a perverse way, I found myself irritated that Lee had been safe and secure while I fretted, and now that he had already gone north, I was again without reprieve. And, too, it seemed ludicrous that while I suffered anxiety attacks he was drinking beer and enjoying a band. There was either something very wrong with this war or with my head. Both were highly suspect.

So Susan and I were a fun pair of inmates for Mrs. Sheldon to warden while she tried to complete the apartment and be on her way back to Tehran to rejoin her husband. Some days Susan did not get out of bed except to recapture Daphne if the devilish cat escaped from our room. Trying to give Susan all the space she needed, I spent my time with Mrs. Sheldon. Because we had grown up in the same region, even if in different generations, we understood each other in ways that left Susan mystified.

"Oh, Linda," Mrs. Sheldon would say with a chuckle and a shake of her head, "you remind me so much of me when I was your age." I was flattered by the comparison although I could read underlying messages that implied naiveté and innocence that I was sure were unfounded.

I was at the PX when it opened on Saturday to pick up the pictures, which I had forgotten were slides and not prints. After buying a miniature viewer, I hurried to the car and inserted frame after frame. And suddenly, there he was—in two-inch-square living color—walking right toward me through a grassy field. His fatigue shirt, with sleeves rolled, was unbuttoned, and dog tags dangled on his bare chest. His empty arms fell at his side as he looked downward to his left.

I followed Lee's gaze and saw what looked like two, maybe three, bodies lying on the ground. I gasped and squinted harder. Yes, there was a foot and clearly a hand. God, why couldn't I make this picture bigger? Our slide projector was uselessly stored in a warehouse in North Carolina, so I had no way of enlarging the scene even when I got home. Surely Lee wouldn't have sent me pictures of wounded Americans, although I recalled he had mailed the film shortly after the booby trap explosion in May.

Disregarding the commissary list, I rushed home. I needed help interpreting what I was seeing and thrust the viewer into Mrs. Sheldon's hands. "Here, look at this," I panted.

She squeezed the light button and peered into the plastic box. "Ah, Linda," she said sweetly, "isn't he cute?"

"No, no. Look around him."

She clutched her chest and gasped, "Jesus, are they dead?"

"What it is now?" Susan asked as she arrived on the scene and took the viewer for herself. The three of us passed it back and forth, searching for an explanation. Lee was in a rice paddy, not a grassy field, they assured me, recognizing the background from their days in the Philippines. We all agreed that the situation must not have been dangerous because Lee was not carrying his rifle. Lee's face, while obviously dirty—we hoped not bloody—was not distraught enough to be looking at dead or wounded men. His walk was too casual, also. After a couple of hours of studying all the slides and this one in particular, we convinced ourselves that surely the platoon was taking a break and that the bodies were napping men, though they still looked peculiar, curled up on the open ground.

Once persuaded that no danger or tragedy existed, I focused on Lee. He had obviously lost weight, his hair was now sun-bleached blond, his olive skin a golden tan, and Mrs. Sheldon was right: he really was cute.

Back to the Presidio PX I went to order this picture enlarged to an eight by ten. I didn't care about the extra money it would cost; I couldn't afford to be without it. Although I admitted it to no one, my memories of Lee were growing dimmer and wispier, and in spite of my best intentions and my ceaseless worry, he was becoming less tangible and more dreamlike. I was beginning to feel as if I were married to an airmail envelope. The picture would help me keep him real.

{Chapter 11}

Our first visitor other than Connie in our Collins Street flat was Susan's brother Miles. Having played football lineman at a small Utah junior college the previous year, Miles was a husky twenty-year-old transferring to San Francisco State and half of the reason the Sheldons were leasing the apartment. It was to be his weekend getaway from school when he needed it.

Miles surveyed the progress we had made and nodded with tentative approval. I sensed that I was watching the proverbial bull just as it stepped into the china shop as he moved around the living and dining rooms, his muscular, sweeping arm motions threatening contrasts to the fragile knick-knacks adorning most of the spaces.

"I think this vase would look better on the small round table over there," he said confidently. "And that screen would do more for the room if it weren't so close to the wall."

He lifted the vase and exchanged it for a flower arrangement with a graceful ease that surprised me. Then he flexed his muscles and gently adjusted the heavy mother-of-pearl and teak tri-fold divider. He was right; they did look better.

Miles continued to be a study of contradictions. His booming voice shook the apartment when he yelled from room to room, shocking our ears that had grown accustomed to subdued conversation. In talking to his mother, though, he was soft-spoken and gracious. To Susan, he was a taunting little brother looking for ways to torment her. If she rose to the occasion, they embroiled themselves in shouting matches that I was sure would terminate their relationship. If she retreated from a confrontation on the brink of emotion, he would quietly comfort her, reassuring her that he understood how tough it was for her to have Tom gone.

When Miles discovered that I could cook chicken-fried steak and make white gravy, I became his buddy, though I didn't understand why he thought that was a special talent; every woman I knew in West Texas did it weekly, if not daily. Having spent less time visiting Rotan than Susan, Miles found the culture there as bizarre and fascinating as I found the one in San Francisco. He mocked my Texas accent with good humor and plied me with questions about growing up on a farm with cattle and horses.

Miles found a hard-hat summer job and moved into the apartment with us until his place near the college was available. Mrs. Sheldon gave him the small bedroom and slept on the hide-a-bed in the living room. Other than his appearance at the evening meal between work and going out, we didn't see much of Miles, except now and then when he brought his friends by.

His friends were an interesting collection themselves. Most were typical college boys, shy and polite around family. One, however, defied categorizing. Randy was a tall average-build fellow with blond hair that constantly fell into his eyes, causing him to arrogantly toss his head to flip the long strands back into place. He moved like a strutting peacock and rolled his shoulders forward when he walked as if he were pushing his way through a disgusting crowd of people slightly shorter than he.

The most intriguing thing about Randy was his clothes. Blessed with more money than taste, Randy spent exorbitant amounts on his apparel, which ranged from the latest tight-fitting European fashions to colored tuxedos and ruffled shirts. Any time Mrs. Sheldon, Susan, and I knew Randy was expected, we found excuses to be in the living room to enjoy the show, for he had more shoes and gold chains than the three of us combined.

Randy never stepped out of character. He always stood within sight of one of the mirrors and constantly combed his hair as he told us about his rock band. I was uncertain if Randy played in the group or simply poured thousands into financing it. Randy could be vague if he thought the truth might tarnish his image.

Miles and his friends always left me perplexed. While Randy was certainly material for amusement, I continued to be struck by the comparison between these boys and Lee, Tom, and the troops in Vietnam. Miles and his friends were the same age as most of the soldiers slogging through the mud and dodging booby traps, yet their lives were happy-go-lucky and carefree. The college boys were well-groomed, or at least expensively groomed, and their biggest worries were about planning activities for Saturday nights while Lee and his platoon were sweaty and muddy with their biggest worries about who would be the next wounded or killed. It wasn't just that these boys were still in college and not yet ready to do their patriotic part. They were never going to Vietnam and made no pretenses otherwise.

Each time Miles introduced Susan and me to a friend and explained that we were waiting wives, I could see a knee-jerk reaction of withdrawal, like someone recoiling from a dangerous snake. Their muscles would stiffen, causing them to all but retract an extended hand before they could overcome their response. The more vocal ones made it clear that they were opposed to the war; the quieter ones said little and eyed us with wary looks, as though getting near a person who knew someone in Vietnam might make them more susceptible.

"Can you imagine Randy in the rice paddies?" I asked Susan one evening as we lingered in the living room after he had picked up Miles. Randy had been wearing his blue tux with blue-edged ruffles on his white shirt. My imagination could advance far enough to see the tux muddy and the blond hair tangled, but I could never bring him into focus in fatigues and a helmet.

"Randy would never go to Vietnam," Susan said, sounding surprised at the absurdity of the idea.

"Oh, I know. But it does seem strange that they are all so unaffected. They make me feel old."

"Randy's your age. You know, they're not wrong not to want to go to Vietnam."

I knew Susan was thinking of Miles; a hint of defensiveness edged her voice.

"No, they're not wrong," I agreed quickly. "They're probably the smart ones. It just seems like the world is out of synch when males of the same age from the same country, I don't know, have such different experiences and different attitudes about obligations."

"Do you resent Miles and his friends?" Susan asked.

"No, not at all," I answered, because resentment had not been my reaction. "They just make me feel old and alien."

"Well," Susan drawled in mock weariness, "you are alien. You're from W-e-s-t Texas. That's about as alien as you can get."

I tossed a pillow across the room at her and laughed, "The only thing stranger is an outsider choosing to marry one of us."

"Yeah, well, I wouldn't have done that if I'd known he was really going to go to Vietnam. Of all the stupid, dumb-assed things Tom has ever done. He could have stayed in graduate school. He didn't have to go."

I considered Tom. He thought he was simply an advisor in the rice paddies of the Mekong Delta when, in fact, he was also a husband in big trouble in San Francisco. Although I did not understand his and Lee's need for adventure that had to include guns, I could fathom it more than I could Susan's anger. But maybe she was right. Maybe I should be angry, too.

Still, the closest I could come to anger were irritations in varying degrees of intensity. One occurred when Lee asked me to look up the San Francisco family of one of his lieutenant friends, "either wife or mother, I'm not sure which. He's a good guy," he had written. Susan and Mrs. Sheldon identified the address as being in the heart of Chinatown. Finding my way to the Presidio was one thing, but I was not yet ready to attempt the hills and narrow streets of the rest of the city. Besides, I thought Lee should get better acquainted with this fellow before I went calling, which was definitely a West Texas thing to do. I wasn't so sure it was a Chinese tradition.

I ignored the visiting instruction until Lee's third mention of the Jongs. By now I knew I was looking for the soldier's mother. So I dutifully looked up the phone number and called, hoping no one would be home so I could write Lee that I had tried. At least maybe he would then stop using up precious space on the pages of his letters telling me to go see this family.

A woman answered, and after a few confusing moments of awkward translations, seemed to confirm that I had the right number. I explained who I was and asked if I could stop by to introduce myself—or something to that effect. Unfortunately, between her heavy Chinese and my Southern/Texas accents, the conversation was two simultaneous one-sided affairs. For my part, I told her that I would arrive in about an hour. I had no idea if she had said "fine" or "don't come."

With great trepidation, I ventured into Chinatown, struggling to watch for streets and addresses amid the colorful linear signs and Asian pedestrians. I would have been no more bewildered had my car been a time machine suddenly depositing me for an unscheduled stop. Cocooned in the metal capsule, I eased slowly through the crowds and vehicles, silently cursing Lee: first, for making a Chinese friend and second, for requesting this mission. I harbored no prejudice against Chinese; I'd never met one. My only problem, aside from trying not to get lost, was that I had seen too many movies where victims were shanghaied from such surroundings.

I parked when I found the correct number and sat for several minutes, collecting myself and wondering why I was there. If Mrs. Jong and I could not communicate over the phone, how were we going to manage face-to-face? Eventually I started the long climb up the steps to the front door and then, huffing and puffing, rang the bell. Waiting anxiously for a couple of heartbeats, I began to feel relieved when there was no answer.

Just as I turned to leave, the door opened and a small woman in a maroon sweater said something that sounded like, "Ah so." Or maybe I had expected her words to sound like that.

Mrs. Jong motioned me inside, and I followed her pantomimed directions to sit, fighting the ridiculous urge to bow repeatedly to compensate for my lack of understanding anything she was saying. She spoke very rapidly, but I did catch "friend" and "Don" and wondered if she knew it was Lee, not me, who knew her son.

Animated and eager, Mrs. Jong darted quickly about the room, fluffing pillows and straightening in-place chairs as she talked. I sat with a frozen smile on my face and tried even harder not to bow. At one point she stopped, patted her abdomen, and pointed at me, smiling happily. At least we had established that I was pregnant. Then she sat down expectantly and waited. Oh, no, I thought, suppose she thinks I've come to tell her news about her son. I didn't have bad news; I had no news at all. Lee had never told me anything except that Lieutenant Jong had a mother. I didn't even know his name was Don until she said it. I had unwittingly assumed that people with family members in Vietnam had some sort of automatic bond. How was I going to get out of this gracefully?

So I just started talking as though Mrs. Jong understood my every word. The discourse was short so I repeated over and over what a great guy my husband thought Don was.

Mrs. Jong sat smiling and bowing—or was that deep nodding—as I talked, her gray-streaked black hair in constant motion. Suddenly she jumped up and said, "You come."

I followed my hostess to the kitchen where a man with an armload of paper bags was entering through the back door. The two of them conversed as I stood back. Mrs. Jong took one of the sacks and began pulling out white butcher paper packages. She smiled and motioned for me to come closer.

Mrs. Jong turned her attention back to the packages and, periodically smiling at me, proceeded to unwrap the goods as she continued to talk, sometimes toward me, sometimes toward the man she seemed to call "Uncle." Obviously pleased, she held up the contents of each for me to see. I recognized nothing I knew as edible, but the smell now wafting through the room was overwhelming. I was growing more nauseated by the minute. I held my breath to keep the pungent and odious smells from penetrating my nostrils and stared at the floor to avoid seeing the bloody and strange carcasses covering the table and counter. "Uncle" grabbed a hatchet and began to chop, releasing more odious smells as he diced the grotesque cadavers into more repulsive globs.

I gasped for breath only to inhale more smells. Covering my mouth and contracting my stomach, I mumbled, "I have to be going. Thank you. Thank you so much."

Mrs. Jong came running around the table as I backed out of the room, protesting and, I thought, insisting I stay for lunch because she kept waving toward the mound of food. "I really must go," I said, exhaling and bowing. Once more in the living room, I breathed again, but the smell had now permeated the house. *Oh, God, I'm going to be sick,* I thought desperately. I bowed again and again as I hurried to the front door. "Thank you again."

Mrs. Jong, who had been wearing a look of distress over my abrupt departure, suddenly smiled, patted her tummy, and nodded her head. "Baby," she said with a knowing look.

I raced down the steps and into the car. Thank goodness Mrs. Jong seemed to understand at least the baby part. We were not able to connect about Vietnam, but the universal propensity for pregnant women to be nauseated by sights and smells had bridged our language gap.

Back at the flat, I related my misadventure to Susan and Mrs. Sheldon, both of whom were holding their sides in fits of laughter by the time I finished.

"I don't even know if the poor woman even knows why I was there," I sighed.

Susan gasped for a breath and suggested, "She probably thought you were telling her that her son had knocked you up before he went to Vietnam. She was just trying to fatten you up on her good food, to take good care of grandbaby-san."

"Oh, no," I moaned. "I hadn't even thought about that. She must be terribly confused."

When Mrs. Sheldon could talk again, she said, wiping tears from her eyes, "Oh, Linda, first you almost get arrested for battering your car and now you've wreaked havoc in Chinatown. What will you do next?"

It was a valid question.

July 1969

{Chapter 12}

The three of us women on Collins Street took turns making the trek downstairs to the garage mail slot, usually more than once a day because our postman was as unpredictable in his delivery time as was our mail supply. Susan and I awaited airmail envelopes from Vietnam; Mrs. Sheldon looked for hers from Tehran. Spotting the red and blue stripes in the box meant someone in the house would be rewarded for her patience—or impatience, as the case might be.

Tom's legal-size envelopes were always thick, and I finally decided it was because he was a writer with bachelor's and master's degrees in journalism. Susan routinely disappeared into the bedroom for a long period each time one arrived. The thicker the letter, the brighter the blaze in her eyes when she reappeared. Really big letters brought an aftermath of door slamming and muttered profanities. Though Susan never said, I suspected those tomes were dissertations on rice growing and agricultural aspects of Vietnam, which intrigued Tom and irritated Susan.

Envelopes for Mrs. Sheldon were identifiable even from their back sides because they were clean and crisp, despite the fact that they had traveled from farther away. She would pop her reading glasses atop the end of her nose and chuckle as she read while sitting at the kitchen table. "Oh, Sus, listen to this," she would say with a laugh and then relay the news item, stopping to fill me in on backgrounds and thus provide more fascinating stories about far away places and sometimes incorrigible characters. The three of us could easily convert one of her letters into a full day's conversation.

Mail from Lee most often arrived in letter-size envelopes that were distinguishable by their muddy smears on both sides. I usually retreated to a chair in the living room to read, translate, and savor them. Whereas before I had been able to estimate the length based solely on thickness, I honed my skills by assessing the state of the envelope. The dirtier it was, the shorter the letter would be.

"I hope this is mud, not blood," Mrs. Sheldon said one morning during the first week of July as she handed me a heavily smudged letter.

I felt the grit on my fingers as I opened the thin envelope, trying to concentrate on my relief at hearing from Lee instead of disappointment at the brevity of his communication. The single page, torn from a small tablet, was so caked with red clay that I had trouble focusing on the words. But this particular little miserable-looking message proved that big surprises really could come in small packages. Lee wrote that he would go back to the brigade main base for seven days, starting on June 28, to act as company executive officer.

I was ecstatic. Seven whole days without worry, I calculated. By now three of the seven were already gone—well, actually, with the date change, closer to four. But that did not matter. I might even get to enjoy the Fourth of July. Yes, I could celebrate, too.

I went running for the kitchen. "Lee's out of the field for seven days!" I shouted, waving the reddened page.

A flash of horror at the sight of the crusted letter crossed Mrs. Sheldon's face before she caught herself.

"It's okay," I reassured her. "He may be muddy, but he's alive. And no one is shooting at him until after the weekend."

Mrs. Sheldon looked at me as though I had lost my mind.

When life is good, life is grand. That afternoon I got a call from Cheryl Hightower, my friend from Bragg and Benning. I was thrilled to hear from her and delighted when she said that she and Steve were in San Francisco, though my heart skipped a beat when I realized why.

"When?" I asked cryptically.

"We have a few more days," Cheryl answered haltingly. Then she cleared her throat and forced her normal voice. "We'd like to take you and your roommate to dinner at the Presidio Officers' Club tomorrow night. Are you free?"

Was I free? She had no idea. The only things on my life's calendar were

2 December 1969: Baby due, and
18 April, 1970: Lee comes home.

In between, I was completely available.

That night as Susan and I sat talking, facing each other across our twin beds that were aligned foot-to-foot along the width of the room, I told Susan about Cheryl and Steve so she would have background for the next night.

If there was one thing Susan loved, it was stories about people—not gossip but the material for analysis. She could become totally absorbed in trying to figure out what made people tick. For her, every person she met was a mystery to be solved, just as the novels she voraciously read were to be finished. A keen observer of human behavior, Susan would, I knew, confirm or contradict everything I told her about the Hightowers.

"Cheryl is truly a sweet person," I said.

"Oh, yuck," Susan grimaced. "I don't know if I can handle 'sweet.'"

"I usually don't like 'sweet' people either," I said, arching an eyebrow at her, "present company included. But you'll like her, even though I hate it when people assure me that I'm going to just love their friends. It's a sure sign I'll find them obnoxious."

"What's her husband like?"

"Steve is quiet and polite, and he's crazy about Cheryl. He must be. He drinks her coffee." Then I told Susan about Cheryl's money-saving grounds, a story she loved and repeated to her mother the next morning.

Susan and I were ready half an hour before the Hightowers were due the following evening. "Well, it's obvious that we have become wallflowers," Susan observed as we sat waiting in the living room. "Look at us. You'd think this was the first time in our lives that we'd been out to dinner."

"In this life, it is, unless you count that terrible meal we had the other night," I pointed out, reminding her of the experience when the three of us had walked the two blocks down the hill to a neighborhood restaurant. The food had been disappointing, if not disgusting, as well as expensive, and we had all felt uncomfortable from the stares three women alone received.

Promptly on time, the doorbell rang. As I reached for the door knob, Susan dashed past me down the hall. "Where are you going?" I asked.

"I don't want them to know I don't have a life," she said and disappeared into the bedroom.

Cheryl and Steve stood grinning on the landing when I opened the door. "Oh, I'm so glad to see you," I said, hugging my friend. "Come in. Come in."

I gave Steve a hug, too, which he didn't seem to mind, though his face turned a little red.

"Let me look at you," Cheryl exclaimed, holding me at arm's length. "You look wonderful pregnant. Look, Steve. Oh, I hope I look this way some day, too, when we have a baby." Steve's face turned redder and we all laughed.

I took their coats and we sat down to catch up. Cheryl and I jabbered while Steve surveyed the room and flipped the car keys in his hand, tolerating our giggles with a patient grace.

"This is a really great place," Steve said.

"All of the stuff belongs to Susan's mother. We invited her to come along with us tonight, but she already had plans."

"Where's your roommate?" Cheryl asked.

"She's hiding in the bedroom," I explained, "giving us time to get reacquainted. I'll get her and we'll go."

Susan came down the hall putting on her earring, which had been in place before the Hightowers arrived. What a ham.

Steve chauffeured their rental car as I gave directions. Cheryl said with awe, "Wow, Linda, I'm impressed. You just got here and you already know your way around."

I laughed while Susan set the record straight when she said, "She can get to the Presidio and back and that's all. Except Chinatown, but that's another story."

Our banter volleyed around the car until we arrived at the officers' club and Steve took the lead in talking with the reservation desk. We all assumed the proper decorum as we were seated in the sedate dining room. All of the officers' clubs I'd been in had the same look and feel—a quiet, understated atmosphere that at one period in history might have been genteel sophistication. Now, however, the muted aura was simply stuffy and condescending, like the senior officers and their wives who frequented the places.

Even so, the dining experience was pleasant, the service excellent, and the food divine. Perhaps the nicest thing about the place was the sense of privacy it afforded, as other diners seemed to pay no attention to us.

"You know, Linda," Susan said, inventorying the room, "we should join this club so we have a nice place to go for dinner without being stared at like freaks."

That struck me as a fine idea, especially since we were having a lovely meal and company. Susan and the Hightowers hit it off immediately, as Susan alternately told them hilarious stories and solicited experiences from them.

Steve asked army-type questions about Lee, and, thanks to the military focus of Lee's letters, I had a supply of answers, complete with the history of the 199th Light Infantry Brigade. I recounted for Steve the platoon's exploits in the Delta, omitting for Cheryl's sake any mention of the booby traps.

"He's in the Xuan Loc area now."

Cheryl shook her head and said, "I don't know how you keep all that straight."

I didn't want to confess that I memorized everything Lee wrote, so I said, "Lee writes love letters to the Army and sends them to me."

Cheryl laughed and said, "You're certainly handling this well. I hope I can be as strong as you." She looked desperately at Steve and squeezed his hand. I saw that he squeezed hers in return and smiled back reassuringly.

"You caught me on a good day," I said lightly. "Lee's the acting executive officer right now so I'm taking advantage of it."

"You should see her the rest of the time," Susan started. I kicked her under the table and shot her a warning look. Without missing a beat, she continued, "She just eats and eats and eats. This is going to be one fat baby."

Without otherwise conspiring to do so, Susan and I continued censoring our comments in front of Cheryl. Nothing would be gained by detailing for her how ungodly long her days were going to be, how agonizingly her lonely nights would stretch, how panic-stricken she might find herself in unguarded minutes, or how empty the hours would feel. She would find out all too quickly for herself. It became important to both

Susan and me that Cheryl be as happy as possible every minute she had left with Steve, as though we could vicariously feel some satisfactions.

For Steve we had mixed feelings. Certainly, we wanted him to be unharmed, not only for Cheryl's sake but also for his own. Yet, there was an underlying resentment toward him for what he was about to do to his wife. We couldn't change the situation, but we could protect Cheryl in every way we knew until the deed was done.

When the Hightowers dropped us off, Susan and I climbed the stairs and wandered into the living room, where we sat for a long while without saying a word. The image of Cheryl's innocence was haunting. I recognized her gestures and looks, the way she constantly touched Steve to reassure herself he was still there. My heart ached for her.

"You're right," Susan said eventually as she continued to stare at the floor. "Cheryl really is sweet and it's so genuine that she pulls it off. As bad as I hate my life right now, I wouldn't trade places with her for anything."

"I don't think I could live through it again," I said simply.

"How can such a fun evening be so depressing?"

We got ready for bed and I pulled out my stationery to write to Lee while Susan found her page in a mystery novel. Our routine, such as it was, continued.

Life for me personally remained upbeat. I got another muddy letter from Lee in which he confirmed the dates he would be at the main base and said that he would try to call me if he got the chance. I was thrilled at the prospect and touched by his closing on the red-streaked page, where he asked, "What about baby names?" Oh, he was wonderful! Here he was, losing his battle against rain, leeches, and heat, and he asked about baby names. And he might get to call me!

I immediately announced that the phone was off limits to all but emergencies for the next forty-eight hours. I was never more than an instant away, both to guard and to answer the phone.

"Mrs. Sheldon," I said as she passed through the foyer where I sat on the floor with the telephone beside me reading a book, "I can't go to your friends' house on the Fourth unless Lee calls first. I hope that's okay."

I jumped every time the phone rang, and it seemed to ring incessantly. Mrs. Sheldon had a million friends and everyone who knew Miles called to find out his plans for the holiday. I made no pretense at being polite. Rather than leave the area, I stayed in place and glared at any prolonged conversation. Fortunately, the Sheldon family was a forgiving one.

The next day I again sat by the phone while Susan and her mother went shopping. When they returned, Susan brought up three envelopes for me. Her look said there were none for her. She went into the bedroom and closed the door.

I began with the thickest envelope, which contained a brief note from Lee telling me that D Company had gotten "cut up bad" the day before and explaining that the enclosed negatives were from his RTO's last pictures in the pineapple fields. He told me to get them developed into slides.

The second letter, dated the day he should have gone to the rear, was less than a half-page long. In it he said only that the jungle was a bitch and repeated that other companies had been in contact. The blue tablet lines were obliterated from the bottom half of the sheet where Lee had rested his wet and muddy wrist.

The third letter was dated two days into Lee's rear time, only it began with "Still in jungle." Crash. My heart plunged into my stomach and I felt ill. I continued reading:

> Overran a big VC Base Camp yesterday—We had one wounded—Got three of them—many more I would guess. We found many documents, etc. that we sent in of very high intelligence value.
>
> I did not go in for XO while he is on R&R. I did not want to leave my Plt.

What a fool I was. Looking at the letters, books, and dishes scattered on the floor around me, I realized I had learned nothing in the weeks Lee had been gone. When would I stop thinking there would be a time when I could relax? Of course, Lee didn't go to the rear when there was action on the front. I hated this goddamned war.

The phone jolted me back into the present. "Linda? Did I wake you?"

I recognized Cheryl's voice and reassured her she had not disturbed me. As we talked, it became obvious that she and Steve would accept an invitation to come over, which they did when I extended it.

Dragging myself up, I cleaned the foyer from my camp-out and put the negatives in my purse. Then I knocked on the bedroom door and let myself in.

"I know you are not having a good day," I said to Susan, who was under the covers reading, "but I need your help. Cheryl and Steve are coming over in about an hour."

"Why?"

"Time's getting short, I think."

"Don't they want to be by themselves?"

"I'd guess they need some relief from the intensity," I speculated, remembering how frantically busy Lee and I tried to stay as the hours slipped by. "So could you help me?"

Susan threw off her glum mood with the covers and came to my rescue. By the time our guests arrived, we had cheerful expressions plastered on our faces and our animation in synch. Susan gave a splendid performance, regaling the Hightowers with family stories and history lessons on the artifacts in the living room. I had now become well enough acquainted with some pieces to add support lines, but Susan carried the show.

In truth, Cheryl and Steve were an easy audience as we sat drinking colas and ignoring what was on everyone's mind. At one point, Cheryl followed me into the kitchen on the pretext of helping. As soon as we were out of Steve's earshot, she asked in dread, "What's it really like?"

I stopped and looked at her distraught face. What did a real friend do in this situation? Did I sit her down and say, "Brace yourself, honey, because you're in for the most horrible experience you can imagine. No matter what anyone's told you, it's worse"? Or did a real friend gloss over the reality? I did not know. The only thing I was sure of was that I would not feed her platitudes.

Finally, I said, "You are strong, Cheryl. You will do fine." I did not add, "Because you have no choice."

Quickly grabbing the refills, I shooed her back to the living room, feeling inadequate, or maybe cowardly. The real truth was that nothing I could say would help. She had to find her own way, and she would probably do so more successfully than I was doing.

When they rose to leave a couple of hours later, I wanted to hold Cheryl and reassure her, but I didn't. I couldn't, because we would both have broken down. Susan and Steve might have joined us, for all I knew. Instead, we were conventional, controlled, and cheerful.

Steve thanked us; Cheryl said she would stop by on her way to R&R in six months; and we wished them well. When I did hug Cheryl goodbye, I felt her tremble through her coat. I gave her an extra squeeze and thought to myself, "You don't know it, but I'm trembling for you, too."

{Chapter 13}

July 4, 1969, was a holiday I lived outside my body. Although I accompanied Mrs. Sheldon and Susan to a lovely home atop one of the Peninsula's grand hills, I had no sense of physically being there. The party played out before my eyes like a snowy late-night TV movie—sound and action but no focus.

Appropriately, fog obscured what I was told was a breathtaking view, leaving us marooned in a fantasy above the real world. The Rolls Royce in the driveway reinforced the dream-like qualities of this American Shangri-La.

As the guests were introduced to me, I recognized names of these women who were gracious with their inquiries, teasingly familiar with each other, and genuinely glad to be together. Susan interacted with them as if they were favorite aunts while I observed the extended family rituals from afar. I was somehow pleased not to be alone but glad to be apart.

Aside from Susan and me, the only other young women there were two sisters, childhood playmates of Susan's and the daughters of one of Mrs. Sheldon's friends. After a buffet lunch, the older sister announced that they were leaving, but their mother protested that they should keep Susan and me company or take us with them.

An awkward moment passed as the four of us struggled to find acceptable reasons to decline both options. With each excuse, the mother grew more adamant. Susan tried to reassure her that we didn't mind their leaving, but her protests went unheeded.

Finally, the younger sister looked directly at her mother and said, "I don't think they would enjoy our friends. We're all against the war, you know. Just because we grew up with Susan doesn't mean we have anything in common now. Her husband's in Vietnam, for God's sake."

No one moved. What had started as an off-hand inconsequential suggestion had turned into a breach of etiquette. While I had no desire to become acquainted with these sisters, I instantly felt officially an outcast, somehow tainted, unacceptable. My concern, though, was for Susan. She shared the sisters' opposition to the war, feeling it more passionately—and personally—yet she was being branded a supporter. And she was being belittled by a superior attitude that suggested that she were somehow less than the sisters because Tom was a soldier in Vietnam.

Mrs. Sheldon had been watching Susan, seeing her face redden and her eyes narrow. She jumped from the sofa and said lightly, "Now you two run along. We understand that you don't want to spend your afternoon with a bunch of old married women."

When the mother opened her mouth to object, Mrs. Sheldon arched her eyebrow and firmly said, "They're young. Married women's gossip doesn't interest them."

I admired how Mrs. Sheldon shifted the emphasis from Vietnam to marital status. The others in the room must have felt the relief, too, for quickly there was an outbreak of unrelated, loud chatter.

"I'm so sorry, Susan," the mother said, biting her lip and fighting back chagrined tears. "I'm terribly embarrassed."

By this time Susan had recovered and said, "It's okay. Linda and I usually don't tell anyone."

"That's what makes their behavior so deplorable," the woman shook her head as she continued. "I was a waiting wife during World War II. I know what it feels like to wait and worry and to be left out of everything."

"How long was your husband gone?" Susan asked, her way of channeling the conversation toward facts and away from emotion. She succeeded and soon all the women were recounting their own waiting-wife experiences, some apparently revealing for the first time the loneliness they had endured. As the memories continued to pour out and the sun set, I felt a kinship with these women, one that they must have felt, too, because for the rest of my time in the Bay Area, they each in turn called to check on

Susan and me, to include us in their activities even after Mrs. Sheldon flew to Tehran, and to offer whatever support they could. Where Susan and I failed to find solace among our own age group, we had found it among wives of another war. The empathy was comforting, but mostly I found this afternoon encouraging. As I looked around the darkening room that day, I saw that women who had once been in a similar circumstance not only survived but also lived whole lifetimes afterward. Maybe there would be life after Vietnam, too.

In the meantime, I returned to my vigil. By the time I next heard from Lee, I had gotten over my disappointment and was rewarded by the longest letter to date. In it he tallied the money in savings, and when I saw the figures of the growing amount in the fund compared to the dwindling amount in my nest egg, I resolved that I would finally tell him I needed more money. I read on:

> It rains at least 3 times a day—We live in mud—We had 3 hot meals in 11 days—Everything stays wet. Have been working in thick jungle—The man we had wounded had to be raised out by a hook from a chopper.

Oh, by the way, Lee, I mentally responded, while you were risking life and limb in the mud, I spent yesterday in a palatial mansion overlooking the Pacific where a Rolls Royce was parked in the driveway. Do send more money. Ha. I knew I wouldn't ask even though he was doing what he wanted to be doing, as he pointed out next:

> Honey, I love and miss you very much. Still I am as happy as I can be under these conditions—Also doing a job that has to be done and doing a fine job of doing it.

I refolded the letter in disgust, not certain if my feelings were directed at Lee or myself. If he was as happy as he could be under the circumstances, maybe he was losing his grip, too. I supposed he had every right to be as wacky as I felt, but the thought was not reassuring. I hoped he wasn't depending on me to be the one maintaining the sanity for the family.

• • •

On many days my goal was getting through twenty-four hours at a time. Any diversion was welcome, including my first visit to the Letterman OB/GYN clinic, though I should have known better.

On the day of my appointment, I dressed in the black maternity smock I made before I left Texas, amused when I remembered that Lee joked that someday I would look sexy in such a garment. Little did he know that there was nothing sexy about this pregnant body. Still, the idea of his saying such a thing made me feel a bit closer to him when I wore the dress.

Mrs. Sheldon looked somewhat startled when she saw me, but I assumed it was because she was surprised to see me dressed so early. She and Susan were going shopping again that morning for her trip back to the Middle East.

I arrived at the high-rise hospital a few minutes prior to my 9:30 A.M. appointment, giving myself time to follow the arrows though the double doors into the clinic. When I checked in, I received a hospital gown and instructions on where to change, what to do with the specimen, and where to take my place in the hallway chairs that were rapidly filling with other gowned and bulging figures. I knew the GYN days were referred to as "cattle calls," but hearing about the herd syndrome and experiencing it were two different things. I modestly tried to keep the back of the gown together behind my back and walked, knees together, to the vacant seat at the end. Each time a name was called, we all got up—back flaps flying—and moved up one chair.

At some point after 11:30, it was finally my turn for the labs, scales, and stirrups without so much as an acknowledgement that there was a person attached to the body. The doctor, who looked suspiciously no older than I, arrived and scanned my chart. Without making eye contact, he asked a series of questions, made notations, and then proceeded to contradict Dr. Hawkins about my anemia—which this man said I did not suffer—and about my diet—which this obstetrician said I was to curtail, especially the salt intake. The only premise he left intact was the due date, though he muttered that such projections were rarely accurate.

He was truly obnoxious; only the opportunity to escape his presence kept me from being angry that I waited more than two and a half hours for the five-minute examination. I chose to ignore most of his advice, rejecting it out-of-hand because he and the whole system were so objectionable. I would continue to take the iron pills Dr. Hawkins prescribed until I ran out, and I would continue to eat what I damn well pleased.

I took several deep breaths of the cool San Francisco air to clear my head and then dropped off the latest negatives Lee had sent, hoping that transforming these into slides would not be too expensive. Before I left the post, I stopped by the commissary to pick up a few groceries. As if some force beyond my control were in effect, I filled the basket with everything the doctor told me to avoid—chocolates, potato chips, and a host of other decadent items I could not afford but now suddenly craved. Then, after waiting in line for almost two hours, I dallied at the post thrift shop, searching through castaway baby items.

It was almost dark when I returned to the flat. Heaving the first sack of groceries up the stairs, I encountered Susan at the door. She took the bag and said, "I'll finish unloading. There's something for you on your bed."

I gladly yielded my load and went quickly to the bedroom, hoping to find a letter from Lee. Instead, on the bed lay a pink-and-white-checkered maternity top and matching pink skirt, one with an elastic panel over the abdominal area. I stared at the clothes.

"Mother and I found this today. We thought it would look great on you," Susan said as she walked into the room a few seconds later. "I hope you like it."

Tears stung my eyes. Susan misread my silence and said with a sigh, "Sorry, I should have told you it wasn't a letter."

"No, no. I love it," I said, fingering the beautifully tailored two-piece suit. "But I can't afford something like this. Can we take it back?"

"No," Susan said as she leaned over the garment. "This is a gift from Mother. I helped her pick it out. How did we do?"

By now Susan was holding up the skirt and examining the panel. "Weird. But it makes sense, I guess. Do you know who first created the first maternity dress?" And she was off on a history lesson. Trivia saved Susan from emotional encounters more than any other person I'd ever met.

I wiped an escaping tear. "But why?"

"Because she wanted you to have it," Susan said, sitting on the bed and crumpling the skirt in her lap. "And if you must know, she couldn't bear to see you wearing black. She said you looked like you were in mourning, and with Lee in Vietnam, it was just too much for her."

When I protested that I couldn't keep it, she said, "Stop being so damned proud. Just model it for her and say thank you."

The suit fit and left growing room. Mrs. Sheldon smiled when she saw me as I pranced into the kitchen and then hugged her. "It's the prettiest outfit I have," I said. "Thank you so much."

"You look nice in pink," said Mrs. Sheldon, who was too gracious to tell me what she thought of the other dress.

I immediately hung the black smock at the back of the closet. I hadn't thought of it as being morbid, but maybe it was. The pink certainly made me feel lighter at heart and saved what was an otherwise distressing day.

{Chapter 14}

With the holiday behind us, our lives on Collins Street fell into as normal a routine as we were likely to attain. Mrs. Sheldon continued working her way through chores she wanted to accomplish while in the States as well as squeezing in visits with friends. Miles exchanged his hard hat for party clothes at the end of each day or else he lay exhausted on the floor and played with the animals. Susan and I did our best to ride the tides of the war that were washing our way, sometimes with poise but mostly not.

My letter from Lee after the weekend jarred me back into living-color terror. His July 5th letter, which reached me more than a week later, related how he had spent his 4th:

> We have been in hell—Delta Co hit an objective on the 3rd—Hit bad—We came up in support—Ended up we were taking on an NVA Battalion Base Camp—We had 9 GIs killed, about 20 WIA—1 CPT, 1Lt WIA—All KIA and wounded officers were from Delta Co.
>
> Bad thing was we could not get the dead out—One man wounded up front was zeroed in by NVA machine guns—Delta lost many trying to get him out—We had to drop back, call in arty and jets—Finally 24 hrs later we hit again—My plt leading—We got bodies out—NVA retreated.
>
> Carrying out 9 US dead is a terrible thing.
>
> First day my plt made it within 30 meters of NVA—Just couldn't push in—Delta was in worst position—We were lucky.
>
> Had to cut out an LZ for MediVac—A hell of a 4th of July Weekend.

I am okay.

I love and miss you very much.

Each combat action Lee wrote about seemed progressively more threatening, I realized with a sickening dread. The frequency and the casualty numbers were escalating by the week. How many more times could he be lucky?

Aside from my anxiety about his physical safety, I now began to worry more about him psychologically. I knew Lee well enough to feel his pain permeating the two pages. For him to have written what he did told me the impact the experience had had on him. His next letters referred to the 4th of July as a watershed date.

Lee wrote that the battle on the 4th had made TV network news. Not in San Francisco, or at least not that I recognized. I watched the news faithfully every evening, but the military designations of corps, brigades, and battalions—always rattled off so quickly—still confused me. I carefully scrutinized each figure on the screen and hoped fervently not to recognize Lee on a stretcher.

Susan continued to handle the war in her inimitable way. She refused to watch the news, preferring instead to stay informed by voraciously reading the weekly news magazines. She dealt with Vietnam almost exclusively as a political topic rather than an emotional issue—when she could get away with it.

Tom still sent Susan thick letters that she rarely discussed. Then one day an envelope arrived for her with a tape reel inside. Susan took a recorder into the bedroom and shut the door. Far too quickly, the door ripped open and Susan raced down the hall with tears streaking her cheeks. Fear gripped Mrs. Sheldon and me when we saw the wild-eyed look in Susan's eyes.

"Sus, what is it?" Mrs. Sheldon asked, grabbing her.

Susan brushed her away and said, "I'm going for a walk."

As she opened the front door, I said in as level a voice as I could muster, "Susan, don't do this."

Susan stopped midway through the door and took a deep breath. Through clenched teeth, she said, "You're right. That's not fair. Tom's okay. He just sent me a goddamned tape with explosions going off in the background. How the hell could he do that to me? I just can't listen to it." She turned and ran down the steps.

I closed the door softly and looked at Mrs. Sheldon. "Oh, Tom, Tom, Tom," she said, shaking her head and rolling her eyes. Then she looked at me and we both laughed, not at Susan's distress, but because we both knew Tom probably thought he had done something terribly clever by sending a tape. His journalistic nature would have prompted him to capture the "real story" as it was happening, to record the events for posterity. Perhaps it was our own relief that made us hysterical, but whatever it was, Mrs. Sheldon and I laughed until tears rolled down our own cheeks, too. Poor Tom. He had no idea what he had done.

• • •

"This is really a shitty way to live," Susan announced as we sat picking over our food at the eatery down the hill a few evenings later. "I hate this diner. Tomorrow I am going to call the Officers' Club. And I'm going to start looking for a job. I just can't stand to live this way any longer."

"I should do that, too," I said. "I need the money."

Both women looked at me. "Linda, who is going to hire a four-months-pregnant woman?" Susan asked.

"Maybe somebody will. After all, Lee and I planned my allotment around my getting a job."

"And what kind of job are you going to look for?" Susan pushed.

I shrugged because I really hadn't thought about employment in realistic terms. "I worked for an insurance company after I graduated from college. I've taught school. Just because I'm pregnant doesn't mean I'm incompetent."

Susan persisted by saying, "Yes, but no employer is going to hire you so you can work for what, four or five months, and then have you go on maternity leave. Besides, you don't have to work. Tell Lee you need more money."

"I can't do that," I insisted. "Especially not after the Fourth."

"I think Susan is right," Mrs. Sheldon added quietly. "I think you will have a hard time finding a job."

I felt trapped between needing money and knowing they were right. I would have to try, even if my heart wasn't in it.

Susan found a job the next week opening mail for a bank credit card department. Under normal circumstances, Susan would never have considered a job like this one. The pay was poor, the bus commute long, and the tasks mindless. But our circumstances were not normal. The war affected us not only emotionally but also psychologically. By the time Susan went job hunting, her morale was scraping bottom, and she could no longer envision herself as the competent, intelligent woman she was.

Before she started her job, Susan called the Presidio's Officers' Club to inquire about membership. She met with a cool reception. The manager told her that the Club was open only to officers stationed at the post. When Susan pointed out that she knew that was not true, the man countered by telling her that the officers could belong to only one club at a time and, because our husbands were stationed elsewhere, they undoubtedly already held membership there. Susan politely told him that Tom was in an isolated region of the Delta and Lee was in the jungle north of Saigon. She assured him that neither currently held officer club memberships. Then the club official grew quiet and finally said that it would be impossible for us to join under the circumstances. When Susan demanded to know just what that meant, he tried dodging the question, suggesting that we probably would not find the club amenable to our needs. By this time, Susan was enraged and asked the man point-blank if the reason for refusing us membership was because we were waiting wives. Cornered, he admitted that it was, telling her that the club could not afford to become known as a place where "unattached" women gathered. That would give the wrong impressions to the young single officers and, well, perhaps others, too, which might cause embarrassing problems.

"Then what you are telling me," I heard Susan hiss into the phone, "is that you're afraid we might try to pick up your officer corps and you must protect them by keeping us out?"

By the way Susan slammed down the phone, I assumed his answer was affirmative. "Bastard," she said through clenched teeth. "If their officers can't take care of themselves in a club, how do you suppose they're going to be able to fend for themselves in a war?"

We were shocked. At the root of our reaction was another sense of injustice. While the scene on the Fourth had not been pleasant, neither had it been truly surprising. We didn't expect civilians to accept or understand us. But to have the military label us as undesirables was another matter altogether. Susan and I had been card-carrying members of the Officers' Club at Bragg, afforded the same treatment as our husbands. Now the message was that we didn't exist without them in residence.

I relayed the tale to Judy the next time I called her at Fort Benning, where she and Jim were now living. "I'm really not surprised," she said. "The clubs here do have a problem with waiting wives hustling the officers."

"All we wanted," I protested, "was a place to have dinner every once in a while."

"I know," she said, "but the truth is a lot of women are making careers out of marrying soldiers headed for Vietnam and then collecting the insurance when they're killed. Some of them have cashed in on three or four."

"So now all waiting wives have a stigma?"

"I'm afraid so," she answered.

In truth, by now the club had come to represent more than just a place to eat. It was now about acceptance, normalcy, and an opportunity for us to get dressed up and enjoy a change of scenery at a place just a short drive away where I could afford the fare and where we found a sense of security.

While I did not want to admit it outright, I was becoming more obsessed about the dangers of getting into a car, worrying about accidents that might harm the baby. I found myself offering excuses when Susan suggested we go down to the Peninsula to see her college friends or when she wanted me to go with her across the city. I knew I was being irrational, but I couldn't stop the dread and fear that seized my stomach each time I ran out of excuses, relented, and agreed to go with her.

I wasn't being fair to Susan. She really had no one else, either. She needed to be busy in her off hours. Out of desperation, she invited herself to one of Miles's friends' parties.

"Come with us," Susan coaxed as she brushed her hair and finished her makeup, rushing to get ready.

"No," I declined from the edge of the bed where I was sitting and watching her. "You go and have fun."

"Are you not feeling well?" she said, stopping to look at me.

"I feel fine," I said, surprised by her question.

"This party is free, you know. It won't cost you anything."

I could feel my face turn red. "It's not the money."

"Then what is it?" She sat down beside me. "You never go anywhere but the Presidio. You need some fun in your life. Come on, I'll introduce you to everyone as my pregnant roommate. That should get some laughs."

"Really," I started, trying to avoid telling her the real reason. "I'd rather stay here. You know these kids. I don't. I don't have anything in common with them. I know you're right about needing some fun in my life, but this wouldn't be fun for me. Please, just go and have a good time."

Suddenly Susan's bubble of energy deflated, and she sighed heavily. "I don't know if I really want to go either. I'm just so sick of having nothing to do. Maybe I should just stay home, too."

"No," I insisted, "go and enjoy. There's nothing wrong with your having some fun yourself." She didn't move. "Listen," I continued, pleading now, "if you aren't going because I'm not, then I'll have to go so you will. And I really don't want to, but you do, at least you kind of do. Please don't say you're staying home."

Susan rolled her eyes in disgust. "God," she moaned, "isn't anything simple any more?"

Susan went to the party and had a good time. Later in the week, she came home from work with a shopping bag.

"I really didn't have the right clothes for the party," she said briskly, clutching the handled sack, "so I got myself a new outfit."

Susan didn't show me or her mother what she had bought. After Mrs. Sheldon left to visit friends in the country a few days later, Susan appeared dressed for another party. Then I understood. The new outfit was a gauzy rendition of the U.S. flag made into a pants suit, the slacks bearing the stripes in blue and white while the front of the top displayed a red field of white stars.

I bit my tongue, knowing by Susan's defiant expression that she was daring me to disapprove. In all honesty, I was shocked. I had only seen pictures of people—protestors, all—wearing the flag. That Susan was now doing so told me loudly that she was making a statement. What good manners and loyalty would not allow her to otherwise express she was now screaming with her clothes.

Carefully, I avoided eye contact and hastily retreated to the bedroom. Approval or disapproval was not the issue. Coming to terms with this side of Susan was. I struggled to understand. I knew she was unhappy, and I knew she resented the Army. But to blatantly disrespect the flag. . . . On one hand, I was aghast that she would dare to have such little regard for the symbol for which her husband was fighting; I found her defiance frightening and unsettling. On the other hand, I admired her fiery spirit and brazen approach. She, by god, did not care who knew that she was displeased with this country. I thought it took a lot of courage to thumb one's nose at the government.

I puzzled over the situation all evening, wishing Mrs. Sheldon were there to explain exactly what all this meant. For all my analysis, I simply ended up feeling naïve, like a child not privy to adult secrets. The result was a need to retreat even further from the unfamiliar into a safe place.

As I tossed and turned that night, I found myself face-to-face again with the issue of God or not. I could have been wrong in the plane over Los Angeles—deeply ingrained beliefs said I was—and the existence of God might be the very factor that was keeping Lee alive. Yet my faith had been shaken to such an extent that I could not pretend to believe things I no longer did. I felt exposed and vulnerable.

I settled on a compromise. Instead of praying, I talked in my head to Lee and beamed my thoughts upward toward where God would be if He existed, hoping my projections would bounce off God, or whatever, at the correct angle to be picked up by Lee on the other side of the world. It was the satellite concept before I knew about such technology. It was also crazy. But it worked as a means of providing some comfort to my confused mind.

When I awoke the next morning, Susan's bed was undisturbed. I found the striped flag pants strewn outside the other bedroom door and the star-spangled top mangled on the back of a kitchen chair. I debated whether to pick them up or leave them as they lay. Was Susan trying to force me to deal with these damned clothes?

Before I could conduct a Freudian analysis, I heard the door to the second bedroom, where Miles usually slept, open; Susan came barreling around the corner and into the kitchen.

"God, I'm going to be late. I overslept." Susan grabbed the top and hurried back down the hall and into the bathroom.

"Where are you going?" I asked, standing outside the closed door.

"Work."

"Susan, it's Saturday."

The door slowly opened. Susan leaned against the wall and said slowly, "I'm losing my mind."

She looked down at the bundle still in her arms and burst out laughing. "They itched like crazy. I couldn't get them off fast enough when I got home. I was so tired I just threw them. I waited at that stupid party for Miles and then he never showed up. I thought I was going to claw myself to death."

I didn't say, "It serves you right," though she probably expected me to. And I swallowed any remarks about what a psychiatrist might say about her own reaction to the costume. Susan and I never discussed her stars and stripes again. She occasionally wore the slacks with another top, which made them look like ordinary striped pants.

{Chapter 15}

I tried to psych myself into a positive frame of mind for my first job interview. My best shot, it seemed to me, was applying at the same insurance company for which I had processed major medical claims in Houston two years earlier. I bypassed the personnel office and contacted the claims supervisor directly. Sounding pleased to hear from an experienced applicant, she scheduled me immediately.

Unfortunately, the office was in the newest downtown skyscraper at the end of a disorienting bus trip that dumped me in the heart of the financial district like Alice into the oversized garden. I felt dwarfed in the shadowed streets and even smaller when I entered the cavernous marble lobby. Standing beside the directory, I fought the urge to turn and run. Only the realization that I didn't know which bus to take home kept me planted in place. That, and the fact that I had a two o'clock appointment with the manager.

I pushed the elevator button and took many deep breaths, reminding myself that if the company had any openings in claims, I was certainly qualified. I threw back my shoulders and prepared to step into the elevator when the bell softly dinged.

Rising more than thirty floors above San Francisco should have been an uneventful whisk to the top. I should then have been able to confidently stride into the interview and stake my own claim on the next available position. Unfortunately, I was in an office building that was not yet completed, unbeknownst to me. Only after I stepped into the elevator and the door closed did I realize that I was not riding in a self-contained box but rather standing on a plywood platform with canvas-draped sides. As I flew upward, I felt my stomach drop through my toes and watched in horror as the canvas rippled in the wind of the shaft, the bottom edge whipping back and forth across the flooring. I couldn't tell if the resulting nausea came from the express ascension or the terror of soaring into space on a piece of plywood. Needing desperately to steady myself, I staggered forward, automatically reaching for the railing—only to jerk my hand back just in time to keep myself from careening into the canvas and smearing my face against the swiftly passing shaft wall.

I was still lurching for balance when the elevator came suddenly to a stop, causing my stomach to snap with such a force I lost my breath. When the door opened, I staggered onto the terra firma of industrial carpeting and clung weakly to the cool marble wall. What was I doing here? I didn't want this damned job—especially if it meant enduring such torture just to get here.

The manager was a woman somewhat younger than I expected. Wearing an inexpensive gray tailored suit with her brown hair pulled pragmatically back into a ponytail at the nape of her neck, she exuded the efficiency and strain typical of her circumstances and no-nonsense position. She smiled pleasantly when I introduced myself, but then as her eyes scanned my blossoming body, the lines on her face fell in reflection.

I knew that she had instantly decided that she would go through the motions of an interview with no intention of making an offer. She asked about my experience, but this encounter had nothing to do with qualifications, as we were both painfully aware. When I made the purposeful point of telling her my husband was in Vietnam, the never-to-be-done deal was sealed. I watched as she bristled.

"I'll certainly keep you in mind," she said. "Thank you for coming in."

At least the interview was over. I could honestly write Lee that I had tried to find a job. This woman's reaction to my condition would only be repeated everywhere I went. What a fool I was to think anyone would hire me. Now I had to summon the courage to spend a few more seconds aboard the raft in the wall and then find the wherewithal to determine which bus to take to Susan's work place.

At the bank I found Susan in her dungeon basement cubby hole. I pushed open the door to find a small windowless room literally flooded shoulder-high in paper. Susan sat hunched over behind stacks of tilting envelopes, robotically gutting them one at a time and separating the innards into overflowing baskets. She and the other haggard-looking women, even younger than we, raised their heads at the noise as the door closed. After a disinterested glance, the others returned to their identical tasks. Susan shrugged in defeat without missing a slicing stroke, "This is only the afternoon mail. You should see what they deliver in the mornings."

I watched, appalled to see how Susan spent her days. Mechanically, unemotionally, Susan moved as though her muscles were part of an assembly line without connection to a human.

"I can't take a break," she said without pause. "All of this has to be cleared before we go home." Her voice, on automatic pilot, too, was the only sound other than the incessant ripping of paper.

"Just tell me which bus to catch," I said quickly.

The apartment never seemed such a safe haven as it did that afternoon. I lay on my bed depleted of energy for the next hour. Distress over my interview fiasco was replaced by the haunting picture of Susan buried in the mounds of paper, beaten, defeated, and lifeless. The Susan I had known at Fort Bragg and had seen on several occasions since I had been in San Francisco—the Susan who was innately curious, industrious, and vigorous—was nowhere to be found since she took this job. Now I understood her insatiable need to find some enlivening activities and why, when she came home in the evenings, she went straight to our room and closed the door, reappeared only for dinner, and spoke only when directly spoken to.

I was surprised that night when Susan initiated a conversation. "How was your interview?" she asked even though she didn't sound particularly interested.

"Oh, I got really lucky," I said lightly.

"You got a job?" She sounded incredulous.

"Not in a million years," I laughed. "I didn't get the job. But I'm lucky because it might have ended up like yours."

Susan's face turned red as she struggled for control.

"I'm being mean on purpose," I said. "You have got to get out of that place."

Susan stared at the floor. "It was all I could find."

"You're letting how you feel interfere with what you're capable of."

"I'm not up to dealing with a demanding job, even if I could find one," she said in a monotone.

"Maybe not. But surely there's a compromise out there somewhere."

"Maybe."

Telling Susan that I was lucky made me begin to believe I was. If I watched every penny, I could cover my expenses for a while longer.

A project was what I needed, so I counted my coins and bought yarn and a pattern book to knit a baby sweater. Bright red for a baby boy seemed a good choice to me, and the miniature size of the garment might be one I could actually finish.

While standing in the PX line to purchase my knitting supplies, I noticed one of the other patrons was wearing a Red Cross uniform. I thought, Why not? I had attended a volunteer training class at Fort Bragg to earn my pin and certificate.

I went home to dig out my training paperwork, and then, feeling exuberant and purposeful, I headed directly to the Red Cross office at Letterman to present my credentials and to volunteer. I didn't want to work around any really blood-gushing areas because of my nausea or in the vicinity of communicable diseases for the baby's sake, but maybe I could help out in other wards, maybe even those where Vietnam veterans were recovering from their wounds, I thought, seeing myself as a Stateside cross between best-intentioned Donut Dollies and Dorothea Dix. Because my time was my own, I could even work twice a week, heck, maybe every day for that matter. I was excited.

Even navigating the maze through Letterman to the Red Cross door didn't dampen my spirits, and I cheerfully presented myself to a steel-eyed woman with an impassive face who looked first at my middle and then into my eyes. Without blinking, she said, "I'm sorry. Perhaps afterward."

I was stunned. When I could find my voice, I asked, "You don't allow pregnant women to volunteer?" I knew I had seen them in the hallways of other military hospitals.

"Only if they have volunteered before their . . ." She cleared her throat. "Well, before."

I handed her my certificate.

"Fort Bragg," she read aloud from the paper. "What's your husbands unit?"

"C Company, 2nd Battalion, 3rd Infantry, 199th Light Infantry Brigade," I recited.

She looked at me through squinted eyes and arched her eyebrows into a frown that further distorted her already unpleasant face.

"Vietnam," I explained before she could ask.

She looked down at my proffering, pushed the papers back toward me, and said without ever raising her eyes again, "Sorry. We have no shortage of volunteers right now. The women of this post provide us with adequate assistance."

I stood speechless. It was the refusal of the Officers' Club all over again. Did the Red Cross think I wanted to hustle the wounded? And it was the rejection of the interview all over again. I couldn't get a paying job, and I couldn't even give my time away. The combination was devastating.

Chagrined, I could feel my face burning even after I stepped into the chill of the afternoon. I wanted to evaporate into the heavy fog that clung to the bay. Was it that I was pregnant or that Lee was in Vietnam? I pulled my raincoat tighter and cursed. Or maybe it was just my personality. Why couldn't I get anything to turn out right?

It was summer. Where was the damned sun anyway? Unlike my misadventures in Chinatown or my job interview, which I had been able to satirize by that night's dinner, I did not mention the Red Cross to Mrs. Sheldon or Susan. I let them suspect a gap in letters was the reason for my quietness during the evening meal.

Mrs. Sheldon and I were reading later in the living room when Susan unexpectedly emerged from the bedroom. "Hey," she said brightly, coming down the hall with her hands suspiciously behind her, "look what I found. Linda, it's your Red Cross certificate. Are you going to volunteer at Letterman?"

"No," I said hastily, regretting that I had not put away the paper that I threw on the dresser in disgust.

"I think it's a great idea, though, don't you?" I hadn't seen Susan this animated in days. Mrs. Sheldon was nodding in agreement.

I shrugged, "I don't even remember the class."

"I'm sure they have more here, too," Susan pressed. "You should go out there tomorrow and sign up. This is the answer. It won't matter that you're pregnant or that Lee is in Vietnam." Which left my personality as the villain.

I tried dodging the issue. But Susan, once engaged, was not to be thwarted. She preached all the merits of doing it and Mrs. Sheldon added more. I saw their enthusiasm turning to frustration as I grew more entrenched in my excuses.

Finally, Susan exploded, "God, I don't understand you. Here's something you can do to be with people instead of staying by yourself all day."

My face was burning again as I faced the choice of the truth or her wrath. I chose the latter. As uncomfortable as her displeasure made me, admitting my failure as a volunteer was harder.

Susan eventually threw up her hands and returned to the bedroom. She was still reading, fully clothed beneath her covers, when I got ready for bed. I brought out my stationary to write Lee and we endured an uneasy silence for several minutes while I scribbled and she flipped pages.

Finally Susan stepped out of bed far enough to reach her nightgown and pulled it under the blanket with her. Sitting and propping the covers beneath her chin, Susan began changing clothes.

"I'm sorry," she said as the bedspread began a ripple of waves from the epicenter of her unseen motions and then garments came flying out one at a time. "What you do with your time is your business. I just worry about you being alone so much."

I was happy to meet her halfway. "And I'm sorry about you in that damn dungeon where you work," I said. "A fine pair we are."

"Just tell me why you won't consider volunteering and I'll leave you alone about it," Susan said as her head disappeared under the covers.

"I'll tell you if you tell me why you change clothes in the bed," I said, knowing I could withhold my humiliating story from her no longer. Besides, I had been fascinated that she so mysteriously dressed and undressed completely under the covers. If modesty was the issue, she could have changed in the bathroom.

"Okay. I'll go first," she said, straightening the shoulders of the gown as she reappeared. "When I went to the Swiss finishing school, we lived in these old drafty castles that didn't have central heat. It was too cold in the winter to get out of bed to dress so I learned to change clothes under the covers. It's actually easy once you get the hang of it."

I gave her a dubious look to which she responded, "Okay, so it's strange, but it's a habit. Now, what about the Red Cross?"

I narrated my day and watched her mouth drop open and her face turn red. When I finished, Susan leapt from the bed, opened the door, and called, "Mother, come here. I want you to hear this."

At Susan's insistence, I repeated the tale again for Mrs. Sheldon with Susan expounding on parts I skipped or played down the second time through. The three of us sat there late into the night discussing the Red Cross woman's attitude. After a while, the rejection no longer mattered to me. I could do without the Red Cross; I could not do without my friends.

The next week Neil Armstrong landed on the moon and took a "small step for man, a giant leap for mankind." Mrs. Sheldon and I avidly watched the events surrounding the space shot in marathon fashion. I clicked the knitting needles in cadence with the commentators' reports, struggling to reconcile the astronauts' technologically advanced exploits with Lee's primitive fight for survival in the muddy jungle—all on the same day at the same point in history. When Armstrong pushed himself away from the ladder and touched the barren surface, I fought an urge to look out the window to see if he had indeed landed in our backyard, for surely my life qualified as the landscape of the moon.

{Chapter 16}

By the latter part of July, I had been in San Francisco long enough to experience reruns of events.

Impatient to see more pictures of Lee, I took my miniature viewer to the Presidio on the day the slides were due. After I waited eagerly in line, the clerk handed me an envelope with the price of $30 marked in red on it. I gasped at the amount. This near to the end of the month, my money was almost gone. As I felt the plastic case through the paper envelope, I knew I couldn't leave without them. I gulped and wrote the check.

In the car, I tore into the package and inserted slide after slide into the viewer, looking for glimpses of Lee. Some of the pictures were so dark that I had difficulty making out the subjects, mostly teenagers with rifles and bandoleers of ammunition, it seemed. Although I studied each, by the time I looked at the last one, I still had not found Lee. Exasperated, I began again, gathering up the frames strewn across the seat. The result was the same. Lee was not in any of those pictures. I couldn't believe it. I had just spent my last dollars to see snapshots of shady jungle and men I didn't know—or know who they were. Why did Lee send me these negatives when he wasn't in the pictures?

Disappointed, I decided to forego my other errands. The car, however, had other ideas. When I turned the key in the ignition, nothing happened. I swore and swung at the steering wheel, hitting the horn and causing everyone in the vicinity to turn and stare.

I raised the hood and took off my shoe. Just as I was about to start pounding, I caught sight of an MP jeep careening around the corner. This time I stood up straight, put my hands on my hips, and watched as the same John Wayne driver slowed to a roll. We locked eyes, his look accusing me of continued mechanical negligence, mine assuring him that I would conk his head instead of the battery if he stopped. He tromped the accelerator and I bent back over the engine.

Since my day had gotten off to such a depressing start, I did not expect alleviation from the mail slot. In the wooden drop box, however, I found two muddy envelopes and huffed up the stairs to read. The first envelope, a suspiciously thick one, contained another set of negatives with a quick note from Lee in which he said that it was easier for him to get sets of negatives from his men than worry with a camera himself, which explained, albeit too late, the photographs I had just picked up. He told me to get the enclosed set developed, too, and let him know how they looked. I stared at the film clips in my lap. Would men take pictures of their platoon leader? Probably not. Was I going to risk what little money I had to find out? Definitely not.

I held my breath when I opened the second envelope. Writing from a base camp where he had been for three days, Lee said they were heading into the jungle again. I read the next paragraph and my heart skipped a beat: "Company X-O leaves in August—I am next in line for it."

August was just days away! Lee would be out of the field in days—hours, really. Executive officers worked in the rear with administrative paperwork and rarely ventured into the action. The worst was almost over!

Of course, Lee's next words wiped the smile off my face and joy from my heart:

> CPT McGinnis asked if I would stay in field—He said he needed me—Also Bn CO said I was needed. So I will be staying in the field. Was told they would get someone with about with 3 months left in-country and job will be mine after I have 6 months in the field. Am not unhappy at all—Feel as though I am needed.

Goddammit! So what if he was needed in the field? I needed him at home, alive and well for the rest of our lives, not just in three-month increments. Let this McGinnis fellow find somebody else. If Lee got himself killed when he didn't have to be out there, I was going to be really angry with him.

In fact, I was angry with him right that minute. It didn't seem that he stopped to ask himself how his decision was going to affect me before he passed the rear job. Did he not think about the baby?

I sighed and let the letter fall to the floor, knowing answers to all the questions I could form. Of course Lee would not transfer to the rear until he had put in his obligatory six months in the field, even when Fate offered him the chance. I told myself I would have been surprised if he had chosen differently. I picked up the letter. At least he had been alive a week ago, which wasn't such a bad consolation prize.

In a strange way, our separation was allowing me to know Lee better than living with him had. His actions bore out his words, for he really was willing to put himself on the line for things he believed in, such as in taking care of his men—evidenced by his decision to stay with them. He obviously cared about me because he never let more than four days go by without writing me even when resupply was unpredictable.

The time apart, too, provided me with other insights into Lee and his behavior which had escaped me during daily exposure. I found a certain comfort, for example, in realizing that at Fort Bragg when Lee had come home at the end of the day and ducked behind a newspaper, he wasn't as much ignoring me as seeking some quiet time. Now I understood it was his way of being alone for a few minutes. Or perhaps, left alone long enough, I could rationalize anything.

Mrs. Sheldon returned home a few minutes later and found me still sitting in the living room with the letters. "Is everything okay?" she asked.

"I'm just so stupid to get my hopes up over the dumbest things." I then told her about the slides and Lee's declining a rear job.

"Oh, Linda," Mrs. Sheldon laughed as she sank down beside me on the couch. "I don't know if I'll ever get back to Tehran. Between you and Susan. . . ." She shook her head and added, "How am I going to leave you two? And Miles? I haven't gotten him back in school yet and I still don't know when Khalifah is coming."

Knowing that I heard earlier references to this young Arab and that he was one of the reasons we had this apartment, I still did not understand his connection. "Tell me who he is again," I said, realizing that his arrival was looming on the horizon.

Mrs. Sheldon explained that he was the nephew of one of her dearest friends. "We've known the family for years," she said, "and we agreed to sponsor Khalifah in this country before we got transferred back to the Middle East. That's one reason we thought it was so great that you and Susan wanted to live out here."

She went on to tell me that Khalifah was already enrolled in nearby San Raphael Military Academy for the fall. "I was hoping he would arrive before I left so Susan wouldn't have to be bothered with any details. But he's decided to extend his stay in London."

"How old is he?"

"About thirteen, I think. Arabs don't count age the way we do, you know. He could be older, but I doubt if he is younger. He will only be here at the apartment for occasional weekends, so I don't think he will be any trouble."

The telephone ended our discussion about Khalifah, whose name I was learning to pronounce. Mrs. Sheldon took the call as I gathered my things and left the room.

When I returned, Mrs. Sheldon said, "Linda, I hope you and Susan are free for dinner because I just accepted for all of us."

"You know what my social calendar looks like," I responded.

"Friends of mine are in town for a couple of days and want us to join them. It's just going to be a bunch of women."

• • •

Susan usually came in from work exhausted so I was surprised when she burst excitedly into the bedroom when I was fixing my hair. "This should be fun," she said, heading for the closet.

"What are you wearing? What should I wear?" I asked.

"I'm wearing my best dress and you should, too. I'll ask Mother if you can borrow her pearls."

The three of us crawled into Susan's Corvair and headed downtown where the lights, traffic, and pedestrians filled the narrow, crooked streets. Finally, Susan pulled into a parking lot, and I looked across the street to see the landmark hotel I recognized from tours Lee and I had taken in April.

"Oh, I know where we are," I said, excited. "Lee and I went to the Fairmont for drinks one night."

"Well, you're going again," Susan laughed and pulled her coat tighter against the brisk breeze as she took off walking at a fast pace. "Come on, Mother. It's cold."

Before we were across the street, Mrs. Sheldon suddenly waved at a small group of women about to enter the building. She hurried ahead, leaving Susan and me to follow.

On the sidewalk, Susan stopped and turned to me. "Listen, there's probably something you should know. I wouldn't tell you, but I don't want you to say anything because you didn't know."

"Are you trying to tell me these are Arab women? I knew that from the names."

"Lebanese," Susan corrected. "Just don't talk politics, okay?"

I was caught off guard. Susan and I had lengthy discussions about the Middle East, about the Arab and Israeli issues, about favorable biases of the American media toward the Jews. With her years in Arab countries, Susan had insights into the controversies ignored by American journalists and commentators.

"Susan," I said, shocked and a little hurt, "I would never insult your friends."

"I know you wouldn't intentionally, but it just doesn't seem fair not to tell you that one of the women is the former first lady of Lebanon," she said and then turned and walked away.

I caught Susan by the sleeve before she got through the door, "Say that again."

"One of mother's friends was the first lady of Lebanon. You know, a Lebanese counterpart to Jackie Kennedy and Pat Nixon."

"I know what a first lady is," I said, sharply. "I just don't know what I'm doing having dinner with one."

"Look, you've got to get used to this. You're going to be living with a Kuwaiti prince in a couple of weeks."

I stood oblivious to the fact that we were blocking the door to the hotel. "Khalifah is a prince?" I asked in a whisper.

"He's a thirteen-year-old boy, but, yes, he's a prince. One of many. His father is the emir's brother, or something like that. Please don't make a big deal over this. Look, they're waiting."

Susan headed toward Mrs. Sheldon and the four exquisitely dressed women at her side. I grabbed the pearls around my neck like worry beads.

When I joined the group, it was apparent that the reservations had gone askew and we could not be seated in the main dining room. Would Jackie Kennedy have been turned away from a Beirut restaurant? I thought not and found myself embarrassed over American ignorance, mine included, about the rest of the world.

Rather than be upset, the ex-first lady waved away the others' concern and asked the maitre d' if the hotel had other dining facilities. Without further ado, we were escorted to a basement restaurant.

I slipped into a chair next to Susan at the end of the oblong table at the point farthest from Mrs. Sheldon and the hostess. After the introductions, I attempted to be only a spectator, intrigued by watching the Lebanese women. They talked and laughed with each other and Mrs. Sheldon like school girls in a cafeteria, gesturing freely and leaning over to whisper amused confidences. Their spontaneity contrasted sharply with their high fashion clothing and bejeweled, manicured fingers.

All of the women, from time to time, turned to include Susan and me in the conversation. Because Susan was closest, she spoke for both of us, which suited me just perfectly. I grew progressively more relaxed and enjoyed the show, captivated by the women's beauty, style, and lack of pretense. If I had any lingering doubt about their authenticity, it was dispelled when the former first lady signaled the waiter at the end of the meal and asked for doggy bags for the uneaten food.

I whispered to Susan, "Do they travel with their animals?"

Before she could answer, the former first lady looked directly at Susan and me and said, "I hope we do not embarrass you, getting these, what, dog bags. But it is senseless to waste this beautiful meat. Here, Marjorie," she said, turning to Mrs. Sheldon, "you take some home, too. There's so much."

When I wrote Lee about that evening, I realized all over again how polarized our lives had become. I had not changed, I was sure, only gained some new perspectives, that was all. But I was not facing death every day. The papers and magazines were filled with articles about tormented Vietnam veterans who were being labeled as crazy. What kind of perspectives was he gaining? While the calendar said that every day brought Lee closer to home, my heart said every night took him farther away.

Depression was contagious. Susan continued gritting her teeth and forcing herself to spend her days in the bank basement. I grew all but despondent without a purpose. Mrs. Sheldon wrung her hands and delayed her departure.

Then Ted Kennedy drove Mary Jo Kopechne off the Chappaquiddick Bridge.

When I first heard about the incident, I paid little attention, irritated the Vietnam news had all but been knocked off the air with the Martha's Vineyard story. According to the early reports, Senator Kennedy had been involved in a late-night accident in which one of his aides, Mary Jo Kopechne, had been killed. Even though the senator had escaped unharmed, having a Kennedy involved in a fatal crash took the headlines.

Susan was mesmerized immediately. "I'll bet you anything there's more to this story than they're telling," she said.

"Come on, Susan," I said. "He's not that stupid. He's a United States Senator, for goodness sake."

I was the gullible public the Kennedy press people prayed for; Susan was the skeptic they feared. With each modification of the original, Susan, now watching the TV news, would yell, "Ah ha! I told you." I grew more disbelieving as it was revealed that not only had the aide died but also had drowned. And then, not only did Kennedy survive the car running off the bridge but also left her there alone and alive to die while he swam away and, rather than getting help, waited to find his people to "handle" the incident.

Susan's willingness to believe unsavory reports about government officials did not surprise me. The shock was how profoundly this distant event affected me. If Kennedy was so unscrupulous, so immoral, how was he being elected? How many more like him were in the Capitol chambers? These were men who authorized President Johnson to send troops to Vietnam.

Susan and I avidly read about the scandal and kept the TV on for any special bulletins, she to confirm her suspicions, I to find rational explanations that would restore my faith in the government and its men. When Kennedy held his tearful press conference, I watched in disgust, now seeing him not only as a coward but also as a liar. I hated him for my sickening awareness that Lee's being in Vietnam might truly in be vain, that the protesters might be right, that my husband might die for no purpose other than to become a statistic of uncaring incompetence.

August 1969

{Chapter 17}

Mrs. Sheldon scheduled her return to Tehran, concluding that life in the Collins Street flat would never be sufficiently normal to leave with an easy conscience. On her last Saturday in San Francisco, she and Susan dashed out to complete her shopping and staggered back at dusk, exhausted and loaded with bags.

Susan, still recounting and reviewing their purchases, insisted on carrying everything upstairs herself. On one trip, she dumped a bag on the table and said, "I got curtains." On the return, she continued, "I'm going to put them up tonight."

"We can surely wait until tomorrow," I suggested.

"No," she said, disappearing again down the steps. "Tonight."

Her hurry made no sense. I looked at Mrs. Sheldon, who shrugged and said, "She's been this way all day."

Then it registered. Susan was facing another separation, this time from her mother who was also truly her best friend. I felt incredibly sorry for Susan and a little sorry for myself, too, as I had come to depend on Mrs. Sheldon for a sense of stability in an unstable world.

While her mother unloaded sacks, Susan climbed up on the kitchen counter and nailed the rod hangers into the wall. "I hope these work," she said. "I got inflammable ones. That's important. Like kids' pajamas."

I glanced from the window to the stove about eight feet away. "I don't know, Susan," I said, "but I think if flames reach the curtains, it's already too late."

Susan hung the miracle curtains, flimsy nylon-looking strips of greenish gray, and jumped off the counter to assess her choice. "Well, they're not great, but they'll do. And we don't have to worry about them catching fire," she said.

The curtains, which looked like two pieces of sooty gauze salvaged from a fire sale, hung suspended over the length of the windows above the sink. "It's nice that they still let the light in," I said, grasping for something complimentary.

Susan called in sick on Monday so she could spend extra time with her mother. It was one of those rare days when air mail envelopes came for all three of us.

Lee wrote, "We have been on some weird missions lately—New Bn CO is trying some new ideas—mostly bad in my opinion." Just what we needed. A new battalion commander trying to make a name for himself with my duty-bound husband as a puppet.

One consistent thing about Lee was that he intuitively knew when he was pushing me too far, and on those occasions he would offer morsels of emotional reinforcements. He must have known this letter would not set well with me because he added a postscript. He wrote, "P.S. Re-read letter—Just thought to myself that I doubt if you know how much I love you and how often I think of you."

Mrs. Sheldon's remaining days evaporated despite the fact that Susan and I tried so hard to stretch the time. Susan, the epitome of efficiency and business all week, was by Friday in a frantic state, attacking every chore she could dream up with a frenzied yet cool energy. The more impersonal and precise she became, the more I retreated, giving her room to deal with anxiety her own way while growing more alarmed about how the two of us would negotiate our differences when our mediator was gone. She shot me occasional looks that suggested she was worried, too.

To make matters worse, I had not heard from Lee since Monday. His last letter said that he was going on another mission, not unusual in itself except that now I knew he had this gung-ho new battalion commander pulling the strings. I wasn't sure which made me feel worse, a commander who spent his time glad-handing the troops like parade field brass or one who wanted to revolutionize modern military tactics. Neither offered me the comfort of believing that Lee's welfare was his top priority.

I checked the mail slot fitfully all morning and finally found a muddy envelope waiting. When I encountered Susan in the hall, I shook my head.

"Did you get one?" she asked.

I nodded.

"Good," Susan said with genuine relief. "You needed it."

I gently extracted the pages. The letter was dated 27 July, five days and a date line ago. Lee started by telling me he had received letters No. 90–92. The fact that I had written No. 100 the night before reminded me that he experienced lag time, too.

The second paragraph read: "This is a very imp. Letter—read carefully." I laughed. Every letter was "very imp." to me and if I read any more carefully, no ink would remain. Still, with this lead-in, I did read more slowly, if not more carefully.

> The Co. has many R&Rs coming up. I feel that in a couple of months I will need one—I can probably get one first part of Oct.—When is the last date that the Drs. will let you travel—Honey, please don't get your hopes up as this may not work out—More than likely I will still be in the field at this time—Co CO has already told me it was fine with him if I took it. Please let me know what you think and/or what Drs. say—

My heart bounced and my spirits rocketed upward. The only black cloud that trailed along was Lee's acknowledging the desire for R&R. His admitting that told me more than he knew—and confirmed that I was not crazy to be scared senseless every day.

Still, to actually see him again . . .

"You look like the cat that ate the canary," Susan said as she strode through the room in pursuit of Daphne. "Not that eating a canary is a bad thing for a cat to do, uh, Daphne?"

I laughed. "R&R in October. That's only two months away."

"Oh," she said, shrugging. "Tom hasn't even been gone that long."

I knew she regretted it the minute she said it. Her face blanched and she bit her lip. "I'm sorry. That was a dumb thing to say. It just popped out."

I sighed. It was true after all. Surely Einstein could have discovered a more encouraging concept of time than its relativity. Tom had been gone forever already.

Even with the niggling worry about Lee's state of mind, the possibility of having an R&R on the horizon helped me through Mrs. Sheldon's departure. I wrote Lee long, long letters describing my excitement about October, so long and so excited that only a heel would not have done everything possible to make it happen. I assured him I would have no problems with medical approval. I felt confident I could find at least one cooperative doctor.

By Saturday, Susan had been so efficient that there was nothing left for us to do except drive her mother to the airport and wait for her flight. In the coffee shop, our conversation was erratic and unnerving, like a scratched record album, playing smoothly for a few beats then leaping forward incongruently. I suspected that what we all wanted to do was sob into our napkins.

"Now, you girls are going to be fine," Mrs. Sheldon repeated for the tenth time. "Lee and Tom will be home before you know it."

With eyes watering, we avoided looking at one another.

"Tell Daddy hello for me," Susan said from deep in her throat.

"When I get to London, I'll have Khalifah's family call you with his itinerary," Mrs. Sheldon said, and then she chuckled mischievously. "I didn't want to tell you, Susan, but I think Khalifah's trying to finagle a diplomatic passport."

Susan's eyes popped open. "I can't be responsible for a thirteen-year-old with diplomatic immunity," she gasped. "That's insane."

Mrs. Sheldon nodded as she pressed her lips together to suppress a grin and then said, "That's what I told his sister."

"Why didn't you tell me this before now?" Susan demanded.

"I don't know," Mrs. Sheldon sighed. "Everything was already too ridiculous. Look at you two, hanging by a thread, waiting for the mail, working a terrible job, having a baby, worrying with two school boys. My God, how can I leave?"

"You're going home because Daddy needs you, too," Susan said calmly. "We'll manage just fine."

When we rose from the booth, I turned to Mrs. Sheldon. "I'll say goodbye here and let Susan walk you to the gate," I said.

Mrs. Sheldon smiled through her misting eyes, "I feel like I've gained another daughter. Now you take good care of that baby and let us know the minute he gets here." She hugged me, patted my abdomen, and then walked away arm-in-arm with Susan.

I wandered through the cavernous building, finding myself suddenly at the door where I had stood the day Lee left. Across the asphalt stood the Greyhound depot and another, or maybe the same, dirty bus belching black plumes. How long ago and far away that horrible day four months ago seemed. I recalled the intensity of the pain I had felt then but now from this distance in time, the hurt was a memory rather than sensation. I felt like a different person from the weeping girl who gasped for breath that day.

That's when I saw a khaki uniform approach the bus and throw his duffle bag into the open luggage compartment. The soldier slipped off the green envelope cap from his head and stepped into the darkened door of the vehicle. Déjà vu. I choked and turned, all but running back through the terminal.

I had time to calm myself before I saw Susan's brisk strides moving purposefully through the crowds. Her head was bowed, but I could see that her face was streaked with tears that she impatiently tried to brush away. I fell in step with her and we marched in silence to the parking lot.

The mood in the car was untenable as we drove away. I watched Susan's jaw-clamped expression set like hardening plaster of Paris. Who could blame her? Sending her mother literally halfway around the world without knowing when she would see her again would be stressful enough under normal circumstances—which, of course, her circumstances were not. As I studied Susan, it occurred to me that were the situation reversed, she would be talking nonstop, plying me with information to distract me.

"Now tell me exactly what it would mean if this Khalifah person got a diplomatic passport," I baited her.

She leapt on the subject with a fury, and I played the devil's advocate, laying out high espionage scenarios, ending up with Russian involvement. The only enemy countries that didn't get any play in my intrigues of misadventure were the two Vietnams. Their roles in our lives were already too significant; they merited no additional air time. Besides, they would have forced reality into a discussion where none was welcome.

By the time we reached Collins Street, Susan was recovering her sense of humor, even cracking a sardonic joke or two. Although my throat was dry and my imagination taxed to its limit, I felt better, too, until we entered the quiet apartment. Emptiness haunted every corner. Oscar, Mrs. Sheldon's lap dog and constant shadow, flopped dejectedly in the middle of the floor, knowing he had been left behind. Only Daphne seemed unaffected, perched on the mantel between the two gold headdresses in wait of a victim. Susan and I silently fell into step straightening the apartment.

I fried steak because Miles would be home for supper. The three of us ate in an awkward hush that he periodically pierced with corny jokes. When he left the table, Susan called him to help with the dishes. He bellowed back an unacceptable response and Susan charged down the hall to confront him. Within seconds, the two were quarreling loudly.

After I cleaned the kitchen, I ventured into the hall. I found the coast clear, and slipped into our bedroom, believing that trying to interrupt and reason with either of them had all the wisdom of stepping between fighting dogs.

The voices in the next room were reaching a crescendo when I heard Susan's angry scream and the slam of a door. The dispute moved to the other end of the apartment as I pulled out my stationary. If they haven't killed each other now, I thought. . . . Dear Lee,. . . .

A couple of hours later, Susan tentatively opened the bedroom door and peeked in. "I'm sorry about that," as she nodded her head toward the front of the apartment. "He makes me so mad sometimes."

Susan's color had returned to her face and a spark was again in her eyes. A free-for-all venting had relaxed her.

"Just as long as there was no bloodshed," I said.

"No, we just get loud. I don't know," she said dropping onto her bed, "maybe I fight with him just to have some excitement. Even old Ted Kennedy is dropping out of the news."

As grim and as horrible as it was to be, Susan should not have worried about losing a point of focus. That night the Charles Manson family went on a rampage in Southern California, and our attempt to solve the brutal murders of actress Sharon Tate and friends held us spellbound for weeks.

{Chapter 18}

When the Tate murders story first broke, Susan was again mesmerized by current events that were far removed from her personal involvement. From the initial headlines that announced the multiple deaths of the pregnant actress, her friend Abigail Folger, and their male companions, she tracked the story with a detective's zeal.

I initially did not pay much attention to the articles about the gruesome crime scene except to be repulsed by the details and distressed about the unborn baby. The butchery and the blood-written messages on the wall frightened me, and I found myself hoping that the cause of the murders was somehow a personalized vendetta toward those particular people, not a random slaughter. The world was scary enough without crazed killers on the loose.

Susan's interest in the mystery made her preoccupation with Ted Kennedy's Chappaquiddick fiasco pale in comparison. She freely speculated with each news release that hit the wires and magazines. As she reiterated the location of the Tate-Polanski home based on a published map, I recalled the afternoon Connie and I had explored the canyons around Los Angeles. Before that time, I would have assumed it impossible for a house to be secluded in such a heavily populated area. Now I knew differently. As I looked at the map, which was not so different from the street vendors' routes to the stars' homes, the story moved a step closer to my soul as I wondered if the killers had been stalking the area two months before.

We read all we could find and Susan, as she had been with the Kennedy story, was desperate enough for information to watch the TV news. We discussed possibilities until each day's reporting went flat and we waited for the next turn of events.

"This is really sick, you, know," I pointed out one night as we sat among clippings and dog-eared magazines.

"What is?" Susan asked without looking up from the paper.

"Our obsession with these gory killings."

She lowered the newsprint and said fatalistically, "Maybe. But it beats the hell out of worrying about Vietnam."

I had my second appointment at the Letterman OB Clinic, this time taking a book for my day in the musical chairs. I grimaced when I weighed in and prepared myself for another lecture. The doctor I drew this time either didn't notice the scale reading or didn't care, which left me feeling that I was getting away with something. He did, however, arch his young eyebrows over my folder and tell me that he, in contrast to the last doctor, considered me borderline anemic and that I should be seen every two weeks instead of monthly.

When he closed the folder, I said, "I want to meet my husband for R&R in early October. Do you see any problem with my flying to Hawaii then?"

"Well, I wouldn't really advise it."

I countered, "But that's not the question. Will it hurt the baby for me to fly to Hawaii in October?"

He grumbled something about my discomfort but didn't seem to think the baby would be in jeopardy. He added, "I hear flight attendants are trained in childbirth."

That was a sobering thought that I considered momentarily. But giving birth in a plane did not seem like something that would happen to me so I stepped light-heartedly out of the hospital and headed for the commissary to stock up on all the goodies the next obstetrician was likely to take away.

Susan, having called in sick again, was home when I returned.

"Is this the beginning of the end?" I teased. She couldn't quit her job anytime too soon for me.

"Probably. But you know, I just realized the other day that there is an insurance corporate office on the corner a block away from here. I'm going to apply."

She did and a week later was working within sight of our flat. The job allowed her to use her mind and it paid better, too. She came home, if not always in a chipper mood, at least in a more agreeable frame of mind.

Within days, we had settled into a new routine. Susan dashed off to work each morning, and I ran my errands at the Presidio or puttered around the house between watching for the mail and starting supper. When Susan came in from the office, she took her news magazines to the tub for a long soak unless there were late-breaking bulletins about the murders. I watched the evening news. Eventually, we convened at the table to discuss the latest in our lives and the Tate murders. Miles joined us at his convenience.

Letters from Lee continued to arrive within a reasonable time frame, and I began to relax a little with the adjustments we were all making. Lee's news that a six-day mission had been canceled helped, even though I still worried about his new battalion commander who had his men "trying a lot of new things." Aside from the company's men suffering from malaria, ringworm, and jungle rot, activity was basically quiet. Of course, I was thrilled every time Lee referred to R&R, especially when he confirmed there would be no trouble with his getting on the roster in early October.

Lee also wrote that he had been chosen Platoon Leader of the Week. This honor merited him a meal at the Commanding General's mess and praise from his own battalion commander. I tried to be pleased for him, but found it absurd that in the middle of war, where the outcome is truly a matter of life and death, the army would have such a juvenile recognition system. Was a man who daily faced fighting for his life really impressed by eating with a general? The war was a puzzling study in contrasts.

The imminent shadow looming over us, unfortunately, was the worry about Jim and Judy's baby due the middle of the month. The doctors would still make no predictions about the consequences of the measles, and we waited anxiously.

However, that concern took a backseat to more immediate alarm when I read Lee's letter written on the eighth of August. Little did I suspect what the envelope held that morning when I happily grabbed it from the box and headed upstairs. Sitting in the living room near the window with the best light, I read Lee's writing, which grew progressively smaller and more difficult to read, Lee's mark of excitement or tension. He wrote that he had been on point with one of his squads on the seventh when they had heard noises. Believing that they had encountered three or four lone Viet Cong, his men had maneuvered into position and opened fire. Instead of a few stray local enemy troops, what Lee and his five men had attacked was a Regular North Vietnamese base camp, complete with fifty to one hundred or more soldiers.

My heart was in my throat. Lee and his followers had been within 75 meters of the NVA when they opened fire, only to discover heavy reinforcements at the target site. *My God!* The NVA then pinned down the squad with return fire and began flanking their position. *They were surrounding them!* The rest of Lee's company could not move to help them. *What the hell were they waiting for?* That's when Lee and his men ran out of ammunition. *Jesus!* They decided to make a run for it. Lee had gone only ten meters when an RPG rocket exploded on the spot he had just left. The concussion knocked him and another man down. If he hadn't moved when he did, if he'd waited another three seconds. . . .

I was shaking so badly that I had to steady my hands against my legs. *Stupid, stupid, how goddamned stupid to get himself into such a situation!* I forced myself to continue reading only to find that the Commanding General of the 199th had pinned a Bronze Star for Valor on Lee the next day—*encouraging his stupidity!*

I sat still. Never had I experienced an anger so cold and of such magnitude. The emotion was too powerful to take the shape of words or tears or any other form of expression. But for the difference of literally three seconds, last week some stiff, military-precision officer would have been handing me a green velvet box with a medal inside, mumbling condolences and telling me how brave and heroically Lee had died. *What bullshit!* I didn't want any posthumous medals. I didn't want a goddamned hero. I just wanted Lee home alive.

I couldn't move, not even to re-read the letter. I was still sitting there when I heard Susan turn the key in the lock in the door. She came charging in, calling out, "What's for dinner? I'm starving for—" She stopped mid-sentence and dropped her purse. "What's wrong?" she asked slowly. "You're as white as a sheet."

I simply held out Lee's letter and she walked across the room to take it. She sank into the chair opposite me without taking off her coat and buried her head into the pages.

Tears began rolling down her cheeks as she read. I envied her ability to cry, although it was only the second time I'd ever seen her do so. Susan looked up finally and whispered, "Jesus, Linda, he could have been killed."

I nodded.

She swallowed and wiped away tears as more took their place. After a long silence, she said, "I guess he's a real bona fide hero now, uh?"

Her words released my fury and I leaped from the chair. "He's not a hero. He's stupid. Stupid, stupid!" I shouted at her.

"They gave him a valor award," she offered tentatively.

"Don't you see? He started it! He's been out there so long he's getting overconfident, arrogant, thinks he's untouchable. He miscalculated. And those goddamned commanders gave him a medal for it. They decorated him for being stupid!"

I paced the floor. Susan, leaning farther back in her chair, said quietly, "I've never seen you this mad."

"I'm furious. What the hell was that squad doing so far from the rest of the company? Even I know how stupid that is. And running out of ammunition? Stupid, stupid, stupid."

"You know, his handwriting is really bad. No wonder it takes you so long to read his letters," Susan teased.

But I was not to be deterred from my tirade. I continued to curse Lee, the new battalion commander, whom I was sure had a hand in this fiasco, and everybody else remotely connected with the episode. To add fuel to the flame, I dug out Lee's previous letter from the sixth. If he had gotten himself killed that next day, that cryptic note would have been my last letter from him. Some farewell.

I was so angry I didn't write Lee that night, one of the few evenings I skipped. I certainly wasn't going to condone his actions or congratulate him. Neither could I tell him what I really thought. I was truly tired of this goddamned war.

I calmed down after a couple of days. I did not, however, forget Lee's near-brush with disaster, nor did I forgive him for it. While his following letters clearly indicated that the experience had gotten his attention, the echo effect left its mark on me as well. As glad as I was to see every envelope with Lee's handwriting, I steeled myself against the possibility of any more heroics as I peeled back the flap. I then proceeded through each letter with caution, as though I might hit a trip wire any minute. He caught me off-guard once; he would not do so again.

{Chapter 19}

The three of us living in the apartment found our footing without Mrs. Sheldon's steadying hand the best we could. Susan made friends with a lovely woman at her new company and began bringing Adrienne by after work. Adrienne's visits were always brief because she was eager to get home to her young son, who spent his days with her mother. Occasionally Susan went out in the evenings with Adrienne, apparently preferring dinners with her friend over parties with Miles. I was always extended an invitation, but I thought it was good for Susan to have time with someone besides me, someone who brought new perspectives to her life and gave her something to talk about other than Vietnam.

Miles continued to work through the remaining weeks of the summer; more often than not, he stayed at home after work those days. I assumed the partying had grown old or that too much fun was taking its toll.

I passed the days in a haze of the mundane, waiting for mail that came too infrequently, traipsing weekly to the commissary, writing letters, and daydreaming about the baby. One day rolled into another during this unusual spell of quiet on the Western Front.

Without Mrs. Sheldon in the picture, Susan and Miles spent more time talking than shouting. It was in the course of one of these conversations that Miles revealed that his partying had dwindled because he had not been able to reciprocate, to host a bash of his own. The flat had been so filled with arriving bodies and settling-in activities during the summer, the opportunity for him to be recognized as one of the occupants had been overcome by other events.

When Susan pointed this out to me, I agreed that she was right, and after all, his having use of the space when he needed it was one of the reasons the Sheldons had leased the flat in the first place. His having access paid a portion of the rent. Both of us readily agreed that he should plan to return the invitations he had received.

On the day of the party, Susan and I cleaned the apartment and prepared the food, actually delighted with the activity and sense of urgency. Susan was excited by the festivities and looked forward to the evening. I withheld any judgments, although I did agree to at least put in an appearance.

A few familiar faces drifted in early. Randy, sporting his most current bib and tucker, assumed the role of co-host and grandly welcomed new arrivals while I kept an eye on the hors d'oeuvre trays as an excuse to stay busy. Each time I reentered the living room from the kitchen, the crowd had doubled again and the noise level tripled. Soon guests were crammed shoulder to shoulder, yelling to each other over the booming music.

Fighting my way back to the kitchen with another empty serving platter, I found Susan by the table, grilling Miles through clamped teeth. "How many people did you invite?"

Miles shrugged innocently, "Just a few, some friends."

Susan whispered furiously, "You don't have this many friends. You don't even know this many people in San Francisco."

Miles retorted, "What's the problem? So some friends brought other friends. It's no big deal." He threw up his hand in greeting to someone he recognized above the heads of the throng and waved them into the room.

"Well, hell," Susan said passively, "we might as well enjoy ourselves, too. Let Miles worry about the food." With that, she grabbed my arm and pulled me into the hallway.

"Excuse me, excuse me," Susan called as she worked her way through the close bodies, "make way for my pregnant roommate."

Susan moved us from one acquaintance to another, introducing me as we inched along. Invariably, when she said "pregnant roommate," eyebrows shot upward into question marks and suppositions formed on faces. Then Susan leaned over to shout into the person's ear that our husbands were in Vietnam. Expressions told me that in 1969, having a child out of wedlock was far more acceptable than having a husband in Vietnam.

• • •

I awoke with a start. "Goddamn it, Miles," Susan was shouting. When I reached the kitchen, Susan was alone, standing with the refrigerator door pulled open. "Do you believe this?" she asked, gesturing inside the appliance. "They ate it all."

The food crammed into the shelves the day before was gone—not only what Miles had bought for the party but also most of the groceries I had stocked up to last us the rest of the month.

"They even drank the two beers I had left," Susan complained, slamming the door and charging toward Miles' room.

This was going to be another screamer, so I ducked down the back stairs and through the garage into the yard. Shivering in my lightweight robe, I sat on the stone ledge and rocked back and forth, trying to decide when it would be safe to return to the house. Intermittent shouts kept me at bay for an hour before I concluded that, quarrels or no, I had to get warm.

By the time I topped the stairs, Susan was cleaning the living room. I dressed and helped her, saying nothing about the fight or the food. We worked in silence until the room regained its former look, and then we started on the kitchen.

"Look, I'm really embarrassed, okay?" Susan said as if in response to an accusation I hadn't made. "He's my only brother, the only family I've got here, and he's young. He and his friends didn't mean anything by eating all our food. Their parents still support them, so they don't understand what it's like not to have money. Miles will pay for the stuff they ate."

I knew I had missed something critical because I didn't understand why she was defending Miles or why she was mad at me. I asked.

"We saw you down in the yard, crying."

"But I wasn't crying," I protested. "I was shivering because it's so damned cold out there. I was just trying to give you two the privacy to fight it out."

Susan stopped in her tracks and stared at me. Slowly she said, "I was mad at him. Then, damn it, I thought you were crying so I got mad at you. I thought 'How goddamned important is a bill of groceries anyway? He's my little brother.' Shit, I don't even know what I'm doing any more. I'm losing my mind."

"Join the crowd," I invited with a laugh.

I used the episode as a pivotal point. I knew that Susan had been angry with Miles because of my financial situation even though she did not say that outright. Besides, I was weary of being poor and feeling as if I was stealing from myself by taking money from savings. In my next letter, I asked Lee to increase my allotment by $100 per month. That wouldn't be enough, but it would help.

The next day's mail brought Lee's response to a picture of myself I had sent: "Wow! Honey, I don't care if you are double that, you will look wonderful in October." I felt tentatively reassured. He said he would be the one who would look bad on R&R, as he had lost twenty to thirty pounds and had jungle rot on his face. I couldn't imagine that any abuse would affect the way I viewed his body. Maybe he felt the same about mine. I looked in the mirror and wondered.

{Chapter 20}

While reading the newspapers for more information about the Tate murders, I could not miss the headlines that announced President Nixon was coming to San Francisco. I had never lived in a place accorded a presidential visit. I found it exciting that I could get a firsthand look at Lee's commander-in-chief when I read that his first stop would be at the Presidio.

Susan, of course, thought I was crazy, declaring that she wouldn't walk across the street to see Nixon. Were she to involve herself in any way with the President's visit, it would be to join the protests during his downtown stop. No way would I have put my body and baby in jeopardy by being part of the throng in the streets, because the protests against the war were growing uglier at a frightening rate.

However, I knew I could count on the military to control the situation at the Presidio. Anyone who looked at all suspicious, especially those with long hair, would be kept outside the installation gates. The Nixon visit to the Presidio would be as safe and sedate as Sunday morning church.

I arrived at the post three hours before Nixon was scheduled to land, determined to get a close-range view. I was so early, in fact, that the troops were still roping off a plot of the asphalt runway as the designated area for the crowd. Selecting what I deemed to be front row center, I took my place as the lone welcoming committee—feeling conspicuous and foolish but also resolved. A few gray-suited men with walkie-talkies shot darting looks at me, determining if my midriff bulge was a baby or a bomb.

During the second hour of my vigil, the ranks of the waiting grew, but not dramatically. The sun was bright and warm; it was a really beautiful day in the Bay area. In fact it was getting downright hot, I realized as I took off my jacket and shifted my weight from one leg to another. I should have eaten breakfast, I thought, as a tingling wave of cool swept over me. I took several deep breaths. I could not, would not, faint here. I threw my jacket onto the asphalt and lowered myself into a sitting position.

By the time the helicopter came into view, the crowd to greet Nixon had grown to a respectable but still conservative size. With the thrill of the President's arrival, I felt revived and stood up. The crowd cheered as the large helicopter touched down and the door slipped open. I found myself smiling and cheering, too. A day to remember, I told myself.

Then Nixon, arms extended overhead and fingers forked into Vs, stepped out and bestowed a toothy grin upon us. I frowned at how much he resembled the caricatures in the editorial pages, but still, I reminded myself, he was Lee's ultimate boss, so I would remain open-minded.

Nixon joined his entourage on the asphalt. My heart sank, and the last of my patriotism vanished. The President of the United States was the smallest man on the tarmac, strutting like a king while his uniformed military greeters stooped to compensate for his lack of stature as they shook his hand.

Nixon paraded before the crowd, passing less than ten feet from me. The top of his head would not have reached my chin. To know from newspapers that he was short and to see it for myself was two different pieces of information. I was appalled.

Then I caught sight of Pat Nixon. Much prettier in person, she carried an aura of serenity—and everlasting sadness. Although she smiled on cue, her expression conveyed no joy, only more sorrow. And even she was taller than her husband.

Nixon performed a token review of the troops, made a short speech, and then prissed his way through the remaining protocol before reboarding his helicopter.

The only other detail that stood out was the sight of NBC reporter Herb Caplow walking by in a madras shirt and khaki pants. I was surprised to see that he limped—another television distortion. Not that it mattered. Anyway, Caplow was more impressive than Nixon, and taller, too.

{Chapter 21}

The impending arrival of the thirteen-year-old Arab boy had been wreaking havoc with our tension levels, making Susan especially nervous about the added responsibilities of supervising a teenager over whom she had no real authority. She was not happy when she learned that Khalifah would be with us for three weeks before his school term began.

"What are we going to do with him?" Susan had demanded of Miles. "He'll be bored out of his mind. I can't just turn him loose in this city." But Miles refused to be concerned.

I, too, had my own anxiety about living, even temporarily, with a Kuwaiti prince. I didn't even know if he spoke English.

When I asked Susan about Khalifah's bilingual ability, she shrugged and said, "I'm sure he speaks English. However, he may not be able to understand you and your Texas accent." She laughed, which did nothing to reassure me.

Late in the day of Khalifah's arrival, I was reading in the living room when the front door opened as Susan heaved a heavy suitcase ahead of her. Miles pushed past her with another large piece that he lowered to the floor with a groan. Leaning back out the door, Susan coaxed, "Come on, Khalifah. Come in."

The boy slipped through the doorway and into the foyer, at once matching what I had expected and, at the same time, taking me by surprise. Khalifah was indeed an Arab teenager with thick, black hair and swarthy skin blemished with acne. It was difficult to judge his height as he shuffled from one foot to the other, though he couldn't have stood more than five-seven upright. He appeared ill at ease yet simultaneously exuded an air of superiority, seeming to have taken it for granted that Susan and Miles would carry his bags while he shouldered only a small tote.

Khalifah looked older than thirteen—more like fifteen or seventeen. Only his eyes betrayed him, downcast but darting nervously at his surroundings like an intimidated child.

Khalifah limply shook my extended hand while I welcomed him and asked about London and his flight. Instead of answering, he looked first to Miles and then to Susan with a puzzled expression.

Susan, of course, laughed gleefully, and said, "I told you he couldn't speak West Texas."

Throughout dinner Khalifah spoke only when spoken to, limited his responses mostly to one syllable, and kept his eyes lowered during the meal, all of which was understandable behavior for a teenage boy in a foreign land being served West Texas fare. The three of us took turns springing from our chairs to fetch additional foodstuff and condiments from the refrigerator and cabinets. While he shyly shook off our attempts to please, Khalifah also managed to convey an attitude that suggested that while he did not require special attention, we were correct to offer it. Life with a prince was going to be interesting.

Susan tried to engage Khalifah in conversation, starting with questions about his sister and relating tales about their experiences together. When that got no response, she switched to London plays and shopping.

The evening ended with Susan and me arching our eyebrows at each other from our opposing headboards after leaving Miles to settle the newest member of our menagerie into the room they were sharing.

In the ensuing days we learned that Khalifah was indeed a loner who liked to leave the house by mid-morning and, we supposed, tour the city until dark. Susan insisted he return for dinner each night. On days when he elected to stay in the flat, he amused himself by listening to the stereo, radio, and TV at their highest decibels, driving all the rest of us into errands we hadn't planned to run.

September 1969

• • •

{Chapter 22}

By the first of September, I had decided that babies never really get born. I had proof: Judy was already two weeks late in delivering hers, and I had been pregnant since before time began.

That was my state of mind when Daddy called to tell me that he and Mother were driving to Tucson to visit Brenda and Danny over the Labor Day weekend. "Why don't you fly down and meet us?" he suggested. A surprising pang of homesickness hit me when I realized they would be together, but knowing I had to monitor every cent in case Lee got his R&R in October, I hesitated. "We'll pay for your ticket if you can get away," he coaxed. I laughed shamelessly at my own transparency and said I thought I could rearrange my schedule. Replacing the receiver, I felt lighthearted at the prospect of an event so near to look forward to.

The first mail from Lee in September, written in late August, reinforced my mood. He wrote that he had been assigned the task of delivering payroll to the battalion's troops hospitalized at Cam Ranh Bay, which translated into a four-day break for him and a relief for me. He also wrote "no sweat" about my request for more money and told me he would increase my allotment by $100 per month, starting with the October payday.

The best news of all, though, came in the middle of the night when I answered the phone, blinking wide awake at the sound of my brother-in-law's drawl. "Well, we've got a baby boy," he announced in a proud voice that was ever so slightly edged with hesitation. I waited for a beat for him to continue, but he didn't.

"Congratulations," I said, delighted yet apprehensive. Rather than ask if the baby had problems, I asked about Judy. He assured me she was fine and that she had been a real trouper during the delivery.

Finally, Jim said, "Well, Linda Ann, looks like we dodged a bullet this time. Baby seems to be okay. 'Course Judy doesn't believe that yet. Don't know if she ever will."

I was flooded with relief that my nephew—nephew!—was normal. But then Jim's terminology of "dodged a bullet" struck a chord of fear in my chest. How many more times could this family dodge the bullets? I was becoming Mrs. Lanning. Still, Lee was the only one now in the land of flying projectiles, and I was never going to like the odds.

Forcing myself to focus on the positive in these wee hours, I asked about the baby's name, which was to be James David, and when mother and baby would be going home. We needed to take joy where we could get it and milk it for all it was worth.

I tried to approach my trip to Tucson with the same attitude—take some joy where I could create it. But nothing was ever just straightforward in my life anymore. This was not a trip I had to take. I was going only because I wanted to enjoy myself. What if traveling when I didn't have to adversely affected *my* baby?

I stopped dead at the realization that enjoying myself had become an absolutely alien feeling, one that now provoked guilt, discomfort, and fear. Standing once more in the door at the San Francisco airport, I took a deep breath, trying to decide how much trouble I would cause everybody if I canceled my tickets. Mother and Daddy were already on the road, Brenda would soon be leaving to pick me up at the other end, and Susan had just pulled away from the curb. I could only rationalize that I was committed as I trudged toward my gate.

Lightheaded with relief when the plane taxied to a stop in Tucson, I fended my way into the aisle and to the jetway entrance only to be blasted by the desert heat. Before I reached the gate, my skin grew taut as my body swelled in reaction to the desert temperature.

Brenda's iridescent smile above the crowd guided me toward my sister. When I stepped out of the throng to greet her, her mouth dropped open and she screamed, "You're huge!"

I sighed, "I feel like a blimp."

By the time we reached the trailer park, my ankles overflowed my shoes; my fingers looked like gloved sausages. Even my face felt stretched. And this was in the dry high desert heat. What would I look like in Hawaii when humidity joined the equation?

When my brother-in-law came home from work, he blinked in astonishment as he surveyed me and said, "Gonna be a big baby."

The visit with my family was fun and familiar, and I was glad that I had not missed it after all. Yet, when the weekend came to an end, I found myself looking forward to going "home" to San Francisco.

• • •

Susan picked me up at the baggage claim curb and handed me three envelopes as she eased her way into the traffic flow. "Here," she said, "I know what you came home for."

I was elated to get the letters, but the stronger emotion was an overwhelming flood of affection for my roommate. I caused her trouble yet offered little of the support she deserved.

I moaned as I read the first letter, "There's a captain from Lee's battalion recuperating at Letterman. I'm supposed to look him up, but I don't think I can pronounce his name."

"Another Chinese?"

"This one looks Italian," I said, scrutinizing Lee's writing.

Susan laughed. "How do you get involved in these things?"

I moved on to the second letter, in which Lee expressed his concern about not yet having heard any news from Georgia. It felt odd to know the baby was almost a week old and Lee still didn't know. How old would our baby be before Lee knew he was a father?

Turning to Susan, I asked, "What's happened here?"

"Tom's fine, Miles is moving out next week, Khalifah can't get a diplomatic passport, thank God, and we're getting a new neighbor. Also, the Whittemores will be back in a couple of days."

I felt like I'd been gone a month.

She explained, "I've spent the weekend working to get the flat above ours leased to Eleanor Morgan, who's a friend of Mother's. Her husband's in Europe for several months. No kids, just poodles."

"And the other people?"

“Oh, the Whittemores,” She continued, “they have a second-floor flat in the building next door. More old friends. They’ve been on vacation since we got here.”

“This is beginning to sound like one of those American compounds you used to live in overseas,” I teased her. “Collins Street, the Sheldon Compound.”

Again I was reminded how little Susan asked from life and how much less than that she was getting. I impulsively suggested, “Let’s go shopping this weekend. We can go to those places down the Peninsula you’ve talked about, or downtown. Anywhere you like.”

Susan shot me a skeptical look, which I countered, saying, “I know, I never want to go, but this weekend will be different. Didn’t you say you needed to buy a baby gift for Gayle Arnovitz?”

“She’s due any day. Okay,” Susan agreed, “we’ll do it.”

I was pleased. Three letters from Lee, a token payback to Susan, new people to meet. Life looked agreeable. In fact, it felt so good to be back that even finding Daphne asleep on my bed and hearing Khalifah crank the radio full blast didn’t faze me.

{Chapter 23}

By early fall, I had become an overachiever in the obstetrics clinic, often arriving before the staff. It did not significantly decrease the actual waiting; I simply waited earlier. Still, it gave me a certain sense of satisfaction to challenge the system.

At my mid-September visit, my arms looked like those of a heroin addict by the time the lab technician finally struck the mother lode, which siphoned off all the new blood I had generated since my last visit. When the lab technician applied the gauze pad, it turned red, so he gave me another. By the time he reached for the fourth one, we were both convinced the vein had no off button.

"Here, hold your arm like this," he instructed, doubling my forearm onto my upper arm and hoisting my elbow above my head.

I had a hell of a time changing from the hospital smock to my street clothes, but the medic was right. As long as I kept my arm bent and my elbow skyward, the bleeding ceased. Each time I brought it down, the blood surged.

I nevertheless located the floor where the Vietnam wounded recuperated, so I could look up Lee's friend, because it occurred to me that this man had seen Lee since I had. I reminded myself that this captain had been wounded in July and, therefore, not seen Lee for almost two months. Still, his time with Lee was more current than mine, which somehow seemed unfair, but I would settle for any additional information I could get.

The minute I stepped off the elevator, my nerve deserted me as an orderly pushed a gurney by me. On it lay an unconscious man. When I looked up, my impression of the open ward was of one of casts in traction, limbs in absentia, warriors bled sheet-white. I thought for a moment that, as with my trek into Chinatown, I would be nauseated both from the hospital smell of disinfectant and the sight of such gross injuries.

I steeled myself and marched forward, finding a nurse and asking for directions. I was not going to fail Lee, and I was not about to prove the Red Cross right about whether I should be in the war recovery wards.

I counted beds until I reached the designated one. Only then did I move my eyes upward where they encountered the cool stare of Bernie Petrocelli. I tried to smile despite the inventory of casts, traction equipment, and other items attached to his body. He did not acknowledge me, which was awkward and unfriendly. But he also did not blink. I waited. Still his eyelids did not move.

A slow dread crept into my stomach. This man was dead, and nobody had noticed. I looked for help, but attracting no attention with my silent plea, I turned back to the body. With great relief, I caught the ever-so-slight rise and fall of the sheet over his chest. I moved around the bed and whispered, "Captain Petrocelli?"

The puffed and bruised face did not respond, and the eyes continued their unrelenting stare toward the foot of the bed. I repeated the name. Nothing. Clearly this man had bigger problems than the broken leg suspended in mid-air. Maybe he couldn't hear. Maybe I had unwittingly stumbled into the psycho ward. These contraptions might be restraining devices.

The groans in the room seemed to be louder than before. Unnerved, I slowly began backing into the center of the ward. The man I had come to visit never moved except to breathe.

When I reached the ward entrance, I met the nurse again. "Did you find Petrocelli?" she asked breezily.

I hesitated. "He didn't seem to hear me. Maybe there's something wrong, you know." I pointed at my ears.

"Nah," she swatted my idea away with the swing of her arm. "Petrocelli hears fine. He's probably asleep."

"But his eyes are open," I explained. "Maybe he doesn't want company right now."

"Sure he does," the nurse countered. "Let's wake him." When I caught up with her, the nurse was shaking her patient.

"Hey, Petrocelli," she said too loudly. "You've got company."

The eyes finally blinked and went instantly from glazed to focused. Bernie Petrocelli slowly rolled his head toward the nurse and then at me. He squinted and closed his eyes as if to correct his vision. I couldn't blame him for not comprehending that there was a gigantically pregnant stranger standing beside his bed.

The nurse pulled a chair around for me and turned to leave. I had just sat down and begun to introduce myself when the nurse leaned back over my shoulder and said, "I should probably warn you, Bernie got his jaw messed up pretty bad. His mouth is wired together so he won't be able to talk much."

I could not disguise my sense of bewilderment, because I had nothing to say to Petrocelli beyond identifying myself as Lee's wife. He was supposed to do the talking, according to my plan. I rubbed my already irritated arm in despair.

When I looked up at him again, I sensed a question in his expression. "I had an appointment this morning. The lab tech got carried away," I explained, holding out both arms for him to see.

He blinked a nod of understanding and then arched his eyebrows. I answered as if asked, "The baby's due in December."

He then furrowed his forehead, which I took to equal, "Who are you and what are you doing here?" I explained that my husband was a lieutenant in Charlie Company of Petrocelli's battalion in Vietnam. He squinted and I repeated Lee's full name. With a rush of disappointment, I realized that the captain couldn't place Lee.

"A lieutenant . . . platoon leader . . . Charlie Company . . . tall . . . tan . . . well, you're all tan, so that doesn't help. From Texas . . . a little arrogant, a bit cocky . . . wears glasses."

There was a flicker of recognition. I wasn't sure if he actually remembered Lee as one of many junior officers who crossed his path or if he only wanted me to think so. But by that time, it didn't matter. We had worked out a system of communication.

Yet another nurse stopped and asked, "So is this the girlfriend?" Petrocelli and I both looked at her in disbelief. She noticed my figure and laughed, "Guess not."

Then we played Twenty Questions about the girlfriend until I figured out that she lived in Los Angeles and flew up on weekends to visit. I actually found myself having a pleasant time. In a way, it was just as well that his jaws were wired shut, because even if Captain Petrocelli remembered Lee vividly, he could not have told me what I wanted to hear. Men don't notice the details that make life worthwhile for women.

When I stood to leave, I told the captain that I had another appointment in two weeks and asked him if I should stop by. His look seemed to indicate he hoped I would.

Images of Captain Petrocelli and the other wounded followed me home to make unexpected appearances in my path like pop-up targets on a rifle range. I had assumed that if Lee came home, he would do so whole. Even though I had obtained my passport in case he was evacuated to Japan, I had not envisioned him actually wounded. I had not had first-hand material for such visions. Now I could see nothing else as I drove home, frowned at the empty mailbox, and made my way up the stairs.

Just as I opened the door, the phone began to ring. I reached for the receiver. I heard static and then I heard Lee's voice. I dropped my purse and grabbed the receiver with both hands, shouting, "Lee!"

But the voice that answered was that of a man giving me instructions on how to conduct an overseas call from Southeast Asia. He repeated that after completing each transmission I was to say, "Over." "Over, over," I complied.

"You don't need to say 'Over' for me, ma'am."

My heart was racing. Lee was on the other end of the line at that very minute.

"Yes, yes, I understand," I said impatiently.

"Now say 'Over,'" he instructed.

Jesus. I did and then I heard Lee laughing. "Hi, Honey. Do you understand that you have to say 'Over' every time you finish talking? Over."

"Lee," I shouted, "is this really you? Are you okay? Where are you? I miss you so much . . ."

"I'm fine," he said as clearly as if he were standing next to me. "But you have to say 'Over' when you finish. Over."

"I know. But I wasn't finished. How are you? Over."

"I'm good. I'm going to a new assignment . . ."

"In the rear?" I jumped hopefully with the question.

"Ma'am, you have to wait until he says, 'Over,' before you can speak," the intermediary lectured.

"You didn't tell me that," I countered. "You only told me I had to say it. Never mind. Lee, are you still there? Over."

"Yes, just listen a minute. I'm taking over a new platoon for the next month or so. Same area, just different mission. Over."

"What kind of platoon? Why? Over."

"Recon platoon. It's a good job. I'll send you the new address but I will still get letters sent to the old one. Keep them coming. How's the baby? Over."

"Lee, I can't believe I'm really talking to you. The baby is fine, and big. Lee, I miss you so much. I don't even know what to say. Over." It was hard to think fast enough and damned disruptive to have the third party overhearing everything, waiting for the maddening "Over."

Lee laughed and said, "Then just listen. I've got the dates for R&R—"

"When?" I screamed.

"You have to wait—" the voice started again.

"Okay, okay. But he doesn't know when I want to talk. Over."

"Linda, will you stop arguing with the operator? Dates are the thirteenth through the nineteenth of October. You got that? Will the doctors still let you travel that late? Over."

"Oh God, Lee, that's only a month. I can't wait to see you. Don't worry about the doctors. But, Lee, I'm really huge—"

"You'll look beautiful to me," Lee said happily. I noticed the operator hadn't reprimanded him for not waiting for the magic word. "I'll send you all the details. Do you have a copy of my orders? You'll need them to get the military discount. Over."

"Is there a particular place you want to stay? Over."

"Anywhere you are is where I want to be. I miss you, too, very much. Over."

"Sorry, your time is up."

"Lee? Are you still there? Over."

"Yes, honey. Take care of the baby and I'll see you in a month. I love you. Over."

"I love you, too. Please take care of yourself. Over."

"Don't worry. Bye, Honey. Over."

"Bye," I whispered into the phone, not knowing if the signal was going to Lee or the operator.

"Transmission complete," the voice announced. "You did real well, ma'am, once you got the hang of it."

"Thanks," I mumbled and then hung up. I went straight to the living room and collapsed into a chair. For the first time since April, I knew Lee was alive this very minute. He sounded so wonderful, his voice making him more real than since he had climbed into that Greyhound bus five months ago. I had never fully expected to talk to him again.

The call had been so sudden. So short. I thought of a million questions I wanted to ask, now that it was too late. He was trying to tell me something important about the new platoon, but I hadn't given him the chance to finish.

Suddenly, I jumped up. I danced, I laughed, I grabbed a calendar, and then I called Susan.

"Hawaii in four weeks and three days," I shouted. "Can you believe it? Where's the nearest travel agency?"

Thirty days and a "wake up." If we could both just hang on for thirty-one more days—him to his life, me to my sanity.

Good grief. I had no clothes to wear in a tropical climate. My hair needed a trim. Suddenly I had a zillion things to do.

{Chapter 24}

The euphoria of talking with Lee and setting into play the plans for R&R could last only so long, of course. This was, after all, war—a war against the VC, a war against the odds, and a war against time. The scorecards did not add up to peace of mind. In this area, Lee was part villain as well as part hero. Since I had visited Petrocelli, I had a new perspective of the real dangers each letter described. I knew that none of those men I had seen at Letterman had intended to end up there. They had all thought they were immortal, and my husband was turning out to be the most delusional of all. When I read Lee's next letter, I found him admitting new ambitions:

> Talked with battalion commander before I came back out. He said the Commanding General needed a new aide and he would recommend me—he also said if I didn't want it that I would have a good chance to be company commander in a few months—I told him I want a company. He said I would stay as platoon leader for another month or so— then work for S-3 in the rear a month or two and take a company possibly in Dec. I will not extend to get a company—but if I can get one during normal tour I will jump at the chance.

I couldn't decide who was worse, Lee or his battalion commander, ultimately preferring to be irritated with the lieutenant colonel because he was obviously a manipulating son of a bitch who knew how to dangle the carrot of command in front of Lee. But I couldn't deny that he was working with easy prey.

Each time I saw light at the end of the proverbial tunnel, the walls collapsed and I had to start digging for hope again.

Susan was stuffing her own letter away one night when I entered the bedroom. "How's Tom?"

"The same. Still spreading rice in the Mekong Delta."

I laughed as I always did when I thought about Tom, son of a Fisher County dry land cotton farmer, teaching the people of the world's rice basket how to improve their native crops. In his advisory role, Tom doubled as a soldier and agriculturalist in the Delta, where the chances were that he was helping the Viet Cong, as well as the "friendlies," produce better crops. His assignment was but one more twist in the tangled intentions of Uncle Sam.

"How's Lee?"

"The same. Still spreading bullets in the jungle."

Susan and I looked at each other and became hysterical at the absurdity that her husband was trying to feed the Vietnamese while mine was trying to kill them, knowing that not one American soldier in ten thousand could accurately tell the difference between a friend and a foe without the props of circumstances or guns.

The next day I pulled out my patterns and material to begin sewing my wardrobe for Hawaii and on Monday hiked up the hill to the nearest travel agency to make arrangements for the trip. The only hotel brochure available in the small office was for the Colony Surf. The pictures looked agreeable, and because I didn't know anything about the island, the location at Diamond Head sounded fine—until the agent quoted me the price per night. I gulped.

"Each room is really a suite," she explained, "with a small kitchen. I think you'll be quite comfortable there."

What the hell? It was only money. Thinking that Lee might like having the convenience of a kitchen, I made the reservations and then wrote the $159 check for my military discount plane ticket.

• • •

Miles moved to his apartment near school and Eleanor Morgan moved in upstairs. Miles's departure left Khalifah even more at a loss during his final week with us, which he handled by leaving even earlier each day and finding yet another higher notch on the TV volume when he came home.

Eleanor, a tall, slender woman with stylish gray hair and crinkles of laugh lines to soften her angular face, brought a flurry of activity and two full-sized jumping poodles that demanded to be the center of attention. All day long the dogs jumped and bounced, making me feel that I lived beneath a gymnasium where basketball players trained. Wimpy little Oscar, who had quickly shifted his allegiance to Susan when Mrs. Sheldon left, might have some redeeming qualities after all. Still, having the energetic and entertaining Eleanor around more than compensated for the irritation of the hyperactive dogs.

Susan introduced me to the Whittemores, a pleasant if fastidious couple who planned each day's activities six months in advance. I envied the trivia they considered worries. Nevertheless, it was comforting to have more reinforcements in the neighborhood, and Don and Jean insisted we call them if we needed anything. With his age and her ill health, I feared they were more likely to need us. Dutifully, Susan exchanged phone numbers with them, recording theirs on the last page of her address book.

At long last, it was time to pack Khalifah off to school, which Susan and I did while trying to conceal our own relief. The nearer we got to San Raphael, the more panicked he appeared. He didn't argue about his destination, though it was obvious he did not relish the idea of being sequestered in the paramilitary environment. I felt as if we were delivering him to prison.

Any guilt that Susan and I felt on the drive home dissolved when we entered the apartment and realized that we finally had the place to ourselves. We began the immediate transfer of her things to her "new" bedroom while I planned how I would arrange what was now my room to accommodate baby furniture when I bought it. While it was wonderful to have more individual space, I found myself apprehensive that Susan's move across the hall would put a distance between us. I need not have worried; that night she propped herself up in her usual spot for a long chat before bedtime.

Now that Susan and I had the apartment to ourselves, we fell into a comfortable routine: She went to work at eight, I sewed through the mornings, she sometimes came home for lunch and often brought along

Adrienne, I put away my projects late afternoon to start dinner, and Susan arrived home by a quarter after five. As before, she went straight for a long soak in the tub while I cooked dinner and watched the evening news.

I began doing my letter writing at the kitchen table while preparations for dinner progressed, which was a vast improvement over trying to balance the paper on my protruding abdomen while propped up in bed. Besides, now the baby kicked so much and so vigorously that he often jarred my pen all over the page.

The Lannings and I exchanged letters every week or so. Writing them was a task, not because I was harboring any ill feelings but because the only thing we had in common was Lee. I repeated positive highlights of his letters and Mrs. Lanning reciprocated by telling me what Lee had written them; I passed along the doctors' prognoses and she reported on the weather.

I also answered Cheryl Hightower's letters in which she told me about living in an apartment in Houston and teaching school. Her cheery notes made her sound well-adjusted except when she mentioned Steve. Her loneliness was evident, too.

Susan got an announcement from Gayle, who had given birth to a baby boy named David. Susan called to congratulate her. It seemed odd to think Gayle and Mike Arnovitz, a couple Susan and Tom had befriended at Fort Bragg, were now parents. Our generation seemed to be moving into the next phase of life—even if the fathers like Lee and Mike were absent from the birthing cycle.

Life finally seemed to have some elements of predictability, which was when time simply stopped. I was twenty-one days away from Lee, and the clocks froze. Each minute lasted an hour and each day a month. I sewed, I cooked, I wrote Lee, I paced, I read. Nothing helped. The next three weeks of my life were going to last longer than the previous five months. How was that possible?

Grateful for any distractions, I was delighted when I answered the doorbell one morning to find an overweight, red-faced man in a company uniform huffing and wiping his brow. At his feet lay a wooden crate about three feet long by four feet wide by eight inches thick. "This better be the right address because I ain't moving this thing another step," the man growled.

"You've got the right place," I said, seeing Susan's name and stepping back to open the door so he could bring the crate inside.

As he headed down the tiled stairs he said sharply, "I told you, I ain't carrying it no farther. Damned thing's all the way from Vietnam. I don't believe in the war anyway."

The delivery man was climbing into his van and driving away when I tried lifting a corner of the crate and found that I couldn't budge it. I grabbed the phone, so excited for Susan's sake that I could hardly stand the delay of going through the switchboard.

"You've got to come home for lunch today," I exclaimed as soon as I heard her voice. "There's something here from Tom."

Susan was at the door within minutes. "What the hell do you suppose he's done now?" she asked, stepping over the crate and into the foyer. "Why is it outside?"

Between us, we finally pushed-pulled the crate into her room where, on its back, it took up all the floor space. I left her alone and waited impatiently.

"He's lost his mind," Susan said, storming out of her room half an hour later. "Or maybe he just never had any sense."

"Are you going to tell me what it is?" I asked.

"I couldn't begin to describe it. Go see for yourself."

Standing on the bed and propped against the wall stood a gigantic landscape painting of farmers working their rice paddies. This, however, was not a typical agrarian scene, though I could not have instantly said why not. The figures—many bending to plant, others leaning against loads, some balancing baskets of cargo—had an unusual quality that defied even an impressionist label. The background, too, seemed odd.

"Isn't that the worst thing you've ever seen?" Susan asked, coming in behind me.

"Well, it's—"

"Horrible. You know what's wrong with it, don't you? It took me a while to figure it out. There are no shadows. Not one."

"Maybe the artist is making a statement or 'plowing new ground,' so to speak," I suggested, trying to help Tom.

"I think the 'artist,' as you call him, had never seen a goddamn paint brush before in his life. I also think my husband is the only idiot who would buy this piece of shit and ship it halfway round the world. And you know how crazy I am about farmers, rice, and Southeast Asia right now, don't you?"

Susan was right. It really was horrible. The only positive point about it was that it had occupied so much of my day.

I talked with Jim and Judy that night. The doctors had found nothing wrong with James David, who was now home and apparently thriving. Judy, however, was still worried, fearful that the effects of the German measles had yet to surface. It occurred to me that maybe worry had simply become a way of life for all of us.

• • •

I returned to Letterman to once again be weighed, lectured, and leeched. After being released from the queue in the OB clinic, I headed for the wounded vet ward.

The miracle two weeks of recovery could effect was astounding. When I arrived bedside, Captain Petrocelli, still bruised but now with a features-distinguishable face, managed a slight smile and greeted me with a stiffly spoken, "Hello."

"Hello again," I responded, feeling myself blush. "I was here a couple of weeks ago. Do you remember?"

"Sure," he said with a stiff jaw. "You're Lieutenant Lanning's wife."

"I'm relieved. I wasn't sure if I should come back."

"I hope I didn't seem unfriendly. Pull up a chair," he directed with his good arm. "How's your husband?"

"Fine. At least he was a couple of weeks ago when he called." Rather than Vietnam news, which I didn't know if he wanted to hear, I gave him narration of the MARS call and my frustration with the operator. He chuckled as if recalling his own experiences.

Then he said, "You don't think I remember your husband, but I do. Big, tall guy. He was already making a name for himself as a good platoon leader before, I, uh, you know, left."

"I'm not the least bit impressed with his making a name for himself. I was furious when he was awarded a Bronze Star."

Captain Petrocelli laughed lightly and rolled his head. "You've got to meet Jeannie. She's still pissed at me and all I did was get on a chopper that crashed." I liked his fiancée already.

With minimal movement of his jaw, the wounded man explained that when the chopper crashed, his face had been smashed, sending bone fragments deep into his flesh and breaking his jaw in multiple places. As he labored to talk, I couldn't help but wonder: if he had improved so drastically in the last two weeks and still looked this battered, what had he looked like two months ago?

We talked for half an hour even though we had nothing in common, no reason to even become acquainted, except for Vietnam. But our conversation skirted that topic as he told me about his family north of the Bay, Jeannie's visits, and his hopes of convalescent leave soon; I talked about the baby, Susan, and the agony of waiting for mail. For him, combat was over, though he would spend months, maybe years, recovering. For me, we didn't yet know. So for both of us, each in our own way, the war continued.

"I've enjoyed the visit, Captain Petrocelli," I said, standing to leave. "Talking to you makes me feel closer to Lee somehow. I guess because you've seen him since I have." I suddenly had a damned lump in my throat.

He stared at the ceiling and sighed, "Yeah, and there's all kinds of things you'd like to hear about him. At least Jeannie said you would. But I just didn't pay enough attention to those kinds of things, I guess. He's a good soldier, if that helps."

"Not at all," I laughed. "Jeannie surely taught you better than that. But thanks anyway."

He smiled and said, "I hope you'll come again, but only on the condition that you call me Bernie. Your husband still has to salute me for a while longer, but you don't."

"Sounds fair to me, Bernie. I'll be back in two weeks."

• • •

That evening, at the end of September, I was sitting at the kitchen table writing Lee about my visit with Bernie when Susan arrived home and poked her head in the kitchen.

"Hi," she said as she peeled off her coat. "What's for dinner? I'm starving."

"Fried steak. It'll be ready by the time you get out of the tub," I answered.

"No hurry," she assured me and left the room.

I spooned the shortening into the skillet and turned on the burner. While the grease melted, I sat down to quickly finish my train of thought about Bernie's recovery.

Suddenly I heard a *whoosh!* behind me. I turned to find flames leaping from the skillet. Damn! I tried to think of what to do as my heart went into overdrive. In case of fire . . . what?

"Susan!" I shouted.

The flame surged upward. I turned off the burner. Now what? Smother the fire. I tried to remember, was it salt or flour or baking soda? I moved to the cabinet and looked. There was more flour than anything else. I grabbed the sack.

"Susan!"

The heat was intensifying. I ripped the top from the sack and, with a heave, sent the flour into the fire. The flames reached for the ceiling. Now the flour was burning, too. Small fires sprang up on the stove where the splashed grease had landed.

"Susan!" Why the hell didn't she hear me?

I backed toward the door, watching the greedy fire lick the flour to brighten the straight column of flames over the skillet. A lid sat on the counter. If I could get it over the pan . . . No, it was too small.

"Susan!" I yelled once more, this time heading down the hall.

Banging on the door, I shouted, "The kitchen's on fire!"

I raced back to find the fire still dancing above the skillet with nothing flammable around to ignite. Maybe we could just let it burn itself out. Smoke was filling the room.

Susan, hair dripping, appeared at the door wrapped in a white towel. "Oh God," she gasped with a cough, taking in the scene, "where's my purse?"

"We don't have to evacuate yet," I said. But Susan was gone.

I found her on her hands and knees by the phone digging through her purse. I watched the fire while she dialed. "This is Susan," she said tersely into the receiver. "We have a fire in the kitchen. We need Don to bring your fire extinguisher." She hung up.

Returning to the kitchen, she explained, "I called the Whittemores. I told Jean to have Don bring the extinguisher. He'll be right here. What do you think we should do?"

"I don't know," I admitted. "The flour only made it worse."

Susan moved toward the counter and picked up the lid. "No," I tried to warn her, "it's too—" Too late. Susan had already half placed, half thrown the lid, jumping back as she did so. The disk landed in the center of the skillet, forcing the fire into a whirl of flame and throwing out more grease. The smoke blackened and belched upward.

"Where the hell is Don?" Susan cursed and ran, holding her towel with one hand and flinging open the front door with the other.

"Shut the door. The fresh air is making it worse," I yelled.

"I'm trying to get rid of the smoke," Susan explained, leaving the door open and rejoining me in the blazing kitchen. "Besides, I don't want Don to have to knock. What's taking him so long? We have to do something," Susan said urgently.

My initial panic had subsided somewhat. Still, a loose fire in the kitchen held disastrous potential. And the wall above the stove was now turning black.

Susan grabbed a potholder and edged toward the flames. "What are you doing?" I asked, my alarm returning.

"I don't know. I think maybe if I could just get it into the sink we could put it out."

"No, no. It's a grease fire. Water won't work."

Before I could stop her, Susan had clamped her elbows against her sides to hold the towel and grabbed the skillet handle in the potholder with both hands. She gently picked up the burning pan and turned toward the sink.

The phone rang.

"That might be Don. Answer it," Susan commanded quietly, concentrating. The flaming grease sloshed dangerously close to the rim, first in one direction and then the other, with each slow-motion step she took.

I grabbed the phone. "Could I speak with Susan please," an older woman's voice asked.

"She can't come to the phone right now."

"Well, this is Mrs. Wilson. I just got a call about a fire in your kitchen. Is it out?"

Even gossip couldn't travel this fast. "Susan's trying to put it out now," I rushed my words to stress my hurry. "She'll call you back." I slammed down the receiver.

"Is Don coming?"

"It was a Mrs. Wilson asking about the fire. How could she know already?"

Susan measured each step carefully.

"It's getting hot," she muttered between clenched teeth, halfway to the sink. "I can't hold it much longer."

"What can I do?"

"Run!" Susan yelled. She took one giant step and threw the pan toward the sink. With a single leap, the flames jumped clear of the skillet and clutched onto the curtains. Ignition! Fire raced upward across the entire width of the window. The blaze was brilliant.

My heart stood still. The whole place was going up in flames! Then, before I could blink, the flames vanished. I couldn't believe my eyes. The flames were gone, and so were the curtains. Susan and I stood staring. From the rod now hung jagged stalactites of charcoaled plastic. Flame retardant curtains really were!

The skillet and lid were still clattering in the sink when Don Whittemore, red-faced and breathless, charged in with an industrial-strength extinguisher that was almost half his size.

"Where's the fire?" he gasped. "I'll put it out. Just show me where it is."

"I think we've got it," Susan said to calm him. "Just sit and catch your breath." She pulled out a chair for him.

"No, no, I should hose it down," he argued while collapsing into the seat. "Just let me figure out how to work this thing."

"Please slow down before you have a heart attack," Susan pleaded. He looked like a qualified candidate if ever anyone did.

"Why didn't you call me?" he asked, still fiddling with the buttons. "I could have put it out."

"I did call," she said dubiously.

"No, Mary Wilson told us."

"She called us, too." I volunteered. "Who is she anyway?"

"Mother's friend I talked to last week. But she lives on the other side of the city. How did she know our kitchen was on fire?'

The phone rang again. I was closest, so I grabbed it. "Is the fire out yet?" asked the same voice.

"Yes, finally. Let me get Susan." I handed off the phone and surveyed the damage. One set of curtains sacrificed, one lid fried somewhere past well-done, one skillet ebonized, one wall slightly scorched. Not bad, all things considered. Globs of smothering coals still puffed faintly on the stove and flour powdered the floor and my clothes.

"Is everybody all right?" I heard another voice behind me. Jean Whittemore staggered into the apartment and stood panting in the doorway, looking prepared to join Don in the coronary unit.

"Sit down, sit down," I said, pulling out another chair.

"I tried to call, but the line was busy. I thought the whole place had gone up because surely no one would be on the phone during a fire. Did you put it out, Don?"

"Hell, no," he muttered. "I don't even know how to use this thing." He was still pulling at every attachment.

I heard Susan laughing hysterically in the hall.

Jean looked at me and asked, "Why didn't Susan call Don?"

"She did."

"No, I called the wrong number," Susan announced from the doorway. "I thought the Whittemores' number was the last one in the book so I didn't even look at the name. I'd forgotten about adding Mrs. Wilson's last week. Poor woman. She gets this call about a fire and has no idea what's going on. Why would I be calling her? So she phoned back. When Linda said there was a fire, she figured out who the Don was that I was trying to call."

We were amazed as the pieces fell into place. Tension melted into laughter as our emergency took on slapstick dimensions, each of us regaling the others with the events from our own perspectives.

"What happened?" Jean Whittemore asked when she finally caught her breath. "How did the fire start?"

"I turned my back on a pan of grease," I confessed, realizing that I had been so frightened and then so relieved that I forgot the whole thing was my fault. "Oh, Susan, I'm so sorry."

"No harm done," she said, "except scaring everybody nearly to death. I thought you were yelling about something on the news and I just didn't want to hear it. I put my head under water. But you kept on. Next time, could you be a little more considerate in your timing? Oh, hell, I'm still in my towel."

Susan went to change and the Whittemores departed with Don still cursing the unusable extinguisher. Left alone, I began shaking. I could have burned down the building, the whole block. All because I wasn't paying attention. The possibilities were even more terrifying than the actual fire. Most terrifying of all was the possibility that if the apartment had been gutted, I might not have been able to go to Hawaii in two weeks.

October 1969

{Chapter 25}

Finally, finally, I could say that I would see Lee "this month" and then "next week." I had my tickets to fly to Honolulu on Sunday the twelfth and return late in the afternoon a week later, allowing me to arrive a day before Lee and depart a few hours after he did. My objective was not to miss a single minute with him.

I now opened each letter from Lee more apprehensively than before, afraid of a change of plans, a delay of days, or a postponement until January. I checked the date as I opened every envelope and then scanned until I found "R&R." Only after assurance that nothing had been altered did I read the rest of the letter. I still did not trust that gung-ho battalion commander.

In one, Lee asked me to calculate the time difference between Hawaii and Texas and let his parents know when and where he would call them. I wrote the Lannings to ask them to be at a friend's house at seven o'clock in the evening their time on the thirteenth. They were to wait an hour. If Lee didn't call that night, he would the next. With so many uncertainties, it was the best I could do.

I secured a prescription for diuretics from a less-than-attentive obstetrician and then popped up to see Bernie. He was sitting on the bed, still in casts but improved.

"I can't stay but a minute," I said after our greetings. "I have a thousand things to do. I'm leaving for Hawaii in three days." I just loved saying it!

He smiled in reminiscence. "Hawaii's wonderful. You'll have a great time."

"Oh, I hope so," I giggled. "I can hardly wait."

Suddenly my face turned red and I bit my lip. Bernie laughed, "Your being pregnant is not going to make any difference, you know."

"You really don't think so?" I was scarlet by now but strangely comfortable with his directness.

"Trust me. What he really wants is just to be with you. Nothing else matters."

"I don't know, Bernie. I didn't look like *this* six months ago. He's going to be shocked."

"Just hold him and tell him you love him. Everything else will take care of itself. Give him some credit. Besides, he's lucky to have a woman like you."

I wasn't sure if we were now talking about Lee and Linda or about Bernie and Jeannie. Maybe Bernie's injuries had realigned his priorities like the surgeons had realigned his face. Maybe he hadn't told Jeannie how important she was when he could have and he had almost lost the chance to ever let her know. Maybe he was just reading my need for reassurance. It didn't matter.

"You're a very nice guy," I said simply.

"Have a good time and come see me when you get back."

• • •

Susan's mood was distant when she drove me to the airport the second Sunday morning in October. I worked to contain my excitement, knowing that my being with Lee all week would only exaggerate her loneliness. Too, I knew she was worried about me. Even in our sequestered life we had managed to hear dreadful stories about pregnant women who went to Hawaii for R&R only to find themselves rejected because their spouses or boyfriends couldn't deal with their condition. Some men had refused to even look at their women; others had taken days to adjust. One soldier had even moved to a different hotel. Of course, there were also the rumors about the pregnant women being sick and unable to leave their rooms. In fact, I had not heard one single story that was encouraging.

"He damned well better be nice to you," she muttered. And then she laughed. "You tell him if I can live with his pregnant wife for six months, he can for a week."

"I'll tell him," I promised, trying to quell my doubts.

When she stopped at the curb, Susan faced me and said, "I'll pick you up right here next Sunday. Tell Lee hello for me and have a good time." She quickly turned her head but not before I saw her watering eyes. I was barely out of the car before she pulled away.

The stewardesses assessed my condition when I boarded the plane. The one nearest my seat asked, "So when's the baby due?"

"Not for another seven weeks," I reassured her and myself simultaneously. Facing five hours over the ocean with no place for an emergency landing was not a situation I wanted to focus on.

The jetway retracted, the plane pushed back, the engines roared, and the nose lifted off. Five months, three weeks, and four days after Lee left for Vietnam, I was finally on my way to see him.

{Chapter 26}

I collapsed on the king-sized bed when I reached my room at the Colony Surf, thankful to have negotiated the arrival, baggage claim, and cab ride without incident other than perspiring profusely and swelling voluminously. The ride from the airport had taken less than half an hour, and the driver, wise to the whys and wherefores of passengers, had pegged my purpose here immediately and pointed out the R&R Center at Fort DeRussey as we drove past.

"You'll want to be there early," he warned. "Never can be sure when those military planes will land." Then, as we continued the drive along the palm-lined streets, he told stories about how some men didn't show up on the planes they were supposed to, how some couples had spent their entire week trying to find each other, how some women came just to tell the men they were divorcing or breaking up with them.

Now propping myself up on my elbows, I surveyed the room with satisfaction. The "suite" was really only one large space with a couch and sitting area several steps from the bed and a kitchen sectioned off to the left. Decorated with cool colors and air conditioned, it was a haven from the sticky humidity.

I caught sight of my enlarged ankles and sighed. I had not been bothered when I could no longer see my toes; I didn't begrudge the necessity of an extended abdomen; but I hated the fat ankles. I took a diuretic.

Next I called the R&R Center, knowing only that Lee had written that he would arrive in Honolulu three hours before he left Long Binh on the same day—which did me no good because he hadn't known his departure time. I asked the soldier who answered when they were expecting planes in from Vietnam the next day.

"The first one is due into Honolulu International around noon and those passengers should be here at Fort DeRussey by twelve-thirty or one o'clock," the male voice answered. Very patiently he asked, "Now, ma'am, did he send you a flight number?"

"No. He didn't know."

"Okay, ma'am, sometimes they don't. Okay, ma'am," the soldier continued in what was an obviously well-rehearsed and often delivered speech, "now you need to come here to the Center in the morning about half an hour before he's due in. Don't, I repeat, do not go to the civilian airport because all arriving men are put on buses and brought directly here. If you go to the airport, you will not be able to see him. Do you understand?"

I was back to the military. "Yes, I understand."

"Good. Now if he's not on that flight, then we've got another one coming in later in the day, and you just keep meeting the buses till he gets here, okay? Sometimes things get messed up on the other end."

Although the soldier was trying to brace me for potential delays or disappointments, he did not dampen my spirits. Everything in my being told me that Lee was already on his way.

With a surge of energy, I drew open the drapes to find a balcony that offered a sweeping vista of the beach and ocean. I inhaled the salty breeze. By this time tomorrow, Lee would be standing there beside me. I was delirious at the prospect.

I unpacked, ironed my clothes, and arranged my cosmetics. I fluffed the pillows. I tapped my toes. I looked at the clock. 3:15. I glanced through the hotel's information. So the balcony was a lanai, huh? 3:22. I examined the kitchen. I rearranged my clothes. 3:27. I paced. 3:31. I turned the clock around.

By dusk, I was exhausted by the sheer anticipation. Shortly thereafter, the pill kicked in and I spent the rest of the night in the bathroom, or so it seemed. Each return trip reinforced my decision, no matter what, to take no more of these capsules. In between, I tossed and turned. *What if Lee wasn't on the plane? What if something had happened to him and the Army didn't know where to find me? What if. . . .* I finally fell into a fitful sleep counting dire "what ifs" as though they were sheep that kept jumping the fences in my mind.

Up before seven and ready before nine, I paced and then studied the mirror until nine-thirty. I had washed and curled my hair, but when I brushed it, the curls sagged in the humidity and limped away. I re-curled to no avail.

Just before ten o'clock, I called a cab and told the driver to take me to Fort DeRussey. "Kinda early, aren't you?" the unshaven man asked, pushing back against his seat rather than turning his head. "Planes don't usually land till around lunch."

When I arrived at the post in the heart of Waikiki, I found a long open-air counter tucked under the low slanted roof of the reception center. Umbrella-shaded tables and chairs filled the patio, making the place look more like a bar at a tropical resort than a military installation. I inquired about the arrival time of the plane and learned that it had refueled in Guam and was still on schedule, due into Honolulu International in two hours.

Eventually a couple more women wandered into the reception area and then a few more. Over the next hour more arrived, usually alone but sometimes in pairs, most nervous and excited, striking up conversations with others and taking animatedly with their hands. A few, however, appeared miserable and withdrawn, eyes downcast and darting. I felt a pang of sympathy for the unsuspecting troops.

By noon the congregation filled the courtyard and the air tingled with giddy laughs and giggles. I was now rigid with apprehension. Never had I seen so many attractive females in one place. Blonde, brunette, tall, short, fair, dark, petite, stout, teenage, mid-life—they came in every description except pregnant. I was the only one with a bulging belly.

"Ladies, ladies," I jumped as I heard a somber public address system voice. "Can I have your attention, please."

The twittering stopped mid-air. The hush was instantaneous.

"Ladies, it is my duty to inform you . . ." the voice drawled and then paused heavily. Suddenly the tone and cadence changed and the voice shouted, "That your husbands have just this minute landed at Honolulu International Airport."

For half a second no one moved, and then a screaming cheer shattered the silence. Touchdown!

"Ladies, ladies," the microphone voice shouted above the elated cheers. Slowly the noise quieted with sporadic laughter still erupting intermittently from one end of the waiting area and then the other. Individual conversations buzzed.

"Now ladies," the voice persisted, "while the plane is taxiing to the terminal, I need your help. If you'll look around, you'll see a whole bunch of women here, somewhere between two and three hundred. Every one of them is just as excited as you are. And if we don't get organized, we'll have a mob scene when your husbands get here and nobody will be able to find anybody."

The possibilities set off another round of snickers and giggles. I smiled, seeing us from an outsider's perspective. We really were in a ridiculous situation, but leave it to the military to find a way to organize and control even the love scenes.

"Ladies," the voice was the same but the sound was different, "now I want you to understand what's going on here."

I followed the stares of the other women, turning to see that the amplified voice was now coming from a bullhorn carried by an officer wearing chaplain's insignia. He paraded toward the center of the group, holding in his other hand a walkie-talkie, and said, "This is a squawk box that allows me to talk directly to our people who are bringing your husbands here. I promise I will keep you informed about where they are at all times. In fact, you will know more about what will happen to them next than they will. So you can all relax and listen to a few things I need to tell you."

The chaplain explained that the men would receive a briefing while still on the aircraft, then deplane, collect their luggage, clear customs, and finally load onto waiting buses. The box squawked and the man lowered his bullhorn to listen.

He looked up smiling, "Okay, ladies, the plane is approaching the terminal and the briefing officer is preparing to board."

I shook my head, astounded at the protocol. The men had been captive on that plane for more than twelve hours. Surely someone could have briefed them between Guam and Hawaii. Besides, how much heed did they really expect three hundred men to pay who hadn't seen their women in six months? Incredible.

The chaplain kept us distracted, lacing his information with jokes that played easily to his eager audience. He was quite good, and tension-relieving laughter fell in with his stand-up comedian timing and delivery.

"Are they off the plane yet?" a woman yelled out. The chaplain conferred with the radio and then said, "Sorry. The briefing is still going." A collective moan hung in the air.

"Aw, shucks," he mimicked. "There goes another ten minutes of your R&R." Louder boos and hisses and more laughter.

"Now to make sure we don't cause any delays on our end, we're going to get ready, right?"

"I'm ready now!" a woman cried, and the chaplain lost his audience. When he finally gained control, there was a teasing rumble of protests while he related he would need us to form two lines along the double-width sidewalk from the street to the pavilion. After we were in place, we were to face inward and not move. Throughout his spiel, he paused to obtain updates, obviously pacing his instruction to us with the progress at the airport.

"Okay, ladies," he said with a big smile, "the first men have cleared customs and are boarding the buses."

Every revelation added another twist of tension for a crowd already wired. Like the others, I could feel my breath becoming shallower with each passing minute.

It was time, he told us, to form the lines. Chairs scraped, heels clicked, purses snapped, and three hundred pent-up women milled and paced. The chaplain cut through the herd, working one group and then another along the sidewalk, bullhorn to his mouth, squawk-box hand waving and guiding. He paced the center, shooing lines against the edge of the walk. When he talked to one end, the other closed in to hear, destroying the formation. He retraced his steps, scolding lightly and reshaping lines—only to find the opposite end had now closed in while his back was turned.

The only time we were all still was when he lowered the bullhorn and raised the radio.

"Ladies, the buses are full and ready to roll. They are now departing the terminal."

Hysteria laid siege to the place and the lines collapsed. The chaplain threatened to withhold all other information if his straight configuration did not reappear.

Finally, choosing a central location and twisting his head back and forth in surveillance, he said, "Now, ladies, the buses are going to unload one at a time. The men have been told they are to walk straight up this sidewalk. You must, I repeat, must stay in your place until your man reaches you. Do not, I repeat, do not go running when you see your man get off the bus. No. If you do, we will have chaos. Stay in your place until he gets even with you and then you can grab him and do whatever you want with him but not until he gets to you. Do I make myself clear? Have you got that?"

There was assenting but dubious laughter and the chaplain walked up to one woman and asked, "Now what are you going to do when you see your man get off the bus?" She screamed.

"Okay," he said, rubbing his ear, "but you can do it from right here, not up there."

"Now seriously, ladies," the chaplain said, "if you don't wait in place, you will not be able to find your man in the crowd. You don't want that to happen to you."

The sun beat down on my head and I found myself wondering if I would recognize Lee. What if he walked by and I missed him? Standing three-quarters of the way down the line, I reassured myself that not many six-foot-five men would make it this far.

The radio crackled with static. Then the chaplain said, "The buses are now three blocks away."

I fought back the tears.

"They're stopped at a traffic light and—wait—green light. Here they come.

"Ladies, it's been a pleasure being with you this afternoon. I hope you have a wonderful week. My people say the first bus is now two blocks away and should be rolling into sight any minute now."

Sure enough, within seconds, the first of the lumbering green army buses chugged into view and slowed to turn the corner, followed in caravan by the others.

The lead bus stopped at the end of the sidewalk and the doors opened. Pandemonium broke loose as the first man stepped off. Women who could see their men shrieked as they jumped in place and tried to obey their instructions. Amazingly, the lines held. The men who walked up the aisle of females looked bewildered as they frantically searched for the right face.

Above the crowd, I watched as the first bus emptied and pulled away. The second vehicle took its place and the screams began anew. I scrutinized every man as he ducked under the door frame and then looked up, bringing his face into full view. After a hundred, and then two hundred, they all began to look alike.

Hugging couples were now moving past me as the other remaining women and I inched closer to the buses. The third bus closed its doors and pulled away. My mind, my emotions, my body, my very being—all were suspended without sensation. The sixth and last bus rolled up and the look-alike heads bobbed up once more.

I suddenly laughed. I knew Lee better than I had remembered. If he was on the plane, he would not have pushed his way to the front. In fact, he would have done just the opposite. I chuckled at his predictability and waited.

The last man off the last bus was mine.

{Chapter 27}

When I saw Lee's lopsided grin, I smiled and waved, wondering how I could have imagined that I wouldn't know that face anywhere under any circumstance.

Lee kissed me and then took me in his arms and held me while the tears rolled down my cheeks as I said, "I knew you'd be the last one off the damn bus."

He held me at arm's length and said, "You sure look pregnant." We laughed and held each other again.

Before we could finish our greetings, we were ushered through the doors of a nearby building. My mind scrambled as I sought to absorb reality. Lee was actually here, actually beside me as we sat holding hands through yet another briefing. In an auditorium filled with reunited couples, I couldn't believe anyone was paying attention to what the uniforms on the platform were saying. For me, only two messages penetrated. The first was the warning that the men were to carry at all times during their stay in Hawaii the small yellow card being distributed. The speaker said that in the event of illness or accident, it was imperative that medical personnel had access to the card. When Lee received his, I read that the bearer of the card was on R&R from Vietnam and had been exposed to malaria, yellow fever, typhus, smallpox, plague, and every other disease known to science. I gulped.

The second message was the ugly reminder that R&R would not last forever. Lee was free until seven o'clock on the morning of the nineteenth, at which time he was to report to the airport for his return flight. I felt panic. We had six months of catching up to do as well as getting a head start on the next half-year, and we had only five days and seventeen hours. But then, I reminded myself, that was more than I ever expected to have with Lee again. We could surely make the best of it.

We hailed a cab and got in. Suddenly we were alone. With so many questions and so much to say, I didn't know where to begin, and Lee seemed to be groping, too, as we traded small talk about the distance to the hotel and my arrival the day before. It didn't matter what he said, though, because all I wanted to do was look at him and convince myself that his hand was really touching mine.

While my eyes were riveted on Lee, his darted about, taking in the towering palms, the postcard beach, and high-rise buildings. He continued to keep his focus on the roadway even after we left the scenic section, and my heart skipped a beat. He was avoiding looking at me. I watched him closely to interpret his signals. He seemed to be searching.

"Is anything wrong?" I asked, thinking that if he was looking for a way out, we might as well get it over with now.

"No, no," he said without taking his eyes off the street, "this is great."

"What are you looking for?"

"Ambushes," he whispered and then caught himself with a laugh. With a sheepish grin, he said, "Habit. I forgot where I was." He visibly relaxed and turned his attention to me.

Seeing him full-face, I studied the changes. His close-clipped hair was sun-bleached and his skin golden brown except for a healing sore on his left cheek.

"Jungle rot," he explained, touching it self-consciously.

When we entered the hotel room, another uncomfortable silence descended upon us as if we were total strangers. Lee was obviously still himself, yet he wasn't the same man I had put on the Greyhound all those months ago. And I, well . . . I knew I had changed, too. Figuring out how those individual differences were to affect our relationship left us both tentative and nervous. So we busied ourselves in touring the suite as if each feature was surprisingly unique and wholly significant. When I found myself showing Lee that the small refrigerator even had a drawer, I knew we had crossed into the absurd. Yet the disconcerting feeling remained.

Lee must have felt the tension, too, because he suddenly said with too much nonchalance, "Oh, I have a message for you."

"A message for me? From who?" I asked suspiciously.

"From the battalion commander," Lee answered without looking at me. Then he turned and said, "He said to tell you that you are married to probably the youngest company commander in Vietnam."

I waited for my mind to assimilate the information but nothing happened. "You're not a company commander," I said.

"I will be in a week," Lee said with a cocky grin. "I take over command of Bravo Company as soon as I get back."

I stared at him, unbelieving and in full denial of what his news meant for me.

Lee continued quickly, "In fact, he wanted me to postpone R&R and take the company this week. But I told him I needed a break."

All I could think about was how many ways I could curse that goddamned battalion commander. That son of a bitch was determined to get Lee killed yet.

"Isn't that great?" Lee asked. I could hear from his tone that he wanted me to be thrilled for him, just as he had when he got his orders for Vietnam. I didn't care that commanding a company was a coup. What it meant for me was more months of terror because now Lee wouldn't be taking a safer job at the rear. But even more immediately, I realized that if I let myself react, this news could spoil our time together, polarize us at opposite ends of the spectrum. I took a deep breath and told myself that many things could happen in a week. Maybe the battalion commander wouldn't be able to wait for Lee's return before putting someone else in the slot. Maybe the war would be over before Lee could get back. Maybe. . . .

As I stood in the middle of the room grasping for an idea to get past this, Lee said from the sofa, "Turn all the way around."

I felt my face burn and said more defensively than I'd intended, "I warned you about how big I am."

"You look wonderful. I just wanted to see you from all sides," he said, grinning. "Wow. Did I do that?"

"You certainly did," I laughed and then grabbed my right side.

"Are you okay?"

"It's just the baby kicking," I explained. In spite of myself, I blushed when I asked, "Do you want to feel?"

Lee looked puzzled but intrigued as he came toward me. "You mean now? It's kicking now? Sure."

I placed his hand high on the right side of my abdomen and felt it bounce against the internal movement. "Wow," Lee said laughing with his wide eyes. "I didn't know it would feel like that."

In that moment, as we stood in the middle of the room with Lee first experiencing the life of our child, all the tension and "what ifs" fell away and we were suddenly, truly together again. And in that moment, too, Lee and the baby fused in my mind as connected entities. Never again would I feel that the baby was mine apart from him as I had felt for so many months.

• • •

At the designated time, I dug through my purse to find the Sylvester phone number so Lee could talk to his parents in Texas. Our get-reacquainted awkwardness behind us, both Lee and I were relaxed and euphoric. I had felt the dread that he might have changed dramatically or be Vietnam-crazy, melt away during the afternoon, and I was basking in relief as I dialed the operator. Lee, meanwhile, was lounging on the bed, pillow propped, hands interlocked behind his head. He was so damned cute.

The operator put me on hold and while I waited, I absorbed the panorama from our windows. The ocean was picture perfect, and into the scene slipped a magnificent sail boat. I was about to tell Lee to look at the vessel when the operator began talking, so I snapped my fingers to get his attention.

Without warning, Lee, who had been so relaxed, suddenly jerked upright, his arms and legs flailing in all directions. He dove for the floor. I watched open-mouthed as he crawled about madly, his right arm violently reaching in groping swings. Oh, God. He *is* crazy, I thought wildly.

I dropped the receiver and stepped back, wondering what the hell I should do. He was having some kind of seizure.

In the next instant, Lee went slack. Then he began to laugh. My alarms were blaring full-blast as I took yet another step away.

"I'm sorry," Lee said as he pushed himself into a sitting position. His face was red and he shook his head in disbelief. "I didn't mean to scare you. It's just that for the last month with the recon platoon, a snap of the fingers meant 'Enemy in sight.' I went for cover. But I couldn't find my damned rifle."

He pushed himself up and grabbed the phone. "Yes, Operator, that's Sylvester, like the cartoon cat," he said, smiling up at me.

Still shaking, I managed a laugh and said, "Everyone told me you would be crazy. I was beginning to believe them."

In spite of Lee's explanation and my relief, I found myself keeping a close eye on him for more unexpected reactions.

"Hi, Mama," Lee shouted into the phone. "Yeah, it's really me . . . It's good to hear your voice, too . . . Oh, I'm fine, just fine . . . Yeah, Linda's here with me."

Lee smiled at me while he listened to his mother. I could hear her excited voice coming through the phone and could picture her intensity on the other end as she talked rapidly. Mrs. Lanning believed telephone conversations should be short.

"Is Pop there?" Lee asked. "Then I want to talk to you again before we hang up, Mama. Hi, Pop. How are you?"

Lee's phone call to his parents lasted less than three minutes. I couldn't imagine how Mrs. Lanning could bear such a brief dialogue with her son after six months, but I was sure that when they hung up, she cried and told Mr. Lanning that all she had needed was to hear Lee's voice for herself.

When Lee called his brother Jim, the first thing he talked about was taking Bravo Company. I could hear once more in Lee's voice the need to have his listener respond enthusiastically. Although I could not hear what Jim said, Lee's reiteration of how lucky he was told me that Jim shared my reservations rather than Lee's excitement.

"What did Jim say?" I asked when Lee hung up.

"He said the battalion commander was not doing me any favors," Lee repeated with a shrug. "I thought for sure Jim would understand."

"Maybe he does," I said, leaving the double meaning to stand.

• • •

On Tuesday morning, we set out for a day of sightseeing. Before we left the hotel, Lee asked with suspicion in his voice, "Are you sure you're up to this?"

I laughed and told him I felt young and alive for the first time in six months, though surely he could see that for himself.

We took a cab to Waikiki and strolled through the tourist sections and into the International Market, holding hands and exchanging humorous, disconnected snippets about our recent experiences. I asked Lee endless questions about the jungle and tried to visualize as he patiently explained triple canopy, elephant grass, and bunker complexes. However, every time I looked into his eyes I lost my concentration. Nothing else seemed real.

"Should we sit down for a while?" Lee asked periodically.

"I'm fine," I reassured him, but after the third time he inquired, I decided that perhaps he was the one who needed a break. "But if you like, we can rest."

We sat at an outdoor table and ordered soft drinks. Before the waiter could deliver them, a loud crash came from inside, sending Lee halfway out of his chair before he caught himself.

"Good reflexes," I teased. He grinned with a red face.

I watched other tourists ambling by, many of them R&R participants. If I had any doubt about my classification of the young men, it was dispelled when a car backfired and I saw the knee-jerk reaction along the street as some males jumped laterally into doorways and others dived head first onto the concrete. For a moment the whole crowd hesitated, as if suddenly suspended, and then action resumed as the men dusted themselves off and laughed with too much macho gusto. When I looked back at Lee, he too was readjusting himself, pulling his legs and arms back into place.

"It's just hard to make the transition," he laughed. "Forty-eight hours ago that sound was gunfire."

"You just keep jumping," I said. "I don't want you out of practice." As disconcerting as the abrupt flailing was, I knew the unquestioned reflex was part of what was keeping him alive.

We stopped at a small grocery store where Lee gleefully stocked up on ice cream, cookies, candy, and fresh fruit—all foodstuff he had been craving for the past six months.

"My doctors would not approve," I told him as I stowed the items in the kitchenette. "Do you want some ice cream now or are we going to a movie?"

"Shouldn't you rest first?"

"Why?" I asked. "I feel wonderful." He was treating me like an invalid, which was out of character. "Look, if you don't want to go back out, just say so and we'll stay here."

"No, I'm okay, but aren't you supposed to be tired or sick or something?" he asked, concerned and confused.

"I don't think so. Should I be?"

"Well, all the guys I heard about who met their pregnant wives on R&R said the women were tired or sick all the time. One of them couldn't even leave the hotel room. So I just figured. . . ."

"Ah ha," I laughed. "You've heard tales, too. Let me tell you one from the women's side, about the guy who moved to another hotel because he was so repulsed by how his pregnant wife looked." We traded stories and laughed about our fears based on situations that bore no resemblance to our experience.

That night we went to see *Midnight Cowboy*, Dustin Hoffman and Jon Voigt's latest film. I was amused that the opening scenes of the movie showed Voigt on a Greyhound bus leaving the Big Spring area, which was about seventy miles from our Texas hometowns.

When we got into bed that night, I was suddenly seized by panic again. Almost thirty-six hours of our time was already gone.

"I resent having to sleep when we have so little time."

Lee chuckled, "We can't stay awake until Sunday."

"But we don't have to go to bed just because it's midnight or eat because it's noon. Let's throw away the clocks and just do what we want when we want. Let's not think about time again."

We talked until the sun came up and then drifted off into restful doses. On Wednesday, we had hamburgers for breakfast and Oreo cookies and butter pecan ice cream for lunch. And then we took an "afternoon" stroll through the market area again, oblivious to the fact that it was almost dusk. As we walked through unhurried crowds, we were accosted by war protestors who were heckling anyone with a military haircut and handing out "Baby Killer" leaflets. I gripped Lee's hand tighter, unsure how he would react to what had become a familiar sight to me in San Francisco. Lee took one of the leaflets, glanced it over, and laughed sardonically before he crumpled it and dropped it into a trash can.

“You’d think they could see I’m more interested in making babies than killing them,” he said with a disgusted laugh. He smiled to reassure me.

An artist did caricatures for each of us and a photographer took our picture, both of which we thought portrayed us as younger than we were.

We continued walking and talking, turning corners and crossing streets with no destination in mind. I gave Lee an animated rendition of my visit to Chinatown and my encounter with Mrs. Jong. He laughed and said, “Yeah, well, Jong thought it was pretty funny you went to see his mother. She doesn’t speak English.”

“You’re telling me this now?” I feigned an indignant pose. “You also neglected to mention that Bernie Petrocelli had his jaws wired together and couldn’t talk at all.”

Then I told him about my visits to the veteran’s ward at Letterman. “What exactly happened to him? I’ve always been reluctant to ask Bernie too many questions.”

Lee sauntered along with his hands in his pockets and said, “He was one of the wounded in Delta Company in June. I think I wrote you about that. The way I heard it, Petrocelli, who was the company commander, took a minor hit to his hand. He got all his wounded dusted off and wanted to stay in the field. But they insisted that he go in to have the wound checked, so he jumped on the last Medivac helicopter. The damned thing was shot down and nearly killed him.”

I could vouch for that, although I found myself censoring descriptions of how Bernie had looked when I first met him.

We continued walking. Lee talked about DeForest, Little, McGinnis, Loeffke, and others whose names I recognized from his letters, but I had difficulty remembering which was the radio man and who was the fellow platoon leader. He talked about Butterfly Hill and the seventh of August, but I couldn’t keep track of which action went with each fight. It was a collage of people and events with no sequential chronology to aid my understanding. Finally, I stopped and stood looking at Lee.

“Tell me what the war is really like.”

We were both somewhat startled to find that we had left the tourist areas and drifted onto a back street. Lee spotted a bar and said, “Come on. I’ll do my best to explain it.”

He opened the bar door and we stepped inside to hear country western music wailing from the jukebox and to meet the uninviting looks of the patrons who appeared to view us as intruders. We ignored the stares and headed for a back booth with its chipped and graffitied black table and worn, red vinyl seats.

Lee ordered a pitcher of beer and began talking, taking me step by step from his arrival in Vietnam. He told me about the different men with whom he lived, laughing at the black humor GIs develop and occasionally wiping away a tear that sprang up as he described the character of his men.

I watched him, spellbound. I still couldn't track each of the events or what men were involved when. I did grasp that DeForest was the radio man who was never more than a step away from Lee, Loeffke was the battalion commander whom I suspected of grandiose schemes and whom Lee defended from my verbal assaults, and Bill Little was a lieutenant buddy from the battalion who had taken over the recon platoon from Lee the day he left for R&R.

"I don't know," Lee said with a shake of his head. "I hope Little does okay with recon. He's good, but he's a kind of overeager, like he's got something to prove."

I laughed. "*He's* overeager?"

Lee smiled and answered, "I got over that my second day in-country. Besides, I don't have anything to prove. I'm just trying to stay alive."

I struggled to comprehend how the six months affected Lee as he allowed me to share in the hurt, fear, humor, and camaraderie he had experienced. We laughed and cried together in the back booth of a back-street bar. The time and distance we had been apart disappeared.

He took a long draw of beer from his glass and smiled. "Somehow talking about all this to you helps the whole thing make more sense," he said quietly. I sat still.

"Little things don't seem important anymore," he continued. "When people start getting all excited about something, I ask myself, 'Is anybody going to die because of this?' If the answer is yes, then it's important. If the answer is no, then it's not."

Lee shook his head fatalistically and took another sip from his glass.

"Everybody who gets killed dies because somebody made a mistake. Him. His buddies. His commander. Somebody." Then he laughed without humor and said, "My job is to not make a mistake and to not let anyone else make one either."

I knew I could never feel closer to Lee that I did at this moment—and that his words about making mistakes would haunt me for the rest of his tour. I now understood that if anything happened to Lee, it would not be God, Fate, or bad luck. It would be because somebody somewhere made a mistake.

We sat quietly for a few more minutes, neither of us wishing to break the spell. Finally, our eyes met, we smiled, and slowly, reluctantly, we left the bar.

Lee bought some ice cream and we wandered back to the hotel. We had experienced an emotional climax and the afterglow lingered.

• • •

The next day, we rented a red Mustang convertible, a wonderful extravagance, I thought, and meandered through the Honolulu traffic and onto the highway to tour the island. Within minutes we were inland among open, bare, cultivated acres that Lee recognized as pineapple fields. I suggested we stop at the Dole headquarters, where I sampled wedges of the fresh fruit. Lee looked at the pineapple with disdain, explaining that he had eaten so much of it in the Delta that he never wanted to taste it again.

On the North Shore, we paused to watch surfers challenging the crashing waves and then followed signs to Captain Cook's landing site. Lee was most intrigued by the talking myna birds, which struck me as a paradox. In many ways, he was still a little boy wandering through the war with grownup responsibilities.

By noon, we were startled to find ourselves back in Honolulu. Our Texas long-distance driving mentality had neglected to realize the compactness of Oahu. We laughed at our misperception and then spent a couple of hours driving through the city, enjoying the sun, the scenery, and each other. In the late afternoon, we returned our jazzy little car to its rental slot and wandered once more through the market so I could buy souvenirs for Susan and my parents.

Lee asked what I wanted to take back. "You," I answered. He suggested a Hawaiian dress instead.

"I never want to be inside a 'fat' dress again," I told him with strong conviction. As colorful and exotic as the native dresses were, their shapeless yardage held no appeal.

"Then what about that one?" he asked, pointing to a floor-length green and white floral fitted garment in the window. Fifteen minutes later we walked out of the store with the dress.

"I'll send you a picture of me in this as soon as the baby's born," I said, hoping that indeed I would someday be that size again.

• • •

On Friday I awoke, sat bolt-right up in the bed, and shook Lee. "I have to have banana cream pie," I said.

Propping himself up on his elbow, Lee squinted and asked, "Is this a craving?"

"I don't know. I've never felt this way, but if I don't get a banana cream pie, I'm going to go crazy."

While Lee dressed, I called the hotel restaurant. No luck. We hopped a cab to the Waikiki area where we began canvassing the coffee shops and cafes. We found key lime, apple, blueberry, chocolate. After a half dozen strike outs, Lee pushed alternatives, suggesting, "Could we go to the grocery store and just get a banana? Maybe you could mash it up in a slice of coconut cream or something."

We spent half the day in search of the elusive pie while I half laughed and half cried, hoping the craving would disappear as abruptly as it had descended. Finally, when we had exhausted the eating places in the beach area, and ourselves in the process, Lee said gently, "If I could get it for you, I would. I just don't know what else to do unless we get a car and drive around."

By late afternoon, the immediate craving had dissipated enough for me to concentrate on other things, one of which was a discussion of baby names. I was adamant that our baby boy be named Lohn, and I had amended his middle name to be Michael instead of my maiden name, Moore—this after having told Mrs. Sheldon my plan and having her say the two names together quickly. Yard equipment had not been what I had intended! And because Lee's first name was Michael, I was pleased with the alternative. Lee had no problems with my choice.

Girls' names were another matter. He favored old-fashioned, traditional ones such as Barbara, Margaret, and Eunice. I preferred more current ones, including combinations of our names. For years we had joked about naming a daughter Reveille because I thought it was a pretty word associated with our past. Not only was the Texas A&M University mascot collie always named Reveille but also we had spotted an exit sign for Reveille Road in Houston. I wanted her name to be Reveille Ann and call her Lee Ann. Lee discouraged the nickname. "Besides, you say you're having a boy. So we don't have to worry."

"Yes," I replied, "but what the hell do I know about these things? Anyway, the best way to be sure it's a boy is to have a great girl's name picked out, you know, like carrying an umbrella so it won't rain."

We spent a few minutes tossing ideas around, each sincerely disliking the other's suggestions. Finally, Lee said, "I guess that settles it. Reveille is the only name we agree on."

"Lee," I admonished him, "we can't name a child after a dog or a road just because we thought it would be funny."

"We can't agree on anything else," Lee shrugged with a grin.

"Then I'll name her what I damn well please," I said and stuck my tongue out at him. "It'll serve you right for not being there."

"Yeah, but I'm here now," he said, and naming the baby gave way to activities upon which there was no disagreement.

• • •

We talked through the night and were still in deep conversation when Saturday's sun rose. This was our last day together, and I touched Lee for reassurance. We never talked about the end of R&R, though its looming presence grew more oppressive each hour. We slept briefly, went out for a meal, and returned to the hotel, which had become a place of retreat and security. We took a late afternoon nap and again talked through the night until it was time to pack for our flights.

I felt it grossly unfair that the one good week in six months should rush past so quickly while the lonely, terror-filled ones dragged on and on. But like Scarlett O'Hara, I willed myself to think about such things tomorrow.

An overwhelming sadness threatened to strangle me as the minutes ticked by. Strangely, however, I did not suffer the anxiety of never seeing Lee again as I had when he left San Francisco. I now experienced a certainty that this time the separation was for six months, not forever. My sadness was for the lonely days we would spend apart.

After showering and shaving, Lee reached into the closet for his khakis, and the final reality of the moment gripped me.

"Not yet," I said softly. "Don't get dressed yet."

Lee looked at me questioningly and then at his watch. I explained, "The minute you put on the damned uniform, you're gone. I don't know why, but you leave me right then, even if we're still together for a while. Let's say our real goodbyes in private now."

Lee laughed lightly and said, "Yeah, I guess when I put on the uniform, I'm ready to move on."

"I know," I said and slid into his arms. "Lee, this has been a wonderful week for me."

"It doesn't get any better than this," he said into my hair.

Tears surged from my eyes. I blinked and swallowed hard, determined. I might cry for the next six months, but I would not spend my last minutes with Lee weeping.

"Hold me a little longer," I coaxed. "Just let me get set."

Lee did as I asked, and when I had collected myself again, I leaned back and looked up at him. "Goodbye," I whispered. He kissed me, and then put on the damned uniform.

• • •

Lee and I took a cab to the airport, dropped off my luggage, and located the waiting lounge, now filling with Vietnam returnees and their women. I spotted a face or two I remembered from the Fort DeRussey "line-up"—which now seemed eons ago—and looked around at the hundreds of others. Where faces had been smiling and eyes sparkling less than a week before, they were now long, dulled, and tear-streaked. I envied the women who sobbed openly.

Lee put his arm around my shoulder and whispered in my ear, "I'm glad you're not crying like that." I smiled up at him, thinking, *if you only knew.*

We stood out on the deck above the plane where soldiers were already boarding. I fought for control. When the flight was called, I reached as far into my soul as I could to find the strength to turn and smile at Lee.

"Please take care of yourself," I said. "Promise me."

He smiled slightly and said, "I will. You take care of yourself. Have the Red Cross send the message immediately."

I nodded. He kissed me and was gone.

I stood on the deck and watched Lee join the line of khakis filing onto the plane. At the top of the ramp, he turned and waved and then ducked into the door and out of sight. R&R was over.

{Chapter 28}

All the feelings I had experienced in April returned as I stood staring at the plane Lee had just boarded: the agony of separation, the unholy fear of the unknown, the gut-wrenching loneliness, and the sense of no control.

The plane bound for Vietnam lurched forward and then taxied away, taking with it my husband and my heart. I felt as if I had been ripped into two again—half of me bled; the other half felt dread.

The tears were ready to roll but I held them as I walked to my gate. I awaited my flight back to San Francisco, if not intact, at least in control.

It was self-preservation. Lee's leaving for Vietnam in April had encompassed certain drama, naïve heroism, and a larger-than-life sense of sacrifice. As horrible as it had been, it had possessed a dash of *life*. This time I knew exactly how many lonely nights six months held; I was all too familiar with precisely how long it took the minute hand of a clock to make a full circle. I knew unexplained terror. I sobbed all the way across the ocean.

Susan was waiting at the gate for me. She rushed to me and grabbed my elbow, asking, "Was it that bad?"

My tears flowed again and I shook my head. When I could speak, I answered, "No. It was that good."

"You look positively ill. I thought Lee had been mean."

"Oh, God, Susan," I wailed, "it's over. And it went so fast."

She turned on her heel and strode ahead of me. By the time we had picked up my luggage and found the car, I was in control again.

"Sorry," I apologized.

"I'm glad you had a good time," she said, starting the engine. "But I really just can't handle hearing about it right now, okay?"

I nodded. I understood. Anyway, I was just as happy to hold the memories in private.

"So what's been happening here?"

Susan clicked off the news as she drove: Tom was okay. Miles had visited and seemed more interested in parties than class. Khalifah had come for the weekend to report that he was plotting to change schools. Work was still boring. Eleanor was deciding on wall paint, the Whittemores had invited Susan over for drinks, and the Thompsons—more Sheldon friends whom I had met briefly during the summer—had asked us to join them for Thanksgiving dinner. The L.A. Police Department had not solved the Tate murders.

So odd, I thought, that the rest of the world had been oblivious to such a special week. Routine was the norm and I had simply stepped outside of time. But nothing had changed, which I found simultaneously comforting and stifling.

Susan came into my room before bedtime and sat in her old place across from me. "How's Lee? Is he different?" she queried.

"Yes and no," I said, trying to define how. "He's basically still himself, but somehow he won't ever be the same again. It's subtle, but it's there."

"I missed you this week," Susan said suddenly. "It was hard knowing every day that you were with Lee. And yet I was glad for you. I think I'm going crazy."

"Sounds like a perfectly sane reaction to me. In a way, you're lucky. R&R almost makes everything worse. I mean, I had gotten used to not being with Lee, not talking to him. Now I feel like I'm starting all over, only this time I know what I'm facing. I don't know if I can do it again. He's getting a company when he gets back. That means he stays in the field."

Susan's face reddened. "Goddammit!" she exploded. "How do you feel about it?"

I shrugged. "Lee's so excited he can hardly stand it. Me? I think he's pushing his luck, though he says the company commander is safer than a platoon leader. That's a relative term. Now he will be surrounded by many radio antennas instead of just one, which makes him a more prominent target."

"How did you like Hawaii?" Susan asked, changing the subject.

"I hardly noticed it, frankly."

"What'd Lee say about your size?" Susan asked with such nonchalance that I knew that was what she had really come to learn.

"'Wow.'" I mimicked Lee.

"He didn't have any trouble with it?"

"No, actually, he sort of found the whole thing interesting. He liked feeling the baby kick." I stopped, my eyes stinging with tears and my throat closing. I looked toward the ceiling.

"I remember when we used to stop over in Honolulu," Susan leap-frogged backward in the conversation and reminisced until I had blinked and gulped through my emotional seizure. Strange, I thought. I had never gotten teary-eyed about the baby before.

But emotional reactions concerning the baby became the norm instead of the exception. After having shared my pregnancy with Lee, I was no longer the sole parent, and that he would only share one week of the embryonic stage assaulted me with an inconsolable sadness.

Even more distressing was the realization that swept through me as I opened the door at Letterman for my next clinic visit: Lee would not be with me when the baby was born, a fact I had known but not felt. I walked down the hallway with tears streaming and sat in the musical chairs sniffling until my turn came.

The doctor, unable to ignore my weeping, asked, "Are you feeling okay? Any unusual symptoms?"

"Only a craving for banana cream pie," I tried to laugh.

"That's a new one. What do you suppose brought that on?"

"Hawaii," I replied.

"R&R?"

Questioning my craving and my tears no further, he gave me a clean bill of health except for the standard admonishments of watching my weight.

I suppressed the lingering loneliness and went to see Bernie Petrocelli, strolling through the double doors of the ward ready to entertain him with highlights of my trip. Standing at the foot of his bed, I was unable to believe my eyes, alarm searing through me with unexpected intensity. The bed was empty. Not only empty but unused. Vacant, like death. I caught my breath. Oh, God! Where was Bernie? He was doing so well, not healed but better every time I came. What could have happened?

I turned to look for a nurse and then I remembered that Bernie had talked about looking forward to being able to go home on convalescence leave. *Oh, please let that be where he was.* When I finally found a nurse to ask, she smiled, as if sharing Bernie's excitement, and said he had gone home for the first time and would be back after the weekend. My knees almost buckled with relief.

It was a sensation that was not to last long, however. After I returned to the flat to find no mail for yet another day and then unloaded groceries, I wandered aimlessly into the living room, checking the clock and seeing that it was too early for Susan to be coming home. Regardless, I drifted toward the large windows and peeked through the opened blinds. It was a beautiful fall afternoon, sunny and reasonably warm. I was admiring the pretty neighborhood, killing time until the dinner hour.

I was about to pop the slat back into place when, out of the corner of my eye, I caught sight of a green Army sedan. I froze. I blinked to clear my vision. Oh, God. It really was an Army green sedan, and it was rolling slowly down the hill. My heart stopped. The car was right in front of our flat. *Oh, not Tom! Oh, Susan!* Those were my first thoughts as I watched the passenger turning his head back and forth as if looking for an address. Our address.

This will kill Susan, I thought wildly. *What do I do?*

Then the cold dread of possibilities hit me. Lee. Was that car looking for *me?* It couldn't be. I stood paralyzed and watched the sedan roll farther down the hill. I would not, could not flag them down. Whether it was Susan or me, they would have to find their prey by themselves. The car rolled out of sight around the corner.

Lee had been in command of his company less than a week, but as always in Vietnam, the most vulnerable days were the first and last ones. I tried to remember what he had said about the new company, cursing myself for not having paid more attention to the details. He had been excited about "turning the company around," I remembered. He had said that Bravo Company had not been aggressive lately. I wondered frantically if that meant the men were inexperienced in combat. And Tom. I did not know specifics about Tom's recent activities, though simply being in the war zone made everyone vulnerable.

Minutes ticked away as I waited, unable to move from the windows. And then I saw the car nose its way into view again, turning this time up Collins from the direction it had gone. Instantly, the certainty that I had felt that Lee would be coming home in six months vaporized, replaced by an equivalent certainty that the notification team was looking for the number forty beside our garage door.

The olive drab vehicle crept up the block. The driver paused directly in front of me and I could see down through the windshield that the two men were studying a map. Then they both nodded and the car pulled forward, the driver appearing to look for a parking place up the hill.

Suddenly, behind me the door burst open, and Susan, breathless, white, and big-eyed, whispered, "There's an army car on our street."

"I know," I whispered back, "I've been watching it."

She dropped her purse and coat and joined me at the window, standing just beyond the drapes on the opposite side.

"How long has it been down there?" she asked quietly.

As though keeping our voices down would prevent their finding us, I answered, "This is the second drive-by I've seen."

"Jesus, it's coming back," Susan gulped. "What's taking them so long?"

"I don't know," I muttered, "but I can't make myself go ask them who they're looking for."

We stood in silence and once more watched the car coast past us down the hill and turn right again. Yet another tortuous time, the sedan reappeared and turned toward us.

"What are they doing?" Susan implored in a whisper.

"Whatever it is, we don't want them to hurry," I responded. "We'll know all too soon."

This time, however, the car moved through our block and the next and then disappeared over the hill.

We waited. We watched for its return. Dusk descended and we scrutinized the vehicles behind the few headlights that drove past, the apartment dark behind us.

Finally Susan turned and said, "I can't stand this anymore." She disappeared down the hall; I continued the vigil. When Susan returned to the window, I sat down. We then alternated watching as we spent the evening mute, without dinner.

The car never returned, but it was the next night before we could talk about it, to speculate about why it had been on our street. We had no answers until one of our neighbors, whom we had never met, stopped Susan on the street a few days later and told her how relieved he had been to learn that the army car had been looking for an officer who had just moved into an apartment a couple of blocks away. He had been afraid it had come for one of us. We had not even known our neighbors knew we were waiting wives. Perhaps our isolation was not as total as it seemed.

I struggled to re-acclimate myself to the agony of waiting and to face the necessity of planning for the future. I bought a baby bed at the Presidio Thrift Shop and wished October into history.

November 1969

{Chapter 29}

"I think we need to talk about this baby," Susan announced one night during the first week of November as we walked into the living room after dinner. Her tone sounded ominous, and I prepared myself for concerns she would voice about an infant in the house.

"What exactly do you know about giving birth?" She leaned forward from her corner on the couch and awaited my response.

I shrugged. "I think it happens no matter what I know or don't know." I didn't feel as cavalier as that sounded, but I had been pregnant so long that I had lost sight of the reason for it all.

"Linda," Susan said, taking a deep breath, "you do realize your baby is due in less than a month. Don't you think you should be more prepared?"

I squirmed, as much from her words as from the kick the baby gave me. "I've still got lots of time," I assured her.

"Less than thirty days," she countered. "In fact, isn't it true that the baby could come early? Like in two weeks or so? Shouldn't you take some kind of childbirth classes? I'm really worried about you."

Her words were hitting the mark, splashing me with guilt. Since returning from Hawaii, I hadn't been interested in anything, even the baby. Lethargy had taken possession of my soul and I hadn't even put up a fight.

"You're right, you're right," I agreed quickly, hoping to change the subject.

"So what are you going to do about it?" she pressed.

I threw up my hands. "I don't know. I don't even know where to find out."

"Call the Red Cross. Surely their local chapter holds classes. Or maybe Letterman."

I unenthusiastically agreed, calling Letterman the next day only to learn I'd missed their November class. As displeased as I was with the Red Cross, I registered for their childbirth orientation class at a community college not far from the house.

I was more than reluctant. I didn't want to go out alone at night, and more to the point, I didn't want to go alone, period. This commitment was forcing me to confront the reality that I would be going through labor alone, too, a fact I wasn't ready to accept. Nevertheless, one night a week later I trudged to a hollow classroom building with three couples and an "instructor." Feeling woefully out of place as the only unescorted mother-to-be, I sat with arms folded while the other couples held hands and made reassuring noises to each other.

When the instructor introduced herself by saying she was there to show us a film that would explain everything, I was relieved that discussions were not to be part of the evening's activities, as I had no inclination to share social chit-chat and exchange body-parts stories with these strangers. I relaxed a little as she lowered the lights and flicked on the projector, my last good feeling of the night.

The grainy film and the syrupy voice of the narrator were an ominous foreshadowing of action to come. I should have departed when I got my first glimpse of the couple whose trek into parenthood we were about to witness—in bright and graphic color, no less. The woman was middle-aged, obviously obese before her pregnancy, and the man was repugnant. With no compassion for either character, I watched as the filmed labor began. The woman positioned herself on all fours on the floor and rocked back and forth. Then she stretched out on the hospital bed where she played cards with her spouse as they watched the clock together. Periodically, she would wince and grimace for a time before relaxing and discarding another card. Beyond that I blocked out most of what I saw—as much as I could anyway. I was not interested in the gory delivery room scenes.

Susan was waiting for me when I returned home. I told her about the class in graphic terms, ranting and pacing the living room as I described what an affront the film had been to all things natural. Susan watched me intently, though amusement danced at the corners of her mouth.

"The woman really got down on all fours when labor started?" Susan asked. "Is that all you're supposed to do?"

"Oh, no," I replied sarcastically. "After the floor exercises, the couple played cards. Periodically, the woman grimaced with pain and then discarded. I guess I'll play solitaire."

"Didn't you learn anything helpful?" Susan asked, this time with sincerity.

"Only that the whole ordeal is messy, disgusting, and I'm not doing it." I choked back the tears of rage and left the room, unwilling to be cajoled out of my anger. When I climbed into bed, the delivery room scenes from the film flickered endlessly through my mind. Fear was not so much what they generated as was degradation. To subject my body to the process was humiliating. The physical exams at Letterman had been bad enough, but apparently in delivery, decorum had no place.

And all the gore would produce a helpless creature dependent on me—me, who knew even less about caring for a baby than I did about giving birth to one. I cursed myself for having created this situation, for thinking I could do it alone, for being in San Francisco—mostly, for ever having met Michael Lee Lanning.

My mood did not improve with the sunrise. I was still morose.

Guiltily I could see that Susan was still concerned about me when she left for work. I was surprised when she and Adrienne showed up for lunch, but then I shouldn't have been. With much finesse and little time, Susan turned the noon-time conversation to the topic of birthing babies. My face flushed red when I thought of my reaction to the process, but Adrienne saved my day when she said with the wave of her hand, "Ugh! It's disgusting. I never want to do that again. Have them knock you out."

Susan pushed Adrienne for support; "Shouldn't she go to more classes?"

Adrienne shook her head, the two of them talking as if I were not there, "Naw, it would just depress her. Leave her alone. You asked for my advice. Leave her alone."

When she returned home after work, Susan held up a deck of cards and said authoritatively, "I've done my part. The rest is up to you. Adrienne says you're perfectly normal. It's hormones. She says one day soon you'll get up and start cleaning everything in sight. I'm putting these cards in my purse so I'm ready at all times."

• • •

Apparently Adrienne was right. My moods swung like a pendulum attached to a rusty clock, without rhythm or rhyme and with no sense of time. Even letters from Lee, or the lack of them, didn't have the power to override the internal chemistry. He continued writing regularly, though less frequently, since he had taken the company. Despite the closeness I had felt with him in Hawaii, the communiqués now had a remote aspect. His style and information had not changed; I was just less submerged in the day-to-day details than before, viewing them distractedly as events to be gotten through so he could come home. Or maybe the axis of priorities had shifted to my more immediate circumstances.

On Saturday morning I was awakened abruptly from a deep sleep. Fear gripped me. Had I just had a psychic experience, my soul knowing something had happened to Lee? I lay paralyzed in the bed. Then I heard the doorbell and hurried footsteps.

I grabbed my robe, wondering who would be visiting at this hour. When I arrived in the foyer, I saw only Susan standing at the door still clutching the knob. She turned slowly to face me, her face whiter than the wall. She mechanically bent her left arm at the elbow to raise a brown envelope clamped in her hand.

"Telegram," she said flatly. Seeing the dismay on my face, she added, "For me."

We stood looking at each other, neither of us moving.

Finally, I said softly, "They don't use telegrams anymore." Seconds ticked by. "Do they?" I asked, now less sure.

"I didn't think so," Susan whispered. "But I've got one."

We continued to stand, looking at each other. Then our eyes moved simultaneously to the envelope. Somehow, if we didn't move, the danger might pass and the evil message might evaporate.

"This is ridiculous," Susan said suddenly, ripping at the envelope angrily. As she unfolded the message, her eyes enlarged, and she gasped, and then she turned to the door, banging her forehead against the wood. "Goddammit," she said softly.

"Susan?" I whispered, hardly daring to find out.

She turned from the door and melted back against the wall, her knees buckling. "How could they do this to me? Of all the stupid things. Didn't they know it would scare the shit out of me?"

Before I could say anything, she explained, "It's a telegram from my parents wishing me a happy birthday."

She pushed herself upright and reread the message, her face turning red. "How could Mother and Daddy not realize what getting a telegram would do to me? Are they so oblivious to the war?"

I could imagine Marjorie Sheldon in Tehran marking the calendar and tipping the Western Union people to ensure the message arrived on the eighth. In all her planning, however, she had, in fact, forgotten what it was like to live with the war every day.

• • •

Despite my attitude toward it, the childbirth class did spur me to seriously consider my lack of preparation for an infant. The second week of November, I traipsed to the Presidio Thrift Shop and found a practically new fold-up portable crib I could afford that would serve nicely as a bassinet while the baby was tiny.

I returned home eager to set it up so I could feel I was making progress. As I climbed the stairs with the contraption clanging behind me, I heard Susan's voice. Maybe she and Adrienne had come home for lunch again. I hurried upward to show them my prize.

But when I opened the door, I saw Susan sitting in a chair in the hallway with the phone gripped against her ear. Tears were streaming down her face. She didn't seem to notice me.

"When did you find out?" she asked hoarsely into the phone.

I froze. In all the time I had known her, I had never seen Susan cry like this. My stomach contracted with dread. I stood motionless as Susan listened and then smeared away more tears.

"Susan," I whispered.

She jerked her head in my direction, read my conclusions, and shook her head, all without losing her concentration on the caller. She sniffled back a sob and handed me a letter that lay in her lap.

I took the pieces of stationery tentatively. Susan pointed and nodded, "Oh, God," she said into the phone, "I'm so sorry."

I glanced quickly over the signature and saw it was signed "Gayle." Good God, Mike Arnovitz was dead. Big, burly, ruddy-faced Mike. The green army sedan had come for Gayle—and hadn't driven past. The baby boy born only weeks before would never see his father. Lee's words came back to haunt me and I speculated on whose mistake had cost Mike his life.

My knees went weak and I sank into the nearest chair, wondering how I had become so complacent, so confident, so detached from the war. My petty aches and pains were nothing, and I couldn't remember when I had begun to think they were important. Those statistics on the news were still real men dying, and one of them had been Mike. Had it been a day when the commentator started his show with "Today in Vietnam, casualties were light"?

The parallels. All I could think about were the similarities between Gayle and me. Both married to infantry lieutenants in the field in Vietnam, both pregnant while our husbands were gone, both friends of Susan, both. . . . With so many things in common, would this fate be mine, too? I could read no more of the letter.

Susan hung up and came into the room to drop onto the couch, "Poor Gayle. I just can't believe it."

"When?"

"He's already been dead for over two months, but Gayle said she just couldn't make herself write anyone about it until now. She says the reality comes and goes. The baby keeps her busy. They had decided to wait until he was born to go on R&R because Mike really wanted to see his son. Then Mike was killed just days after David was born."

We sat in a deadening silence, each of us lost in our own thoughts. Then Susan said abruptly, "I invited her to come out here for a few days."

I must have blanched because Susan added quickly, "Maybe I shouldn't have."

"Of course you should have," I said, at once eager to befriend Gayle and yet panicked at the thought of facing her, as if by having my husband alive, I had committed some grievous wrong against her. "Is it going to be awkward?"

"I didn't even think about that," Susan said wearily. "Their R&R had been scheduled for next week. San Francisco seemed better than nothing. She and the baby will be here Wednesday."

• • •

In the meantime, I made my bi-monthly trip to the OB clinic where I encountered yet another new doctor, this one older and sterner. He lectured me severely about my weight, told me I was to now make a weekly appointment, and ordered a battery of blood tests for the next day. He was so unapproachable that I didn't demand explanations except to meekly ask, "Is there something wrong?"

"Your red blood cell count looks low." End of discussion. He closed my folder and walked out.

I tried to toss off the nagging thoughts that followed me to Bernie's ward. If anything were seriously wrong, I concluded, surely the doctor would have said so.

Bernie was back in place, which was reassuring. For him, however, the return was grim, with another operation on the horizon. We chatted for a few minutes, but neither of us was in a social frame of mind. Too much had happened since Hawaii for me to reconstruct my excitement, and I was not inclined to mention Gayle's forthcoming visit; he was having difficulty readjusting from leave. Nothing seemed right with the world.

I went back to the hospital on Friday to submit to a significant loss of blood drawn into vials by a mute technician. Back home, I brooded. Throughout my pregnancy, there had been disagreement among the doctors about my anemia. Yet, because I had never seen the same one twice, no one had tracked the condition. I should have been paying more attention. Red blood cells carried oxygen. Oxygen was vital to the development of brain cells. Did too few red blood cells mean too little oxygen had reached the baby's brain? Oh, God, my baby was going to be brain damaged.

By the time Susan came home, I was in a state of hysteria, sobbing uncontrollably. "Oh, no, what's wrong now?" she asked.

I cried harder. "Look, being this upset can't be good for the baby. Tell me what's wrong and maybe we can do something about it," she coaxed with forced patience.

I told her about the blood tests and my line of logic. She assessed the information while we tried to create sensible order out our chaotic medical ignorance. By eight o'clock, I had persuaded her to be alarmed rather than her having calmed me.

"We're going to the emergency room," she declared.

I protested but Susan insisted, driving me to the post and then pulling me by the coat sleeve through the halls of Letterman until we found the emergency desk at the back of the building. Susan demanded to talk to a doctor who could explain human reproduction and blood in terms we could understand. By the time she had turned the idle staff on its ear, I was flushed with recriminations, feeling that I was the brain-damaged one, not the baby. I sat weeping in the waiting room while Susan, slayer of dragons and military bureaucracy, located and coerced a doctor into talking to me. He sat beside me and patted my arm. "I'm sure the tests are precautionary."

Susan plied him with questions that he patiently answered. I depended on her to pay attention because I couldn't do anything but sniffle, partly out of fear for the baby and partly out of humiliation for being such an idiotic crybaby myself. Eventually, however, the comforting tone of authority de-escalated my hysteria to a low-grade worry, and Susan and I returned home.

{Chapter 30}

On Wednesday night Susan went to the airport to pick up Gayle. I drew a breath of apprehension when I heard the garage open and watched the petite blonde climb toward me with a sleeping baby cradled in her arms. I mimed a greeting and motioned for Gayle to follow so she could put David down.

By the time Susan had emptied the car, the hallway was crammed wall to wall with luggage and infant trappings. Gayle stepped out of Susan's room and gently closed the door. "Where's the baby bed?" she asked expectantly.

"It's still in the garage," I answered. "We put the crib in there for you. Did you see it?"

"Yes, but I don't think it's sturdy enough for David," she observed pointedly, "I assumed you'd have everything set up, but I guess we can get by."

I bit my tongue. Sympathy for Gayle had eclipsed my memory of her sharp, Eastern style of communication, which was a major reason, from my point of view, why she and I were acquaintances rather than friends. I excused myself and went to the bedroom where I dallied for as long as I dared.

When I returned, Susan and Gayle had settled in the living room where their conversation skittered from topic to topic like nervous birds lighting on one tree branch and then another. Susan plied Gayle with questions about David—birth weight, current weight, length—queries she explained were intended to enlighten me. Gayle answered with a restlessness that exposed a pent-up energy. It was as though she were wired for action, and the tension I felt in the room told me she might spring loose at any moment, though I had no idea if the result would be hysterical tears or scathing sarcasm.

Finally deciding Gayle resented my presence, I said goodnight and escaped to bed. It was going to be a long five days, an assessment that made me feel guilty and tired.

• • •

The next morning I found Gayle in the kitchen with David strapped into an infant seat in the middle of the table. "Since you don't have a high chair, I'm having to improvise here," she said as she poked a tiny spoonful of cereal into the baby's mouth. I watched as he rolled it around on his tongue and forced it back out. She scooped up the bite and reinserted it no less than four times before I stopped counting.

"Make yourself at home," I said, having decided to ignore her opening remarks. "Just let us know what you need. I have a doctor's appointment, but Susan is taking the day off."

"What time do you think she'll be up? I want to see San Francisco," she said between coos to David, who was a divinely beautiful baby with fat cereal-caked cheeks and blue eyes too big to bring into focus. "Mike says it's a wonderful city." I jerked to attention but supposed that the adjustment to his death would cause inconsistent slips.

"Oh, you're such a cute boy," Gayle baby-talked to David. "You look just like your daddy."

I almost dropped my cup, instead clattering it against the counter. This would be a good morning to be extra early at the clinic, I decided.

At the hospital, I found my medical folder in the hands of a meek little obstetrician. I badgered him into a detailed explanation I couldn't begin to comprehend, but his ultimate message was clear: the baby had never been in jeopardy. The tests had been to predict my body's ability to handle the delivery without undue loss of blood. I believed him, I supposed, but my mind had locked into an alarm about the baby's health like a tracking device and nothing seemed to deter it from its course.

• • •

When I arrived back at the apartment, I heard Gayle announce at the top of the stairs, "Oh good, Linda's home."

By the time I completed the climb, she was standing in the hall with her purse on one shoulder and David on the other. "Here you go," she said, transferring the wiggling baby into my arms before I could close the door. "He should go down for a nap in an hour or so. His juice is in the refrigerator. Be sure you burp him so he doesn't get colicky. Okay, Susan, let's go."

"We won't be too long," Susan assured me with a worried look as she followed Gayle. She knew how little I knew about babies.

I couldn't even remember the last time I had held an infant. As I stared at this little human entrusted into my unskilled care, I was relieved to see that he looked sturdy.

That afternoon I honed what skills I had in diaper changing, nicking myself numerous times with the pin while managing to shield David from my unschooled dexterity; deduced that he did not like his juice cold; succeeded in burping him just short of knocking the breath out of him; and rocked him to sleep in a chair with no rockers. The only trick I could not master was getting him into the crib without his waking. So I held him through his nap and then started the whole care process over.

We finished the second cycle, including another unauthorized nap, and Susan and Gayle still had not returned. David grew fussy and displeased with my techniques. I jostled, I sang, I bounced, I rocked. He wailed. I offered more juice, which he rejected with a spit. He was hungry for mother's milk and refused my reasoned explanations. By the time his mother arrived, David was shrieking, and I was ready to join him.

Susan came flying in the door while Gayle followed calmly, recognizing her offspring's message for what it was. She took him to the bedroom and, within seconds, blessed silence filled the house. I collapsed on the couch sucking my pin-pricked finger.

"I'm sorry we were gone so long," Susan said, distressed. "I kept telling her we had to get back because you didn't know anything about babies. What's wrong with your finger?"

"I've got to get better at diapers," I said, showing her the stab wounds.

And more practice I got. Susan and Gayle spent the next three days in a whirlwind of sightseeing, leaving early and returning only at night when David had to be nursed. I grew quickly proficient at tending him and developed an adoring affection for the happy baby. We were at odds only when I offered him the formula Gayle had left. Otherwise our days were pleasant exchanges of learning experiences.

Nights were another matter altogether. Susan, worn to a frazzle in her attempts to provide distractions, struggled to keep the evening conversations light and fun. Gayle responded in kind for the most part as they recounted each day for me. Looking at Gayle made me feel guilty somehow, relieved not to be in her shoes, fearful I would be any day; sorry Mike had been killed but glad it hadn't been Lee; ashamed to admit that I kept personalizing her tragedy. Susan and I avoided discussing the situation, but each day, I could feel the tension turned up another notch.

It was Gayle's comments that were unnerving. She started almost every sentence with "Mike says" or "Mike thinks" or "Mike believes." Her words were apparently not slips, for I never heard her use the past tense. The longer she stayed, the more disconcerting her usage became.

Also difficult were those occasions when the young widow would unexpectedly erupt into emotional outbursts. Not being able to discover what specifically caused them elevated our anxiety. The conversation would be flowing along and suddenly Gayle's eyes would water in an undisguised raging hatred and she would storm from the room. On the second night of her visit, we all had been sitting in the living room chatting. I made some inane comment and Gayle suddenly stiffened in her chair, her eyes growing narrow. She sent me a piercing look and said bitterly, "That's easy for you to say." With great indignation, she stomped down the hall.

I was aghast. "I'm sorry Susan," I said quickly, never intending to offend her friend. "What did I say?"

"I don't know," Susan shrugged as she stared down the hall. "I think maybe it's because our husbands are still alive."

Had Gayle periodically burst into tears over Mike, her broken heart, or her fatherless child, I could have coped. Grief I understood. The anger, the hatred, the animosity, I did not. I didn't blame Gayle; I just did not know how to react.

Learning to keep my mouth shut did not solve the problem. If I was too quiet, Gayle would pin me with her eyes and say, "Oh, I know what you're thinking." And off she would storm again. Susan and I would look at each other but say nothing, not daring to share our thoughts for fear of never being able to conceal them again. Eventually, Gayle would return as though nothing unusual had occurred and conversation would resume.

With almost the same frequency as the outbursts, Gale would become maudlin, grateful for our hospitality. "I just can't tell you how much coming here has helped," she would begin and then elaborate her appreciation until I felt like a complete heel for being irritated by her demands and style. Then, as often as not, she would transition into broad, undisguised hints that she would entertain the thought of staying longer if asked. Each time she said she had no reason to hurry back to Pennsylvania I held my breath, sure that Susan would suggest she stay on for a while.

By Gayle's last night, I could stand it no longer. When Susan came to bed, I accosted her. "Have you noticed how she always talks about Mike in the present tense, like he's still alive? Does she talk about his death? Does she acknowledge it?"

"In a very detached way. She says she doesn't want to think about it while she's here. Maybe she just wants to pretend when she's around us. I don't know. But it makes me jumpy as hell and I never know when she's going to be set off by something."

"Yeah," I concurred. "On the one hand, the whole thing makes me so sad I could cry all day, but on the other, I think if she weren't leaving tomorrow, I'd go crazy. Not nice, am I?"

"Me either, I guess," Susan said, reaching for her night gown and then jettisoning clothes from under the covers. How familiar her idiosyncrasies had become.

"Susan," I ventured, "you know she doesn't want to go home."

"Yeah, and every time she hints about wanting to stay, I'm scared to death I'm going to ask her to."

"Are you?"

"No, I already told her we have to get ready for your baby. I've been moving up the due date. You can't keep lugging that big baby around. And I'm really sorry you've been left to do all the babysitting."

"That's been the best part," I said with a smile. "I think I've decided to have my baby after all."

Susan reloaded all the baby paraphernalia into her car on Monday morning and returned Gayle and David to the airport. I stood watching them drive away with mixed emotions—glad that I no longer had to walk on conversational eggshells; sad that I might never see the sweet baby again; sorry for Gayle and the grief she had to endure; guilty for being so glad I wasn't in her place; angry that Mike had allowed this to happen to his wife and child; regretful that a Vietnam widow had so few people who cared or even noticed what had happened to her.

But mostly I was exhausted. I went upstairs and flopped on the couch, where Susan found me when she returned. She sank into a chair and slipped off her shoes. Gravity seemed to have increased its force tenfold; we were too weak to move against it.

"Well," Susan said after several minutes, "that's one of the worst weeks I've ever been through."

{Chapter 31}

With a burst of energy, excited about having a baby and suddenly ready to prepare for it, I went to the PX to purchase the critical items—baby powder, oil, shampoo, diapers, pins, and other sundries Gayle had for David. I looked longingly at the sweet layette things I could not afford, but the sacrifice didn't depress me. I could thank Gayle for my new perspective.

I came to the card section and perused the packaged birth announcements in search of the right look. With dismay I realized that they were either too cute, too sappy, or too frilly, so I decided to make my own and bought plain white note cards, a calligraphy pen, and a bottle of ink.

At home, I sketched ideas for the birth announcements that could be adapted to my limited artistic skills. I designed a stick-figure prototype in which a stork was departing the scene after having delivered a basket onto the front steps of a building whose sign read "Lanning Recruiting Center." Inside, I designated a space for "recruit's" name, date of enlistment, physical description, and commanders. I was either a clever woman or else an idiot with too much time on my hands.

I sat at the table practically every waking moment for two days, repeating pen strokes onto the individual cards. I was nearing the bottom of the stack late one afternoon when the doorbell rang. Assuming Susan had forgotten her key, I swung the door open to find a young couple.

"Is Susan here?" the boy asked nervously, as the girl turned away. I thought I recognized them as Miles's friends, a couple whose names had been inseparable.

"She should be home any minute. Come on in."

They looked at me and then at each other before reluctantly crossing the threshold. The young woman brushed past me with her arms crossed and her companion followed with an embarrassed smile.

"Sit down," I invited. They sat stiffly on the couch, careful not to touch, I noticed. Something was terribly wrong.

"We don't want to keep you," the boy said, shifting.

"You're not. I was just finishing up announcements for the baby," I said with a laugh, hoping to lighten up the atmosphere. "It's due in a couple of weeks, and I'm running out of time."

The girl grimaced and pushed herself deeper into the sofa. Her hostility toward me was now blatant. I suddenly knew why.

At that moment Susan appeared, and her arrival seemed to ease the tension. The boy cleared his throat and mumbled, "Miles said we should talk to you." He sent a worried look in my direction.

"I'll get you something to drink," I said, leaving the room.

I dawdled in the kitchen and then served the soft drinks. Susan was on the phone when I deposited the glasses in front of the couple, neither of whom acknowledged me.

I tiptoed back to the kitchen. Susan came in, her face filled with distress, and announced quietly, "She's pregnant."

"I figured that out. She can't even look at me."

Casting a quick look over her shoulder, Susan whispered, "What am I supposed to do? Miles said he'd lend them money."

"What can you do?" I asked with a sigh.

Susan squared her shoulders decisively. "Come on. We should at least talk them out of being impulsive."

When I followed Susan into the living room, she quelled their glances by saying, "She knows. But I'm not signing the check until we talk this through."

For the next four hours, Susan and I grilled the couple on their options and listed the consequences of abortion. Once I might have viewed parental disapproval, embarrassment, and financial struggle with the same catastrophic potential as did this couple. I had spent so much of my energy concentrating on the continuation of life; now I was an unwilling party to an unnecessary end to it. Susan, who had wanted a baby so badly herself, pleaded with them to reconsider the temporary inconvenience and see the broader scope. Our arguments went unheeded.

Wearily, Susan signed the check and the two meekly left. She and I looked at each other, knowing we had failed.

Suddenly Susan laughed. "Boy, they must have been shocked when you opened the door."

We got hysterical as we took turns narrating from the couple's perspective. But as abruptly as our laughter had started, it died. There had not been one single funny thing about the evening.

"Oh, the irony of it all," I observed, leaning my head back against the chair and closing my eyes. "Mister and Miss Civilian All-Star American, son and daughter of the Establishment, are going to abort their child, and the protestors call our husbands 'baby killers.' There's something wrong with the system."

• • •

Indeed the system was in jeopardy, and the war protesters were gaining even more momentum. The first "Moratorium Against the War" had been staged in San Francisco while I was in Hawaii. Now a second was planned for the following weekend, and the thought of it sickened me with fear, for it seemed that each time the protesters created another large-scale organized rally, the government became less certain about its commitments in Vietnam, which ultimately translated into more inconsistent orders in the field, leaving those in the boonies hanging out on the proverbial limb.

Susan and I acknowledged the upcoming protests, but we didn't venture beyond the cursory facts of date and time. She favored the protests, if they were not violent, as a way to effect change.

"Come in here. I've got to talk to you," Susan said as she walked from the kitchen into the living room after dinner on Friday night. I dried my hands, gave the cabinet one more swipe with the cup towel, and followed.

"Listen, Susan," I said before she could start, "I'm not going to any more classes. And if Gayle is coming back, I don't want to know. Miles can tell the rest of his friends to go elsewhere for money or counseling. I have to tell you, I cannot deal with another crisis right now."

Susan let me finish without interruption. "This is different. But I'm just not sure I should tell you."

"Oh, please," I sighed with more exasperation than I felt. "What now?"

"Well, Eleanor and I have been planning a baby shower for you, but I have this problem."

I laughed, understanding her dilemma. "There's no one to invite because I don't know anyone here. Don't worry about it, Susan. I appreciate the thought."

"No, no. The guests are all invited and everyone is coming to Eleanor's tomorrow afternoon. My job is to get you there without suspecting anything because it's a surprise."

I waited. She continued, "You know, I'm supposed to make you think we're going somewhere and then decide to pop up to Eleanor's on our way out. Something like that. Only you're such a pain in the ass, I can't ever get you to go anywhere. Besides, tomorrow is the Moratorium and I don't think we dare go out into the streets. But if I just drag you up there on some pretext, you won't be dressed or have your hair done. So I decided you'd rather know and look nice than be surprised. You can just pretend."

"But it is a surprise," I said. "The thought never crossed my mind."

"Why?" Susan asked. "You think you shouldn't have a shower like every other normal pregnant woman just because your husband is in Vietnam and you live like an outcast from society?"

"I don't know what to say."

"Then don't say anything except about how surprised you are when you walk in there tomorrow. Now, which dress still fits?"

On Saturday afternoon, as Susan and I readied ourselves for the party, we repeatedly heard sirens racing on the major streets on either side of us. San Francisco was a city under siege, as if war had come to our doorstep. Had the door suddenly crashed open and tie-dyed, sandal-footed protesters arrived to arrest us for being waiting wives, the scene would have been more believable than climbing up the back steps to Eleanor's, which we did at the appointed hour.

"I feel like a fool," I whispered as Susan turned the knob.

"Just don't overplay it," she warned as we stepped inside to find a roomful of chattering women. At least the group did not yell "Surprise" and force me into a gushing, fake response. Instead, when Eleanor invited us in, I surveyed the faces and said, "My goodness, this is the first time I've known everybody since I've been in San Francisco," which was true. The women chuckled and let me figure the game out for myself.

Most of the guests were Mrs. Sheldon's and Susan's friends I'd met during the summer, such as Mrs. Johnson, who had entertained us on the Fourth of July; Mrs. Turner, whose daughters had wanted to flee that holiday gathering; Mrs. Thompson, who was hosting us next week for Thanksgiving; Jeanne Whittemore, who had survived our kitchen fire. Adrienne was there, too, smiling and asking if I was going to go through with having the baby after all. As I talked with each of them in turn, I was overwhelmed with emotion and deeply touched. While the surprise may have been based on pretense, the affection I felt for the group was genuine.

And so was the thrill as I opened each package—wonderfully practical baby gifts, cued by Susan, I was sure. A diaper bag, jumpsuits, blankets, and an adorable silver-plated piggy bank. As I sat looking at the bounty, I bit my lip, thinking how fortunate I was to have these people in my life and wishing that Lee could see the presents for his baby.

• • •

Still in my expansive, "all's right with the world" mood, I waddled downstairs on Monday morning to get the mail, where I delighted in finding an airmail envelope with Lee's handwriting. Settling into my favorite chair upstairs, I peeled back the flap to read the November 15 letter.

Dearest Linda—

Well, we are back in the jungle—3 days ago my old recon platoon hit a base camp. Platoon leader, LT Little, was killed. We were in C Company together and saw each other at Cam Ranh Bay.

Recon could not get the body out—C Co., Recon, and B Co hit the base camp 3 times—finally ran gooks out—B Co was first in—still searching it at this time.

I knew Little better than anyone in the Battalion, I guess—a sad thing carrying his body out of there. Contact is at highest peak I've seen in VN—but we are doing good.

Old familiar dread wrenched my stomach, squeezing away all my euphoria. I wanted to hold Lee and weep with him for the loss of his best friend in Vietnam. Though his letter was factual, I had seen him talk about his buddy, and I remembered his misgivings because he thought Little was a bit too eager to prove something. I knew Lee would harbor a sense of guilt as well as grief. I also knew from the way he had written that he was not allowing himself to feel the death, or much of anything else.

I felt tired and defeated as I sat wondering where I would get the strength to endure knowing "contact is at highest peak." Then a flash of anger burned through me, demanding to know why Lee couldn't just sit in a safe place for a couple of weeks until I delivered this baby. Was it asking too much to have only one major crisis at a time? I wanted to withdraw from the world.

• • •

"Exactly how far down the Peninsula do the Thompsons live?" I asked Susan in reference to the Thanksgiving invitation.

"About an hour and a half. Are you afraid of being that far away from the hospital?"

"Not really, I guess."

"You don't want to go, do you?"

"Not really."

Susan was quiet for a moment and then said, "I'll call Mrs. Thompson and tell her we can't come because Khalifah will be home for the holidays."

Susan came back from the phone, throwing up her hands and saying, "She's so excited about the dinner that when I told her about Khalifah, she said, 'Oh, wonderful. Bring him, too.' I don't know if he will want to go or not."

"Well, he won't want to spend Thanksgiving alone."

"Linda," Susan said in mock disgust, "he's from Kuwait. Thanksgiving is just another day to him."

"Right," I said, reminding myself. I guessed that in reality it was just another day to me, too. Only now it was a day when the postman wouldn't come and I had no chance for a letter.

The day before Thanksgiving, I once more trudged to Letterman and managed to remain dry-eyed for the first time since R&R. A nurse gave me a booklet containing details I would need to prepare for my stay in the hospital and space for me to provide vital statistics and other pertinent information for the birth certificate.

"Fill in all the blanks," she instructed. "And be sure you bring the completed book back with you."

Bernie was on leave again so I returned home and studied the blue booklet, which reminded me of the blue books I'd used for college exams. Following the checklists, I packed the suitcase with my things and those of the baby. For the first time, I realized the miracle, that one would go into the hospital and two would come out. Absolutely amazing.

Following the list of articles I was to bring to the hospital was a page dedicated to vital statistics necessary for the birth certificate. Glaring out at me at the top of the page were blanks for the baby's name, one for a girl, the other for a boy. I filled in "Lohn Michael Lanning" with a flourish, skipped the girl's blank, and then proceeded down the page, completing the data about Lee and me. Then I went back to the gaping hole on the page. What was I going to do about a girl's name? Oh, Lee, I thought despairingly, we really need to talk about this. If I could have only a minute or two!

While I was tempted to fill in the blank with my preferences, I just couldn't do it. I started to print her name when I realized I didn't know exactly how to spell it. Good God, what kind of mother was I going to be? I went in search of a dictionary, where I found the French spelling of Reveille. I studied the letters and concluded that I would just substitute an *e* for the last 1 so that her name would end in "lee" and therefore we could call her LeeAnn after all. Besides, she would be in college before she could learn to spell Reveilee. I closed the booklet with relief and finality. I wouldn't have to worry about coping with a girl, anyway.

Anticipating Thanksgiving dinner held my interest for a couple of days before the holiday arrived. I salivated as I remembered my grandmother's dressing, hoping that Mrs. Thompson was somewhere nearly as good a cook as my mother's mother. By the time we all piled into the car for a drive down the Peninsula, I was imagining not only the sage cornbread dressing but also the pumpkin and pecan pies with whipped cream that topped off such a festive meal. I was so eager to dive into the food that I overcame my anxiety about how far we were traveling from Letterman Hospital.

The Thompsons greeted us warmly and welcomed Khalifah with open arms. With the ease of a gifted guest, Susan smoothed our entrance with humorous snippets from our trip down. When Susan mentioned my growing anxiety as the distance from my hospital increased, Mrs. Thompson assured me that we were not far from Stanford University Hospital and that she had personally clocked the trip in miles and time in the event my labor began prematurely. Just knowing that she had been so thoughtful eased my concern.

"I'm not due for another week," I assured her.

"Just the same," she said, "I would rather be prepared. We can hope that it won't happen."

The aromas of the meal in progress filled the house, and my appetite grew voraciously. Mr. Thompson took drink orders of bourbon for Susan, cola for Khalifah, and milk for me. We had just settled into an easy conversation when the doorbell rang and the host rose to answer it.

"We've invited some other guests, too," Mrs. Thompson said as she followed her husband out of the room. The three of us exchanged shrugs and Khalifah excused himself to find the bathroom.

Moments later the Thompsons returned with the new arrivals, a dark-haired, slightly exotic-looking young couple, meticulously groomed. Out of the corner of my eye, I saw Susan blanch as introductions were made. I didn't catch the names but smiled on cue and wondered about Susan's reaction.

"They didn't have any family in the area, either, since they just moved here from New York," Mrs. Thompson was explaining as Khalifah reappeared. Instantly the air electrified like that first split second when a dog and cat unexpectedly find themselves occupying the same space. God, I was stupid. This couple was Jewish, which Susan had immediately known.

Khalifah's face turned purple and the woman's hair bristled along the back of her neck beneath her chignon. Mrs. Thompson preempted the shock by charging on with a gutsy commentary. She merrily told the couple that Khalifah was a member of the royal family and to him she elaborated on how the two Israelis had once lived in a kibbutz. "So, see? You have something in common already. You've lived in the same part of the world."

I didn't dare to move even my eyeballs. Mrs. Thompson, an intelligent woman who had spent years overseas, must have known when Susan called about Khalifah that this moment was inevitable.

Khalifah, like a cornered animal, looked to Susan, then gave a quick nod of acknowledgement to the couple and sat down, keeping his eyes on the floor. The Israelis exchanged searching looks. With indecision hanging in the air, Mr. Thompson calmly asked what they would like to drink. When each finally answered in turn, we Americans breathed a collective sigh of relief, thankful indeed that the worst seemed to have passed.

As though oblivious to the crisis just averted, Mrs. Thompson turned the couple's attention to Susan and me, telling them that our husbands were in Vietnam.

The woman's neck reddened again as she straightened her shoulders self-righteously and pronounced, "We are very much opposed to the war."

I didn't look directly at Susan, though I could see color rising in her face. "So am I," she said, laughing tentatively and trying to avert another scene for the Thompsons' sake.

"How can you say that?" the woman demanded stubbornly, "when you let your husband be part of it?" This female was trouble, I decided. Khalifah was behaving admirably, and Susan was trying valiantly to deflect a confrontation. I concluded that my best course of action was to keep my mouth shut.

Fortunately, Mr. Thompson arrived with the drinks before Susan and the woman could complete their staring contest.

"Well," Mrs. Thompson declared, rubbing her hands together with relish, "I hope everyone is hungry. We have enough here to feed an army." A poor choice of words, given the warring factions in the room, but it passed.

"Linda hasn't been able to talk about anything else for weeks," Susan exaggerated. "She can hardly wait for the stuffing, even if she does call it 'dressing.'"

"We have crouton stuffing or oyster."

Oyster! Stuffing? Crouton? My heart plummeted. Social tensions were one thing, but messing around with Thanksgiving dinner was another matter altogether. My mouth watered for my grandmother's cornbread dressing, which my family in Texas would have devoured hours ago. I was suddenly homesick.

I caught myself, realizing that I had an opportunity to keep the conversation on a safe track by focusing on the food. "Everything smells divine. Can we help?"

"No, no. I have it under control. The turkey is ready and the ham will be out of the oven in a minute." We all froze. I could see Mrs. Thompson stiffen as she realized the affront the ham would be to the Arab and the Jews. At least they had a disdain for pork in common, if nothing else, but I wondered if we would make it through the American observance without an international incident.

Mrs. Thompson's seating arrangements, for better or worse, positioned the three of us from Collins Street across the table from the Jewish couple, like enemy camps aligned on either side of a demilitarized zone. The white linen tablecloth, fine china, and crystal goblets proved a poor divider.

I assessed the crouton concoction and, while consoling myself over my disappointment, looked up to see the Jewish woman jabbing her finger at Susan as she asked, "How can you live with yourself, knowing your husband is killing innocent women and children?"

The woman had obviously been watching too much television. I interceded before Susan could respond. "Actually," I said politely, "Susan's husband is an advisor, and an important part of his job is to teach the Vietnamese to grow better rice crops—to feed all those innocent women and children. It's my husband who's in combat, and I doubt that he has shot *back* at a single innocent woman or child." Her hostile gaze shifted to me.

"Then you actually support the war."

"Excuse me," I said, gently laying my fork across my plate, "but do you really think that you are more concerned about the war than Susan and I are?"

"Well, I must be. I protest it. I go to the demonstrations," she said with great pride. Her husband, who had not participated until now, added, "Yes, we think it is important to protest."

At least I now knew where her rhetoric had been framed. Pleasantly I asked, "Has it ever occurred to you that the protests might be prolonging the war?"

She looked shocked. "Surely you are joking." The Thompsons exchanged looks down the length of the table.

"Without the support of the protesters, Hanoi might have taken a different tactic and the war might have been over years ago. We'll never know, will we? Susan, would you pass the salt?"

"You're not supposed to have this," she reminded me as she put the shaker in my hand. To everyone else she announced, "Linda's doctor says she has to cut back on her salt intake."

"But this is such a special occasion, I think I'll just celebrate and indulge." Surely we were through with the war as a dinner topic. "Everything is delicious, Mrs. Thompson." I picked up my fork and speared a honeyed yam, pleased at my restraint for not stabbing the woman across from us through the heart.

"Who needs seconds?" our hostess inquired, seeming relieved. I surveyed the plates to note that the Jewish couple had seemed so intent on expressing their political views that neither had touched their food; Khalifah was miserably stirring his to give the appearance of having ingested a bit; Susan gulped quick bites but the glaze over her eyes told me she was tasting nothing; I had only sampled before losing my appetite.

"You are wrong about the protest demonstrations," the woman began again, even more authoritatively. "The protesters want the war to end. We work hard to stop it, and it is very important to us."

I saw Susan's jaws flex and sensed her desire to rearrange the woman's face. Even though years of etiquette had been instilled, I didn't think Emily Post stood a chance so I reacted first.

"Excuse me," I said again, looking first at our hostess and then our host, evaluating their attitudes, which now seemed to be "What the hell, there's no saving this evening."

"Exactly how is it you propose to stop the war?" I asked.

"We must persuade the soldiers to just put down their weapons. If everyone does that, then there is no more war. We are only trying to save the soldiers," the woman said as she cocked her head self-righteously.

I looked her square in the eye and asked quietly, "Which of us at this table do you suppose has the most interest in saving soldiers? Who do you suppose cares the most? You? Or Susan? Or me? Who do you think wants the shooting to stop more: you, or the soldier being shot at? Huh? Who? And what do you suppose would happen to our soldiers if they simply put down their weapons? Do you honestly think the North Vietnamese would say, 'Oh, what a fine idea,' and then lay theirs down, too? Do you not know that they would just blow our men away?"

She looked daggers at me, especially when I smiled condescendingly at her ignorance and asked if I could help with dessert.

Susan followed me into the kitchen and whispered conspiringly, "Couldn't you just go into labor about now? It would be a really good time."

"What? And miss all this fun?" I asked.

Susan swore under her breath as she left the kitchen and then she swore profusely as we drove home. Before we reached Collins, however, Susan and I were hysterical at the circumstances of our memorial Thanksgiving. Even Khalifah chuckled at the whole mismatched evening.

As we pulled up into the garage, I checked off the one holiday that had stood between me and the baby. I knew that December, just days away, would bring incredible changes to my life, but as our day of gratitude came to an end, I had no idea just how significant those changes would be.

December 1969

{Chapter 32}

December did finally arrive, taking its own, sweet time. Before the first dawned, I had washed and folded all the baby's clothing and blankets. I had fussed with the crib; I had padded the portable bed. I was as ready as I was going to get.

I talked with Mother and Daddy, reassuring them that I was fine. We talked about their impending visit, scheduled around the baby's birth. Daddy told me he was impatient, and Mother confirmed that he had been whistling for a week, a sure sign that he was happy about something. I promised them I would call when I headed for the hospital.

I sat down to wait. The second of December arrived, but the baby did not. While that was no surprise, really, I was astonished that I felt no different, no closer to delivery. Once more I became convinced that this child was never coming, so I decided to make one more run to the commissary to supply the kitchen for company. Mother and Daddy would need to eat, after all, and Susan shouldn't have to worry about feeding them while I was in the hospital.

After wielding my basket through the enormous warehouse that had become so familiar to me, I joined the wraparound line of shoppers, prepared yet again to wait an hour or more to get through the checkout line. Before I could dig my book out of my purse, however, the woman in front of me turned to strike up a conversation. When she saw my bulging figure, she asked when the baby was due.

"Today," I said.

"Today? You shouldn't be standing in line, for goodness sake. Here, you go ahead of me."

Faster than my protest, the harried woman in worn slacks and buttoned blouse, which no longer quite met at the hem, had pulled her cart out of line and pushed mine forward. She angled her cart back into the line behind mine and brushed past me to approach the woman now in front of me. I saw her confer in whispers, and then she motioned me forward indicating that the other woman was also willing to let me go ahead of her.

Without waiting, the woman continued working up the row. With each new customer she pointed at me while she talked ever louder, saying, "There's this poor pregnant woman back there whose baby is due today. I said she shouldn't be on her feet and told her to go ahead of me. Would you mind if she cut in?"

I was so embarrassed by all the heads now turning that I literally hid my face behind my hand. When I dared to peep through my fingers, the woman had reached the curve at the front of the aisle and turned out of sight down the home stretch. Now everyone was watching me. I turned around to discover that those who had arrived after me were passing the word in the other direction.

I didn't want special treatment; all I wanted was to grab my groceries and to run, neither of which I was capable of doing.

Within minutes, the woman rounded the aisle and headed back to me, stopping at each basket to update the participants, "She's going to the head of the line. Not a single person said no."

She grabbed my cart and pushed it herself while I meekly followed, trying to smile my appreciation.

"Here you go," the woman said triumphantly as we arrived at the register. "Now don't you carry these. Have your husband unload them when he gets home."

I didn't dare tell her Lee was in Vietnam; she might have arranged a military escort for me.

"Thank you," I said. "That was very kind of you." She beamed, and I was struck by the notion that when she had been pregnant, probably no one had done such a thing for her. This was her way of righting a little part of the world.

"Now you go home and take care of yourself," she instructed as she turned to walk back to her own hour-and-a-half wait.

She had nothing to worry about. I had just made my last public appearance as a pregnant woman. Home was indeed where I was going and where I would stay.

As I made trips up the stairs with the groceries, I stopped to peer into the mail bin once more. Much to my surprise, an envelope lay angled on the chute, deposited by either late delivery or some thoughtful soul who had found it in the wrong box.

The packet was thick and I hurried upstairs. First I read that Lee's unit was getting a new battalion commander. While I had not been happy with the exploits of the current one, at least he had not gotten Lee killed thus far. In Hawaii, Lee had displayed a high regard for his commander, which had generated a begrudging respect for the man on my part. It was unsettling to have the Army tampering with a functional equation.

Lee also said that his unit was scheduled for a "standdown" for the next few days, which sent my calculations into action to conclude that he might have had a holiday, too. By now, though, he would be back in the field.

I was weary of living behind the curve of time, but I realized that he was probably experiencing the same thing. Today was supposed to be "baby day" and there was no sign of our new family member. I wanted desperately to let him know that everything was fine. No news simply meant no news. I hated having him suffer through the unknowns as I had for so many months. That was not a fate I would wish on anyone, especially someone I loved.

But he would get to wait along with me this time—which is what I did through the next two days: Wait. No change. No baby. The hours dragged. Susan spent the evenings scrutinizing me with squinted eyes, trying to ferret out any change, any progress. I just threw up my hands in hopelessness.

By the fourth of December, I was back to believing I would never have the baby—or at least not for another couple of weeks. I picked up John Haley's new book *Airport* and read. In fact, I got so caught up in the book that I read until two o'clock in the morning just to finish it.

I had just put the book down and turned out the light when I both felt and heard my water break. I raced first to the bathroom and then to Susan's door where I pounded and yelled, "Susan! It's time for the baby."

Behind the door I heard a muffled sound and then silence. I banged and shouted again before returning to my room, trying to decide what I needed to do. After so many months of waiting, I was suddenly clueless about where to begin. I took a deep breath to calm my growing excitement. I was about to have a baby!

Susan dragged herself to my door frame and complained, "What time is it? Couldn't you do this in the morning? I'm too tired."

"Come on, Susan," I coaxed. "It really is time, I think. My water broke."

Suddenly Susan was on full alert. "Okay. Okay. What do we do first? I've got to call Adrienne. She'll know."

"It's three in the morning. You can't call Adrienne," I protested. "Let's just go to the hospital."

But Susan was already dialing. I dressed while she awoke Adrienne for a second opinion.

Susan drove my car because I could no longer squeeze into her Corvair. "Are you having contractions yet?" she asked grimly.

"No, I don't think so."

"Don't you know?" she quizzed without taking her eyes from the road. "Do you feel different? Is this false labor?"

"Susan, I've never had a baby before. I just don't know."

"What did they tell you in the film you saw? Huh? Aren't you supposed to have contractions first and then your water breaks?"

When we arrived at the now-familiar emergency room entrance, I was coerced into a wheelchair and taken to the maternity ward while Susan took care of admission.

"Well, we weren't expecting any visitors tonight," the nurse said with a sleepy smile when I arrived at the ward. "The doctor's taking a little siesta, but we'll get him." With that, she wheeled me away to the exam room, where, several minutes later, a tall, husky young doctor arrived, rubbing his face. Following a mighty stretch and gaping yawn, he shook his head violently and then smiled through a mock indignation, "Do you know what time it is? Couldn't you have waited, oh, say, three hours? I'm not done with my beauty sleep."

"You sound like my roommate," I said.

"Your roommate?" he asked, arching his eyebrows dramatically, and then proceeded as he examined me to solicit the story of how I happened to be accompanied by a roommate rather than a husband. His casual manner was calming, and I wondered why I'd never had the good fortune of finding him during my clinic visits.

"Have you had any contractions yet?"

"No, just some cramping sensations very once in a while."

"Well," he said through another yawn, "those are contractions, but just warm-ups for the big ones. You might keep an eye on how often they occur. Everything looks fine, but you can relax. We're many hours away from a baby. I'll have the nurses put you in a room. Meanwhile, I'm going back to sleep."

I was rolled to a room at the end of the hall, transferred to a bed, and left to stare at the ceiling, which I did for half an hour before Susan found me.

"What are you doing in here by yourself?" she asked, winded from her rush through the hospital.

I explained that we were in for a long wait, and she described her battles to get me admitted. "I filled out the forms like they asked," she said, dragging a chair to the bed, "and where it said 'next of kin,' I put Lee's name. I just wrote 'Vietnam' as his address. But they wouldn't accept that. They said they had to have a 'next of kin' they could contact, so I put down your dad's name and address. But when they saw 'Texas,' that was no good either. To make a long story short, I am officially your next of kin. So do this right and don't embarrass me, okay?"

Susan began digging in her purse and eventually rooted out a pad, pencil, and—I couldn't believe my eyes—the deck of cards. "Okay," she said authoritatively, "the Red Cross says play cards, so we're going to play."

"They didn't say we had to keep score," I pointed out.

"The pad is for taking notes," she corrected. "I thought I'd write down the time of your contractions so Lee could know about the night his baby was born. Have you had one yet?"

"Yeah, a little one a couple of minutes ago."

As Susan glanced at the large round clock face on the wall and scratched on the pad, I said, "And here comes another one."

"Tell me when it's over," she instructed clinically. "I want to get all of this down."

Then she dealt the cards. The thought of playing cards struck me not only as totally absurd but also as slightly irritating. But Susan insisted, determined to do her part, and coaxed me through one hand of rummy, though we had to stop every two or three minutes for her to note another contraction, each of which increased my irritability level.

Susan studied the list of times and durations. "You're not doing this right," she informed me. "The contractions are supposed to be fifteen minutes apart and then ten and down to five and so forth. Yours are jumping around all over the place, and it's too soon for them to be this close together."

I looked at her plaintively. Unabashed, she continued her analysis. "In fact, you're not doing it right at all. I think I'll go show the doctor."

She was gone with her chart before I could protest or tell her that the man in white was asleep. With a sinking feeling, I was afraid she was right. Instead of experiencing knife-like stabs of pain as I had expected, I was enduring these damned cramping seizures that were making me cross as hell. I was sleepy and more and more angry with myself for not having had the good sense to go into this ordeal well rested. Besides, the walls of the room were plastered with diagrams of the dilation process, and who the hell wanted to look at those?

By the time Susan returned, my mood had deteriorated considerably, although she was in high spirits. "I showed the nurse. She's going to get the doctor."

Settling back into her chair, Susan reached for the cards. "So much as touch those," I said menacingly, "and you'll be playing fifty-two pick-up—alone."

Startled, Susan looked up, quickly reassessing the situation. "Oh, I see we're getting grumpy now."

"No," I corrected urgently. "I'm going to be sick. Get me something quick."

"Ugh, I didn't know being sick was part of it," she complained, hurriedly handing me a stainless steel bowl and turning away in disgust.

What goodwill I had remaining departed as I retched.

"You can leave," I told Susan weakly.

"No, I have to time your contractions for Lee."

"If he'd wanted to know about the contractions," I said between gritted teeth, "he damned well should have been here himself."

Just then two doctors and a nurse entered and Susan stepped up to detail my progress. After her clinical descriptions, she added, "Besides, she's getting crabby."

The doctors executed their examination, and Dr. Sleepy from earlier this morning looked at me and said, "I knew you were going to be trouble the minute I saw you. For this to be your first baby, you're really moving along. Which is good and bad. Good, because you'll be done sooner, but bad because you've already dilated too much for the mild sedative we usually give early on. Now you'll have to wait until it's baby time for the other drugs."

"Is that why she's sick?" Susan asked in obvious dismay about the latest development.

"Nah," the doctor shook his head. "She's just doing that to bother you." He grinned and they departed.

For the next hour or so, Susan continued to time my grimaces, growing chattier and more nervous as I became crankier and sicker. She made teasing, disparaging comments about my techniques to a nurse who eventually arrived to conduct a check on my progress. Susan showed her the sheet of paper, which the nurse eyed suspiciously before dashing out the door.

"They don't think you're doing it right, either," Susan concluded as she drew a deep breath.

Somewhere from the deep recesses of the person I had once been, there was a feeling of sympathy for Susan, a friend who avoided emotions, unpleasantness, and pain at all costs. Yet she stood there and endured her phobias for me, a fact for which I was not ungrateful. But it was a gratitude that could not compete with my overriding sense of irritation at everything that moved or made noise, including, and maybe especially, Susan.

Suddenly the door flew open and a crew of white uniforms descended. "Time to change rooms," the nurse announced as I was once more transferred to a gurney and whipped down the hall, a nauseating sensation that caused more retching as I rolled.

When I was situated in the labor room, Susan appeared, shouldering our purses and still clutching her pad of paper. I was beyond caring about what was happening except for a concern about the baby. But Susan, highly intrigued now that we were in a place of medical apparatus, asked thousands of questions, it seemed, of Dr. Sleepy and his colleague.

I paid little attention to the buzz of conversation until the doctor wheeled a cart carrying a large black box about the size of a small TV screen beside the bed. "Your roommate says you're worried about the baby," he said as he tinkered with wires from the box, reminding me of the parking lot "mechanics" who had fiddled with the engine when my car wouldn't start. His indecisive scrutiny of the wires and machine did nothing to instill confidence, but he distractedly tried to reassure me. "What we have here, when I get it figured out, is a new device that will allow you to watch your baby's heartbeat. Then you can see for yourself that the little fellow is doing fine."

Finally satisfied, he attached a small suction-cup-looking device to the soft spot of the baby's head and, like magic, I could watch the quick little bleeps of green that indicated my baby's heartbeat. Relief flooded through me as I lay mesmerized by the signals from a separate, and soon to be independent, human being. I experienced an overwhelming pang of regret that Lee was not with me, that he could not see this miracle, too.

"Now she's crying," Susan reported to the obstetrician.

"Don't worry," he said off-handedly, "women in labor go through all kinds of emotions. Babies get born anyway."

The next thing I knew I was startled awake. Seized with panic, I looked around to find myself still in the labor room, Susan still talking and laughing with the staff, and the clock indicating that I had slept less than a minute. I couldn't fathom how I could have dropped off so soundly in so little time, but surely it was a bad sign, though the green blimps were steady. The kid was doing a better job of consistency than I was.

"Okay," the doctor said strolling over to me, "time for the epidural." He explained the medication, assuring me that within minutes, I would feel no more cramping or pressure. He rolled me to my side and injected the painkiller.

The next time the doctor strolled by, Susan hailed him to ask how soon I should feel numb. He furrowed his brow and pulled a safety pin from his coat pocket. He began pricking at my ankle, working his way up my leg. When he reached just above the knee cap, I yelled. He jumped and jabbed himself with the pin. With his bleeding finger pressed against his lips, he stood deliberating.

"How tall are you?" Susan asked him.

Puzzled, he looked at her and answered, "Six-five. Why?"

"How long were you when you were born?"

"I don't know," he frowned deeper, "why?"

"Because her husband is six-five and she's five-eleven. I'm just wondering how long this baby will be."

Only Susan, I thought, would be asking these questions.

The doctor jerked his finger from his mouth and stared down at me from toe to head. Looking at Susan as though I weren't in the room, he asked, "How tall did you say she is?"

"Five-eleven."

"Well, no wonder," he said. "This medication numbs from the toes upward. She's too tall for the regular dosage."

With that he picked up another needle. Less than five minutes later, I felt my last discomfort. My good humor returned and I, too, could be fascinated with the process. I never took my eyes off the monitor, though, as I grew increasingly thrilled.

In a flurry at 10:15, I was surrounded again and whisked to the delivery room. Susan waved goodbye after giving my shoulder a squeeze. She looked exhausted and I thought she might cry.

I, on the other hand, was ecstatic, inspecting the green-gowned professionals as they busied themselves and set a mirror in place so I could watch my baby arrive. Feeling very much an outside observer, I watched the preparations and heard the doctor's instructions: "We have a machine that tells us when you're having a contraction. Push when I tell you."

The lower half of my body was missing as far as my nervous system was concerned, and I wasn't sure how I could cooperate. But I wasn't worried about it so long as I could see the blipping green monitor light and be reassured that the baby was fine.

"Get the forceps ready," I heard the doctor say.

"No," I raised my head to speak. "Don't use forceps."

Dr. Now-Awake looked at me over his mask and wiggled his eyebrows. "Who's delivering this baby? You or me?"

I laughed. "It's your delivery, Doc. But it's my baby. Don't use the forceps."

His eyes smiled. "Trouble right to the end, aren't you? Well, I'll have the forceps handy just in case. Get ready. Push."

I checked the clock. 10:33. I focused on the blimps and concentrated.

"Okay—" the doctor's voice was excited. "Here comes the head."

I looked into the mirror and watched spellbound as my baby slipped into the waiting hands of the doctor who announced through the muffling of his mask, "It's a girl."

I lay back on the pillow and laughed aloud. "I should have known," I said and laughed again. I couldn't imagine why I'd ever thought I was having a boy. What was Lee going to say? I laughed once more at the thought of his surprise.

"Let me see her," I said, raising my head and realizing that I had not heard her cry. "Is she okay?"

"Just a minute," the doctor said. A nurse held the baby and worked a suction cup over her mouth. God, why didn't they hang her upside down and smack her bottom to get her to cry? I waited, suspended. Then the baby gasped and yelled her protests while I chuckled in relief.

The nurse laid my black-haired baby girl on my chest, and I gently touched her clinched fist. My daughter was the most amazing thing I had ever seen.

"What are you going to name her?" the nurse asked.

"You wouldn't believe me if I told you," I laughed, kissing the baby's fist before she was lifted away.

I felt euphoric as the orderly rolled me out of the double doors of the delivery room. Looking down the short hallway, I saw Lee, grinning ear-to-ear, near the window. I was so surprised—not only that he was there but that he was wearing a shirt which had been his favorite in high school—that it took my breath. I raised my head to smile in return. But when I blinked, he was gone. The corridor was empty. Tears stung my eyes.

Just then Susan stepped from a doorway and joined my moving bed. "She's got Lee's ears," she proclaimed with a laugh.

"You've seen her?" I asked, surprised. But, of course, Susan would have seen her by now. She was on a first-name basis with everybody on the floor.

"They held her up for me when they brought her out," she explained. "What's Lee going to say about having a baby girl?"

"I have no idea," I said, thrilled with the baby but still haunted by Lee's appearance and disappearance from the hallway. "But would you go tell the Red Cross so they can send the message to Lee that she's here and that we're both fine? I know he's wondering what's going on. All the information about his unit is in that little blue book in my bag."

By now we had reached the recovery room and Susan stood tentatively at my latest parking place. "What about the name?" she asked. "Are you really going to name her Reveilee Ann?"

"Oh, I don't know," I wailed and then laughed. "It's no more absurd than anything else in my life, I guess."

Susan stood waiting while I considered. I continued, "Well, telling Lee her name is Reveilee doesn't really make it official yet. I don't have to decide for sure until I sign the birth certificate. Just get the message off. But first," I insisted, grabbing her arm before she could turn away, "please get me something to eat. I'm starving to death."

"Ugh," she moaned, "how can you go from being sick to being hungry so fast? I'm never having kids, I can tell you that."

"I'm going to have a dozen more," I smiled, "just as soon as I get something to eat."

"You're drugged," she concluded and left on her errands.

• • •

"The Red Cross guy thought I was a lunatic," Susan reported. "You better think about that name. I called your parents, and they are going to let Lee's parents know. And I called Jim and Judy. Everybody's thrilled. And everybody thinks you're crazy with the name and nobody can spell it. But I think the damage may be done. Poor little thing. Lee's ears and a name like Reveilee."

"The important thing is that she's healthy and she's beautiful," I said, feeling full of energy and optimism. "Did the Red Cross say when Lee would get the message?"

"It will go out of San Francisco today but the guy didn't know how it would be routed when it got to Vietnam since Lee's in the field. Maybe in twenty-four hours or so."

I wished I could see Lee's face when he learned she was a girl. I didn't think Lee had ever considered the possibility.

{Chapter 33}

"Didn't you just deliver this morning?"

I turned from the nursery window to see a nurse beside me, her brow crinkled into a frown.

"Yes," I said. "That's my baby in the incubator. Isn't she beautiful?"

"Yep," the older woman said with a cursory look toward the glass, "she's a cutie. But you've been up too long."

"I just love to look at her," I protested.

Checking the hallway, the nurse asked, "Where's your husband?" She sounded as though she wanted someone to take charge of me.

Without taking my eyes off the baby, I answered, "Vietnam."

I heard her quick intake of breath and felt her pat my back as she walked away, saying, "Well, you just look at her all you want."

A few minutes later, the recovery room nurse appeared at my side and scolded, "Here you are. I thought I'd lost a patient."

She escorted me to a room with two beds, a close-up view of the Golden Gate Bridge, and an array of floral arrangements.

"Are these all for me?" I asked, amazed.

"You and that baby girl of yours," the nurse answered as I pulled cards from the bouquets.

Mother and Daddy. Jim and Judy. Brenda and Danny. Eleanor Morgan. Mr. and Mrs. Lanning.

Until I saw their card, I hadn't thought about the Lannings' reaction to a granddaughter. Mr. Lanning would be pleased, and Mrs. Lanning would need a few days to decide.

Emotion rushed to my eyes. If only Lee could be here, I thought. Not that he would have cared about the flowers, but he, too, would have appreciated the sentiments. I knew, however, that had Lee been there, he would not have been the attentive husband hovering over me. He would have been pacing the floor with boredom, demanding to hold his kid. I laughed to myself as I wiped my tears. Given a choice, Lee would take the jungle over a maternity ward any day.

I sensed an impending lull, like the letdown after Christmas presents have been opened or the last of the company has departed. I knew if I gave in to the denouement, I would be racked with grief that Lee was missing the first minutes of his daughter's life, with worry that our baby down the hall might not even have a living father, with self-pity that my husband wasn't at my side when I needed him. The only way for me to avoid being overcome was to outrun those emotions with activity. I straightened my shoulders, swallowed hard, and went to find a telephone.

After talking with Mother and Daddy, I returned to the nursery to watch my baby, who was now in her own crib. I was watching the slight rise of the blanket as she drew each breath when another new mother, slightly younger than I, shuffled to the window. We exchanged smiles; I asked, "Which one is yours?"

She pointed to a crib and said, "That one."

"Oh, lucky you, you had a girl, too."

'Yeah, it's been all girls here for several days," she said with a sigh. "Is your husband disappointed, too?"

"What?" I asked, astonished. It hadn't occurred to me that Lee would be disappointed, only surprised.

"My husband's real disappointed that we didn't get a boy," the woman said sadly, leaning her head against the glass above her child's crib. "I think she's sweet myself, but he's pretty upset."

Looking down at her tiny newborn, I was outraged that anyone—especially the father—could be disappointed. It was unthinkable.

"What did yours say?" she asked.

"He doesn't know yet," I answered. "Maybe tomorrow."

"Why so long?" she queried, curiosity replacing depression.

"He's in Vietnam."

"Oh, I'm sorry," she mumbled, as uncomfortable as if she'd discovered he were dead. With a nervous look over her shoulder, she quickly retreated down the hall. I was engulfed once more by a sense of isolation, in this case not because of anti-war stances but because I represented a possibility too close for comfort.

• • •

By early Sunday afternoon, I had adapted to the hospital environs, sharing the room with a Norwegian woman whose husband turned out to be, of all things, a Letterman obstetrician. Only occasionally did I catch her staring sympathetically at me, usually just after her husband had been in to visit.

I had continued to spend my time since Friday at the nursery window, impatient for each chance to hold and nurse the baby. The only strange thing about my child was that, like a kitten, she refused to open her eyes even when I knew she wasn't sleeping.

I wrote Lee pages and pages of minutiae describing her. Still, my words were inadequate, for I suffered the delusions of certainty that I was the only woman in the history of the world to ever experience motherhood so completely.

I had also filled in the blanks on the birth announcements. While the Lanning Recruiting Center cards had seemed terribly clever when I designed them, I was less sure now that people would appreciate either my artistry or my sense of humor, especially when the recruit's name was Reveilee. I sealed and stamped them before I changed my mind.

Emotions were difficult to keep at bay as I watched uniformed men uninhibitedly make goo-goo noises to their babies at the nursery window, when I saw couples strolling arm-in-arm, when I passed rooms where men sat cradling their newborns in awkward poses, when I caught a woman whispering to her husband and pointing at me, and when I wondered if Lee even knew yet.

On that Sunday afternoon I was waiting for Mother and Daddy to arrive from Texas when a motion near the door caught my eye, and I turned to find Bernie Petrocelli balancing lightly on a cane, his face alight with a smile.

"Yep, this is it," he said into the hallway and, as he limped into the room, an attractive red-headed woman followed. "Hey, congratulations! I hear it's a girl," he said with a laugh.

Surprised, I stammered, "How did you know?"

"I've been on leave, but your roommate stopped by the ward and left word. I wanted Jeannie to meet you."

"I'm delighted," I said, extending my hand. "Bernie talks about you all the time."

"I've heard a lot about you, too. Congratulations," she echoed softly as she briefly shook my hand, flashing a quick smile that held a trace of reluctance—or was it resentment? I had the impression that just as Bernie had been a link to Lee for me, I was a link for Jeannie—a link to Vietnam, a war she would never forgive. She stepped quickly back to Bernie's side where the top of her head barely reached his shoulder and stood with her arms crossed, her freckled face impassive. Even so, Jeannie was a strikingly attractive woman, and I suspected that her green eyes glittered when she was pleased. At present, however, she was not.

I might have dwelt on Jeannie's attitude except that I was to glad to see my recovering friend. "Gosh, Bernie," I laughed, "we've traded places. Here you are in street clothes and I'm in the hospital bed. Who would have thought we'd ever make it to this day? Would you like to see the baby?"

As we stood at the nursery, Bernie looked at me and then back at the baby. "Isn't that amazing?" he whispered. Jeannie leaned her forehead against the glass and then swiveled it to cast a meaningful look at him. He blushed and I laughed.

Just then Reveilee came to life with an obvious cry that we couldn't hear. She threw her tiny fists and her face went red.

"She's got her father's temper, I see," Bernie observed.

I chuckled, "Bernie, you don't know Lee well enough to know if he has a temper or not. But it's nice of you to try."

• • •

Mother and Daddy flew into San Francisco late Sunday afternoon, and Susan brought them directly to the hospital. Mother lit up with a grin when she saw her granddaughter in the nursery while Daddy paced the halls, hardly able to contain his impatience to hold her. At the end of visiting hours, Susan shepherded the new grandparents away so they could get a good night's rest before returning the next day.

As far as the doctors were concerned, Baby Lanning and I were free to leave after rounds on Monday morning. The hospital had other ideas. First, I had to complete the paperwork for the birth certificate. I wavered. Goddammit, I needed to talk to Lee just long enough to tell him we couldn't do this to our child. She would be in grade school before she could pronounce her name and graduating from college before she could spell it. How long it would take her to learn to live with it, I did not know. I was able to sign the paper only when I decided we could always go to court to change it.

Another hospital requirement was that I attend a birth control class. When I suggested to the nurse that I had no immediate need for the training, she shrugged and reminded me that this was, after all, the military and rules were rules. I sat through the session, once more the lone woman among couples.

I had but one more task to perform. Clutching my checkbook, I went downstairs to pay my bill. The clerk handed me the tally, and I smiled. This was the first thing I had actually been able to afford since Lee left, and I happily wrote the check for $5.25, the charge for my meals. Some days, the military system had its merits.

While I dressed the baby and packed, Mother and Daddy went to get the car. As I finished bundling her up, I was seized with panic, wondering if the hospital personnel were actually going to let me leave with this defenseless child. It seemed incredible that, with all the attention and equipment devoted to ensuring her safe arrival, they would entrust her unquestioningly to my care. I kept waiting for someone to accuse me of ineptitude so I could confess. Instead, an orderly appeared with a wheelchair, in which I was required to ride, even though I had just gone downstairs unaided to the cashier. As he rolled me toward the elevator, I sensed that the hospital had its priorities wrong.

Daddy cautiously steered us through the streets while I kept my eyes glued to the baby. The farther he drove, the smaller she became. By the time we had completed the drive to Collins Street, Reveilee Lanning had gone from a robust infant who filled my arms to a fragile newborn who fit in the palm of my hand.

What a fool I had been to think that finally having the baby would alleviate any of my worries and fears! Instead, they had quadrupled. Now, not only did I still have to live with the dread of Lee's being killed at any moment, but also I now had become solely responsible for the life of another human being. I wondered if I would survive seeing to the survival of the other two.

Susan swung the door open and greeted us. "Welcome home," she said, reaching to pull the blanket off the baby's face. "Daphne loves the baby bed. She's not going to want to share."

"Susan," I cried in horror. I could see the damned cat suffocating the baby.

She laughed, "It's okay. I told her she could use it only until you got home. I've got to go back to work now. I'll see you tonight. There's mail from Lee on the mantle."

I knew before I opened the first letter that it had been written days before the baby was born, let alone before Lee could have received word of her arrival. Still, disappointment gripped my chest as I read his description of Thanksgiving dinner in the field. His words seemed to have been written in a century past for all the immediacy they had. When Lee scribbled the letter he was still counting days until the baby was born; when I read it, we had a three-day-old child. The gap between us seemed to widen, the space filling with depression.

The second letter unsettled me further. His company had killed two enemy soldiers and activity was on the upswing again. I wondered how my life could have changed so drastically in the last week and yet still be exactly the same.

I felt the urge to run away. Mother and Daddy could take care of the baby better than I could, and Lee was going to get himself killed no matter what I did. I would disappear and we would all live and die happily ever after. Instead, I took a deep breath and went to face the tasks at hand.

Reveilee was a sweet, lazy baby who insisted on nursing every two hours around the clock. Still refusing to open her eyes, she could fret herself into a cry, rather unconvincing but enough to persuade me she needed to be fed. By the second day, however, I was growing blurry-eyed from lack of prolonged sleep. Mother suggested if she fussed longer, she would be hungrier, nurse more, and sleep for lengthier periods. That didn't work, either.

Then Mother cautiously presented another possibility, which I instantly interpreted as a failure on my part. "You know," she said gently, sensing my defensiveness, "mothers under stress don't produce much milk. You're worried about Lee all the time, and you have the responsibility for this baby. Maybe she needs a formula supplement."

I looked down at my nursing baby, so beautiful and so perfect—except for the lack of eyelashes. Maybe if I'd listened to the doctors and not gained so much weight, she would have had lashes. Or maybe it was the salt that I refused to do without which had caused this flaw. Whatever the explanation, it was my fault. Now I couldn't even provide her with enough nourishment. I fought back the tears and agreed.

This seemed a sensible solution until the next day when the baby began to scream with all her might and draw up into a ball. Nothing we did or offered appeased her. I was beside myself, demanding a diagnosis.

"I just don't know," Mother said, bouncing her squalling granddaughter. "She doesn't seem to have a fever."

Daddy was pacing the floor, almost as unnerved as I was after a couple of unrelenting hours of the painful cries. "Do you have a baby book that might help?" he asked, brightening.

"You mean like a Dr. Spock?"

"Exactly," he said, snapping his fingers. "That's what we need. I'll bet it will tell us what's wrong."

I stopped in my tracks. "I don't have one," I confessed, avoiding his inquiring blue eyes. "Spock is a war protester and I could never make myself buy one of his books."

Daddy drew a deep breath, sucking in oxygen and patience. "Well, then. Do you have one written by someone else?"

I shook my head and continued to avoid his eyes. Feeling like an irrational teenager who had shown marginal judgment after bad, I admitted, "Spock's is supposed to be the best. I didn't want anything less than the best, so I didn't get any."

Daddy executed an exasperated laugh and then reasoned, "Listen Hon, I don't think a little advice from an expert would make Lee's baby a pacifist. I think we need to help her."

I grabbed the Yellow Pages and searched, finding a perfect compromise to my dilemma. "There's a used books store just two blocks from here."

Daddy elected to go on foot rather than drive. From the window I watched him seat his Stetson firmly on his head as he headed out from the apartment. He looked more ready to face the range than to brave the city elements, but his determined gait said he was riding to the rescue, nevertheless.

Mother and I took turns jostling the screaming baby until Daddy returned, a smile on his face. "I think I know what's wrong," he announced and held open a page for me to read. Every symptom fit; we had our diagnosis: colic.

Knowing that the baby was in danger of nothing worse than indigestion reduced the trauma her cries created. Within minutes of our relief, the baby found her own and fell peacefully to sleep while we adults plunged into exhaustion.

We were still collapsed when Susan arrived home from work. She had wisely chosen to bunk upstairs with Eleanor while my folks were in the city, but she stopped in each afternoon to monitor the three-ringed circus we were operating, clucking her tongue at the inability of three grownups to manage one baby.

Susan didn't stay long, dashing to her room to collect a few more things and stopping briefly to tease Mother and Daddy. I was disappointed when she headed upstairs so soon, for I found myself missing her even in the middle of the chaos. She didn't seem to want to talk to me though, as if I now made her uncomfortable. The rejection stung, but I hoped it was a temporary reaction that would disappear when Mother and Daddy left at the end of the week.

I was shocked the next morning when my daughter suddenly opened her eyes, as if on cue from some internal clock, and took an unfocused look around. Her irises, so brown they appeared black, seemed to tell me she would do all things in her own time.

Not only was I thrilled that she had decided to visually join the world, but also I was ecstatic to discover that curled into the furrows of her eyelids lay fine, soft lashes—ready to wear and quick to flutter. I kissed her perfect puffy cheeks.

Remarkably, we fell into a mini-routine with the baby nursing every two hours, Mother and Daddy watching over her while I grabbed what sleep I could, and Susan popping in briefly each afternoon after work. I was comforted by having my parents, veterans of three babies' survival, at my side to help me deal with what should have been the simplest of things, such as sterilizing the baby bottles—and remembering to do that each day—and turning unfamiliar tasks into smooth gestures. I was thankful I had had practice with baby David when he visited, but there was a difference being a stand-in sitter and a full-time mother.

Amidst all the baby focus, I began to feel myself fading from existence. My wants and desires no longer took priority; the baby's did. And she was the total focus of her grandparents, about which I was pleased. Yet without Lee there to talk to as another adult and without Susan's constant company, I felt myself slipping away as an entity, and such feelings generated even more feelings—of guilt, inadequacy.

I missed Susan terribly during this time, but she was obviously keeping her distance. I did overhear her talking with my folks one evening about postpartum depression, a topic she abandoned instantly when I entered the room. I felt even worse.

Once more life was not turning out as planned—or more accurately, the plan was turning out not to have the prescribed outcomes. I guess I had thought the baby would simply erase any and all other worries because I would be so happy to have her that nothing else could touch me. While I was ecstatic about this incredible infant, I was not out of the reach of life, which I had to face once more when Susan came in late in the week and said we needed to talk.

My heart was in my throat. Susan avoided eye contact and then she started talking without pause, saying, "I just hate this, but there's nothing I can do about it. Here's the situation. Miles got his mid-term grades and when Daddy saw them, he had a fit. Miles is smart but he's not studying. Anyway, Mother—she's thrilled it's a girl, by the way—well, Mother and Daddy have been on the phone to Miles and to me for days now, ever since you went into the hospital. I think if Daddy were here, he would yell at Miles and raise hell for a few days and that would be the end of it. But he's in Tehran, probably feeling like he has no control. So the long and the short of it is that Daddy says Miles has to get his grades up and he thinks the only way that will happen is if Miles moves back in here, you know, away from all the parties and stuff. Mother and I tried telling him he wasn't being fair—not to us or to Miles, but Daddy says he's paying a portion of the rent here and that if 'Miles, by God, wants to go to school, he will move back.'"

My head was reeling from the collision of two different reactions. I was relieved that Susan had not decided that she hated me or the baby, on the one side, and stunned at the idea of having Miles back the apartment on the other.

Susan now looked directly at me, shrugged, and lowered her eyes again. "Anyway," she continued, "I thought you ought to know while your folks are here, so you can decide what you want to do."

"I have to leave? Is that what you're telling me?" I asked, trying to understand.

"No," she said quickly. "You don't have to leave, you know that. You live here, too. And I don't want you to go, but you may decide it's best. Remember this summer when Miles was here? The parties? You may not want to go through that again, especially while trying to take care of Reveilee by yourself. I mean, Miles and his friends are noisy and they're sometimes inconsiderate. They'd wake the baby. I just don't know how it would work."

I stared at Susan, trying to read between her words at the same time I attempted to comprehend the full impact of the unfolding events. Despite her reassurances, I felt as if I were being evicted.

"Are you worried about the baby being in the way?" I asked.

"No, the other way around. Miles is a big boy. He can take care of his own needs. Reveilee Ann can't."

We sat in silence. I tried envisioning the apartment, as spacious as it was, being large enough to house a college student, a working woman, and a mother and baby, all of whom operated on divergent schedules. A crying baby would keep the other two awake when they needed their sleep; loud music on weekends would play havoc with the baby's schedule. It seemed that Susan would be the only non-trouble person.

But leave San Francisco? I had finally managed to make it feel like home, I realized too late, and now I would have to face displacement all over again, and with a baby in tow, too.

I became aware of my heavy sighs only when Susan repeated, "I'm really sorry about this. Do you think we can make it work?"

I shook my head slowly, knowing that from the minute Susan had started talking that this conclusion was inevitable.

“I’ve had all week to think about it,” she said quietly. “Eleanor and I have racked our brains, but we’re at a dead end. I don’t want you to be unhappy, and I’m afraid you would be.”

“Thank you for not waiting any longer to tell me,” I said, brushing away a tear. “And for not telling me sooner. Maybe Mother and Daddy can cancel their flight and drive us to Texas. I mean, I guess I’ll go back there. I don’t have anywhere else.”

“Shit,” Susan swore with a hiss.

“No, I didn’t mean it like that. I just meant that I automatically assumed I’d go there. Do you think they’ll mind having their granddaughter around for the next four months?” I asked with a half-hearted laugh. At least somebody would be happy with the latest developments.

“I think they will be ecstatic,” Susan said, brightening as we passed the awkward point. I had the inclination to tell her how much she meant to me as a friend, but I knew she would fend off my efforts. The best thing I could do was show her by not giving way to my emotions and by making her feel that I was okay with leaving, though I was far from it.

• • •

Sleep evaded me as I lay in my darkened room an arm’s length from my infant. Part of me felt an immeasurable relief that I would have experienced help in caring for her. But another, more troublesome aspect stabbed at my soul—disappointment in losing the opportunity to see if I could withstand the challenges of completing the year on my own. Returning to Texas seemed a defeat of sorts. Even in the black clouds of despair at my failings, I could see great strips of silver linings luring me to follow the obvious path back.

Mother and Daddy saw no black clouds of despair at the news that Reveilee and I would be going back to Texas with them. Indeed, their eyes glinted bright when I delivered the news and asked if they would cancel their flights and drive us. Daddy went immediately for a U-Haul trailer to attach to my car and Mother and I began packing.

Worry had been my constant companion for so long that I no longer thought of it as separate from me. It was simply an appendage that changed form from time to time. Now it took the shape of concern over the advisability of taking a nine-day-old baby on a three-day car ride. My mind was assailed by all sorts of possible mishaps—blown tires, reckless drivers, deer in the headlights.

But the idea that kept pounding at me was that I was totally responsible for the welfare of this child. Not having Lee there to share the decisions was more daunting than I could have imagined. In reality, he would not have been particularly helpful in dealing with most trivial matters, but the fact that I could not discuss my plans with him left me feeling I had the burden of the world in my hands—and no clear instructions on how to proceed. Though I would never have admitted it, even I suspected postpartum hormones were sometimes to blame. Still, I made Daddy check and re-check all the safety aspects of the trip until even his patience was almost at end.

When we pulled away from 40 Collins Street, I felt myself once more adrift. I was leaving before I had received a letter from Lee telling me he knew he had a daughter. Believing that such a letter would arrive any day made it incredibly difficult to leave, but I could ask Mother and Daddy to wait no longer. Sitting in the back seat next to Reveilee Ann's portable crib, I felt like a passenger in my own life.

But I was not a silent passenger. All the way from San Francisco to Roby, I continually voiced my concern over Reveilee's safety, constantly fretted over irregular car noises, and elevated backseat driving to an art form as we covered the relentless miles of interstate highway. Daddy was a saint who seemed to think having his granddaughter around was worth even my unrelenting worry.

To pass the time, Mother reminisced about when she and Daddy had taken me, as a six-week-old, from Texas to California. "You were very good on the trip," she grinned, turning her head over her shoulder to me, "but when we got there, you cried for a week."

"Where did I ride?" I asked.

"On a pillow right here in the front seat between us," she answered. "We didn't know then to worry about seat belts."

Mother's strategy of talking about the past worked. For the next hour I contemplated the replay of history. I had been born during a war, as had my daughter. My father had learned about my birth through a telegram, which was still in my baby book, and Lee would learn about his daughter over a field radio, in all probability. Daddy did not see me until I was six weeks old; Lee would not see his daughter for sixteen weeks, give or take a few days. I was taken from Texas to California as an infant; now I was reversing the route for my daughter. I wondered at the similarities and debated whether I had unwittingly set any of the repeat performances into play.

Despite my fixations on impending doom, Daddy chauffeured us without mishap, and at the end of three days' travel, we pulled up at their house. I felt not so much a sense of coming home as a sense of deliverance. We had made it. Reveilee Ann Lanning was alive and intact. Her mother, however, was a basket case.

• • •

Early the next morning, I called Marina Babb, the post mistress at Sylvester, and asked her to relay a message to Mr. Lanning that Reveilee Ann and I were in Roby, where he and Mrs. Lanning were welcome to see their granddaughter.

"They'll be here by nine-fifteen," I told Mother when I got off the phone. "By my calculations, he will be at the post office about eight, get the message, go back home to pick up Mrs. Lanning, and come straight here."

A few minutes later, the phone rang and Mother handed the receiver to me with a frown, "It's the post office. Something about flowers."

In an excited voice, Violet Upshaw, the Roby post mistress, started talking, giving me no chance to respond: "Linda, we've got a special delivery for you all the way from Hawaii. It just came in and, I don't know, I think from the return address that it's flowers. We don't have any place to keep them cool. With the heater on, it's too hot in here. I've got the box sitting outside. What do you want me to do?"

"I don't know anyone in Hawaii," I responded, confused.

But she reiterated the information, again requesting instructions. I told her I would be right there, knowing that she was, above all else, dying of curiosity.

Frankly, I was curious myself, trying to sort out the puzzle as Daddy drove. I laughed when I saw a lone, slender box propped up along the side of the building. Only in a small town, I thought, would I get such service and attention. By the time I reached the box, the door was open and Violet, along with four mail carriers, stood waiting.

The package was plastered with labels, routing slips to and from San Francisco, and instructions to "Keep in Cool Place." Much to my surprise, my name was all over it.

"We've got scissors if you want to open it now," Violet offered hopefully. Thinking it unfair to take my booty and run, I went inside. It was not every day that special delivery packages arrived in this part of the country.

I cut through yards of tape as several pairs of hands assisted me in removing the lid. Green florist's tissue paper concealed the contents. When I peeled it back, I found a bouquet of Hawaiian flowers—orchids, birds of paradise, and exotic specimens I could not identify—arranged around ferns and monkey pods. I looked for a card among the wilting pedals and eagerly opened it. It read, "My love, Lee."

Now I was really confused. Lee was in the jungle fighting a war. It did not make sense for him to send me flowers, especially when he wouldn't have thought to do so if he'd been stateside living next door to a flower shop. Part of me gushed with warm feelings while a larger part of me was highly suspicious about the origin of these blossoms. But the people at the post office loved the romance of it, and the story added spice to their day. And in truth, it added some sparkle to my own, despite my lingering misgivings. The most exciting aspect was that the flowers, however they had come to me, must mean that Lee knew about the baby.

I missed my prediction about my in-laws' arrival by five minutes. I saw the Lanning's brown pickup truck pull up and my father-in-law walk briskly toward the back door without waiting for his wife. Mrs. Lanning, her face set in grim dread, was still getting out of the vehicle as I went to let them in. When I opened the door, Mr. Lanning clapped his hands together and, eagerly rubbing them back and forth, asked, "Where's my granddaughter?"

"Right this way," I said, pointing inside with one hand and holding the door for my mother-in-law with the other. "Hello, Mrs. Lanning."

"You certainly surprised us," Lee's mother said as she kissed my cheek. "We had no idea you were coming back."

"Neither did I," I responded without elaboration.

I led the way up the two steps to the port-a-crib placed next to the kitchen table with Mr. Lanning close behind. I watched as he leaned forward, his face softening into a smile and his eyes watering as he stared down at Lee's baby.

I looked back to the den to see Mrs. Lanning engrossed in conversation with Mother and Daddy, hands gesturing in support of whatever she was saying, obviously ignoring the reason she was here. She would see the baby when she was ready.

I reached into the crib and lifted my sleeping infant, who did not so much as even flinch, and passed her into Mr. Lanning's enormous waiting arms. She fit like a peg to its hole and his face lit up as if she were his electrical source. He ever so gently began to bounce her, and I could tell it was all he could do not to coo and coddle her with baby talk.

Mrs. Lanning, still in animated discussion, was now sitting on the couch, never glancing toward the kitchen. I turned back to hide my laughter, wondering just how long she could pretend that there was nothing of interest in the next room.

"Alice," Mr. Lanning called to his wife, "look what I've got."

But Alice was engrossed in the details of the last rain in Fisher County, recounting to a tenth of an inch how much had fallen at their house. Alice was not yet ready.

Mr. Lanning and I exchanged looks. His said, "Be patient with the old gal." Mine answered, "She has no idea what she's missing."

Aloud I said to him, "I think she looks like Lee."

He answered without lifting his eyes from the baby, "She's the spitting image of him at this age." His eyes watered again.

I felt a warm bond with my father-in-law at that moment. "You said you wanted a girl. You got her."

"And she's a little princess, too," he grinned, swaying her back and forth. "Hi, there, Princess," he said to the oblivious baby.

"Alice," Mr. Lanning said, louder this time.

Mrs. Lanning had crossed her legs and turned her shoulder toward the kitchen, a virtual body language barrier. This woman was unbelievable—and incredibly consistent, I had to admit, admiring her fortitude. She did not want to deal with this baby.

Mother stood but vacillated, not wanting to be rude and not wanting to be in the way. I crossed my arms to watch the drama unfold as Mrs. Lanning turned her head toward her husband.

"Can I take her to her grandmother?" Mr. Lanning asked me.

"Of course," I smiled.

Mr. Lanning carefully negotiated the two steps down to the den and crossed to the couch. Mrs. Lanning reluctantly uncrossed her leg and turned center-front, taking a deep breath of preparation. But as much as she was trying to act uninterested, the new grandmother could not sustain her show. Before Mr. Lanning could position himself beside the arm of the couch and lower the baby, Mrs. Lanning was reaching upward to pull down on the blanket. When the baby came into full view, Lee's mother melted. Like a gigantic iceberg, Mrs. Lanning's resistance thawed with the speed of a single snowflake against the skin, releasing waves of emotion she could not hide. Now she could not get the baby into her lap fast enough. Mesmerized, she sat and stared. The only sound was a quick inhalation of awe.

"My God," Mrs. Lanning said finally, "she looks just like Lee did as a baby." I knew then the die had been cast; this child would always hold a special place in her grandmother's heart.

My biggest regret at the moment was that Lee could not see the pure love his mother and father surrendered instantly and unconditionally to his child. It was a mirror of the way they felt about their son, condensed and amplified at the same time. The tender moment reminded me that once Lee had been their baby.

{Chapter 34}

Reveilee Ann Lanning was two weeks and one day old when I received the letter from Lee that told me he knew about her birth. The wait had been torturous, but when I opened the letter on December twentieth, the morning of our second wedding anniversary, I knew we had survived another phase of the war and the waiting.

7 Dec 69

My Darling Wife and Daughter—

Got word on the radio from Battalion Commander
at 1555 yesterday deep in the jungle. Radio congratulations
came in from other companies, etc.—A very proud moment.

All the word I got is: a girl 8 ½ lbs, wife and daughter doing fine—hope to get more word in on resupply tomorrow.

My feelings are fantastic—unbelievable. I didn't know how much I would want to see the baby—Send pictures as soon as possible.

Word came at a hell of a time. The Co and Bn have been in nearly daily heavy contact for the last week—but we are fine and things have calmed down again.

I think standdown has been put off till 16 Dec.

My pride and love for you both is beyond words—

Much to do

I love you both

Lee

Is the name Reville Ann?—I don't even think I know how to spell it.

At long last, I *knew* that he *knew* that he had a daughter. The letter was the most wonderful anniversary present I could have received. I was so excited by Lee's letter telling me that he had been notified that I headed for the Lannings to tell them. When I turned into their yard, I saw Jim and Judy's car and felt yet another boost to my spirits. That my brother-in-law and sister-in-law were already home for the holidays made the Christmas season feel real despite the eighty-degree weather.

I played out the arrival ritual, and everyone piled out of the house to help me with the baby and accompanying paraphernalia. Once we were back inside, the greetings and conversations continued with hearty voices and exaggerated movements as I made a fuss over how big and healthy Jim David was and Judy sighed over the sweetness of a baby girl. The whole family kept up the momentum as though if we all talked loudly enough and moved quickly enough, no one would notice Lee was not among us. Such efforts, of course, only underscored his absence. And watching Jim hold his own child was almost my undoing.

The time spent visiting that day put me into the Christmas spirit. Now that I had received the treasured letter from Lee and spent a congenial day with his family, I was ready to celebrate.

While the Christmas season was filled with temptations to wallow in self-pity, I sternly reminded myself that I had a living husband and a healthy baby; wishing for anything more seemed greedy. Feeling lonely and apart from most of the festivities was simply something I had to endure, though I was grateful for any occasion that made me feel otherwise.

Such was the occasion when one of mother's friends knocked on the back door.

"Come in," I invited. "Mother's in the kitchen."

"No, thanks, but I can't stay," she said standing in the doorway, self-consciously straightening the scarf covering her curlers with one hand and holding out a package with the other. "I just wanted to drop off a little something for the baby."

"Thank you so much," I said, taking the beautifully wrapped present. "Are you sure you can't come in?"

"No, I got to run," she answered, waving out the door.

I untied the white ribbon and loosened the heavy silver paper. When

I opened the box, I found a frilly white dotted Swiss dress trimmed with lace and bows. I knew instantly that it would be the perfect dress for Reveilee to wear when her daddy first saw her.

I was still determined the next day to be upbeat when I received a thick envelope from Lee. Expecting documents, I wearily peeled into the packet to find a six-page letter. Alarm bells went off. Counting the flowers, this was the second out-of-character action by Lee this week. I went to my bedroom, closed the door, and instinctively prepared myself for bad news.

Lee's handwriting was crimped as he began telling me about two major contacts his company had had since his last letter. They were averaging heavy engagements every other day now, and the recon platoon had suffered a KIA two days before. He repeated to me the praise he had received on the performance of his company. There was an inconsistency, though, in what he wrote and the way his handwriting relayed it. Usually when Lee was boosting of his triumphs, his words were large and bold. These were tight and pressed into the paper.

By the bottom of the second page, his script grew larger and his revelations more open. I read on with a growing dread:

> One thing I hesitate to write about, honey, but I feel I should—Don't take it wrong and don't worry please. As we both well know I have been out for 8 months. In the last two months my nerves have really gotten screwed up. I am still calm and don't lose control in contact. However, I am aware and so are Higher-ups that a man can't stay out forever. I understand I will get a job in the rear in a month or so. This does not make me unhappy at all. My job is complete—I made the worst into the best. A man can just stay out so long and he gets a little screwy. Nothing to worry about—nothing permanent. You just get a little edgy.
>
> I have gotten to the point I take absolutely no chances. Honey please don't worry. I still haven't changed—except a little more arrogant and conceited—Being a father has added to that.

The fact that Lee told me not to worry three times within two pages told me it was time to be hysterical. That he had admitted his nerves were shot warned that not only should I be frantic with worry but also that he was himself worried. His confessions to being a "little screwy" meant he felt a lot screwy. I sensed that he was tottering on the edge of some line, and crossing that line meant something irrevocable. I was more frightened that I had ever been.

My helplessness turned to fury. If everybody knew a man couldn't stay out forever, why the hell was he still there? And if he was burnt out, why would they wait another month to replace him?

Taking "absolutely no chances" seemed as dangerous to me as taking too many. Besides, Lee's code of conduct would never permit him not to take action—he would now just be taking it with less confidence, which would make him more vulnerable to those mistakes he had said cost lives. MacArthur may have been right about what happens to "old soldiers." Young ones who excelled at their jobs, however, did not get the chance to fade away—they were blown to smithereens at the hands of field grade officers who wanted the glory of the highest body count. Lee's enemy may have been the Viet Cong and North Vietnamese Regulars; my nemesis was the goddamned United States Army.

My anger was replaced by an utter sense of defeat. I had convinced myself that things were getting better. Just a few days ago, "contact" had seemed less tangible—or had I only been paying less attention? Had Lee been focused on the baby, or had I wanted to see only that? With each passing day, his tour had been growing shorter and my attitude more optimistic.

In Hawaii, Lee had persuaded me that he was handling the side effects of the war. Perhaps I had believed that because it was easier for me. So much for Lee's reassurances that being a company commander would be safer than being a platoon leader. He might not have been in as much physical danger, but he obviously was more susceptible to psychological peril.

I finished the letter: "On the baby—I think you wanted a boy. I thought I did too till I got news of our girl. Now I know I wanted a girl. I couldn't be happier."

As if the admission that his nerves were shot was a catharsis, Lee finished his letter in his normal handwriting and seemingly in an alleviated mood. It was almost as if he and I had talked and the crisis for him had passed. I felt at that moment, perhaps for the first time during this separation, that Lee really needed me.

I grappled with the effect of the letter until I had my emotions under control, deciding that my finest gift to both our families would be keeping the contents to myself.

When anyone asked about Lee, I cited only his words from the latter part of the letter and did my best to convincingly go through the motions of the season, making Reveilee's first Christmas special. She, of course, was oblivious. My actions were to fill my needs, not hers. Still, the pretense during the day helped me divert my thoughts from those that haunted me in the quiet of the night. It would have been a good time to pray, and it would have been nice had Santa Claus been real.

On Christmas Eve, Connie, who was visiting her parents in Sylvester for the holidays, came over. "I want to see the baby," she said without preamble when I opened the front door. She headed straight for the crib and stood staring for minutes.

"So this is Reveilee," she said finally. Then looking up at me, she continued, "I just can't believe it. I mean, I knew you were having a baby. I saw you when you were out to here. But you just can't imagine how astonishing it is that she really exists. All these years of knowing you and Lee, and now you have a baby. It's the most amazing thing I've ever seen."

She never took her eyes off the baby while we exchanged news about her holiday plans, my trip back to Texas, Susan and Miles, and our extended families. Finally, she stood and said, "Well, she's just amazing."

Then with a penetrating look, she asked, "How's Lee?"

I could have used a confidante. I needed to tell her how he really was, just to help me process everything. But it was Christmas, and she couldn't have changed things anyway. I said simply, "Fine, the last time I heard from him."

• • •

I looked forward with a passion to New Year's Eve. I could hardly wait for the clock to strike midnight because on the other side of twelve o'clock, I could finally claim a small victory—that Lee would be coming home "this year."

January–February 1970

{Chapter 35}

January was the winter of my wait in every sense of the word. Northers blew into West Texas, dumping snow and bringing freezing temperatures that lasted for days. But the chill I felt came from cold fear that shivered deep inside me.

Lee was in trouble and I knew it. I scrutinized every letter even more carefully now for clues to his psychological well being. The standdown in mid-December seemed to have helped temporarily, because for the next couple of letters, he wrote more like himself. I was not naïve enough, however, to think that a three-day break could cure the trauma of eight months in combat. By now, cheerful letters were as terrifying as grim ones, because they hinted at a hysterical euphoria, and notes that said he was fine and didn't mind now how much longer he stayed in the field smacked of fatalism.

In each of his letters, Lee continued to say that he expected to be replaced soon. I had learned not to believe that. Yet no matter how hard I tried to steel myself against hope, I found that I tore into each new letter with expectation. A full thirty days after Lee first wrote that he would give up command "in a month or so," he was still writing the exact words.

The contents of his letters reinforced my growing alarm. December, I learned in January, had been a bloody month for Bravo Company. In fact, the last week of 1969 had been the worst combat Lee had endured. On December 29, he wrote:

> Yesterday at about 1000 hours we set up a large perimeter and sent some squad-size ambushes out—One of my ambushes was ambushed themselves—Took 1 WIA. After we hit the area with

gunships we went back in—only to have the entire company hit by gooks in a bunker complex. We finally had to get arty, gunships, and air strikes to pull out. We ended up with 9 WIA—4 of them in very bad shape. However, they are still alive this morning at the hospital so they should make it.

Was the worst fight I've been in.

I wanted Lee out of the field, and I wanted him out now. But Lee was not done with command or the toll of its responsibilities. In his next letter, he recounted how he ended 1969:

New Year's Eve

The last 3 days have been bad. Since the last letter about the 9 WIA we've been in nearly constant contact—lost 3 more WIA and 1 KIA. We hit a large element—or rather they hit us—with machine guns etc—In last 3 days I've used over 500 rounds of artillery, 8 gunships, 6 air strikes. Bn finally, finally pulled us out. Evidently we hit a couple of companies. What I've heard is it was the heaviest contact over 3 days the area has had in some time.

I lost men out of every plt. Lost more in one day than I had lost in 9 months—My feelings are hard to put into words—a deep loss. I just asked one of my plt leaders how to put it in words. He said "The most violent action the Battalion has seen." I agree.

As far as the contact goes, it was bad. However my company's actions were beyond belief. For 3 days we slept little, ate nothing. Battalion and Brigade say we accomplished a great deal—I wonder. I dusted men off with wounds that will disable them the rest of their lives. I dusted a dead man off I had chewed out a week before. I am realizing the burdens of being a company commander.

Enough on what happened. Now for my actions and feelings now. Honey, I've done my job. I've kept the men going. I've shown no emotion. No one but you knows my deep hurt on the WIA and KIA.

I feel I've lost a great deal—I've hardened a lot. But now this action is over. I read back on this, honey, and I have matured, as only a soldier can. My nerves are if anything steadier. I even feel good—even happy. I am alive. More important, more of my men are alive than for any reason should be.

Once again we have proven Bravo is the best. Okay—enough of this.

The more I look back, the better I feel. This whole letter I've just been talking to you—same as we used to do. Some of it probably should be scratched out. However, I will leave it.

More news—Talked to the Bn CO today. The S-3 Air, another cpt's position, is vacant the end of Jan. I am to be the new S-3 Air.

I told Bn CO I would not leave Bravo unless he had a damn good replacement. He said he did. So about 1 more month in field.

I look back and say disregard letter of worry. Also add I did no heroics in any of the 3 day contact. I only did my job.

I am happy. For the first time in some months I am satisfied. I am in command of the best fighting unit in Vietnam.

Enough of this—

"Enough of this" was right. I knew Lee's repeated refrain was aimed at his continued writing about the contact, but in my best Freudian analysis, I concluded that what he was really doing was screaming "Enough of this" about his part in the war.

I was frantic—not only about the horrors of what five hundred rounds of artillery and ten wounded and dead really meant but also about Lee's state of mind. He had matured; he was pleased with himself for showing no emotion; he was happy. Or so he said. My estimation was that he had gone around the bend into the jungle, not of triple canopy, but of madness. To me it seemed crystal clear that he was losing his mind and his grip on reality.

I wanted to scream that I did not understand why Lee's commanders did not replace him. But I did understand. It was the Army system of "Use 'em up" and "If ain't broke, don't fix it." Lee wasn't broken—yet. And with his stupid military bravado, he wasn't allowing anyone to see the fissures spreading through his façade. Of course, if any higher-ranking officer had been paying the least bit of attention, he would have spotted the signs. But as long as Lee and Bravo Company were producing body count, no one was going to look very closely. In fact, it was my theory that all concerned would look the other way if they suspected a crack. According to what Lee had said in Hawaii, being "crazy" was perfectly acceptable in a combat zone. And so long as one did his job, such lunacy was applauded and encouraged.

The wait for letters had started at Mother and Daddy's house and to their house it had returned. My frantic panics about mail last summer now seemed superficial, juvenile, and melodramatic. How little I had understood then what this year would be like. By comparison, I could see that I had grown up in some ways, or maybe it was only my worries that had matured. For by January my sense of apprehension had developed into a quieter, more deep-seated dread. I was no longer a girl hysterically anxious about her inexperienced second lieutenant; I was a woman, old beyond her years, fearful for her exhausted, war-weary husband.

In San Francisco, I had realized how difficult I had made life for Mother and Daddy when I was here before, dragging them along on my roller coaster ride. I tried to appear cheerful, less subject to emotional over-rides, sometimes more successfully than others. Without Susan to talk to, I withdrew more and more into myself.

Yet we all fell easily into a routine with Reveilee as the central focus, placed each day in her port-a-crib beside the kitchen table. She began to spend progressively more time awake and extended her feeding intervals from two to four hours. Her cheeks grew fat and her kicks stronger. Every move she made was wonderful—and observed by somebody hovering nearby. Grandmother found incredibly creative reasons to need to come over: to bring us a pecan pie she had just baked or to return Mother's bowl that had been in Grandmother's cabinet for three years.

"You don't have to have a reason to come over," I would tell her with a laugh and hug as I took yet another warm pie from her. "You can come see the baby just because you want to."

"Well, I don't want to be a bother," she would answer, heading for the crib to kiss the baby's fists. "Just look at those wonderful little hands."

The Lannings, too, suddenly had a lot of business in Roby and naturally thought they would drop by. One morning, as I returned from the kitchen with a cup of coffee for her, I found Mrs. Lanning holding Reveilee in her lap, stretching the baby's arms out in either direction, as if she were dissecting the infant.

I must have frowned because my mother-in-law quickly said, "I was just measuring. When Lee was this age, I made him a shirt and embroidered little ducks on it. I thought I'd make a dress and put the same little ducks on it. I remember exactly how I did it."

Sure enough, a couple of days later, the Lannings returned with a frock adorned with ducks for Reveilee. I immediately dressed her in it to encourage letting the baby become the bridge we needed to cross over the gap in our relationship.

• • •

At night, I nursed Reveilee before bedtime and again at her two o'clock feeding, keeping her beside my bed in the port-a-crib even though Daddy had assembled her bed. She still seemed too little to sleep all the way across the room.

When Reveilee began to fuss for her six o'clock feeding, Mother would slip into the room and take her to the kitchen, where she and Daddy would give her a bottle. In my drowsiness, I could hear them talking and giggling; the indistinguishable but steady conversation made me feel safe and reassured.

Through it all, I felt polarized—terrified for Lee on the one hand, fascinated by the baby on the other. In the middle, I scrambled the poles, displacing my fears for Lee onto Reveilee. I became obsessive about her safety, never allowing more than a few steps to separate us. When I worked in the den, I moved her crib. When I cooked, she came back to the kitchen. When anyone else held her, I was within arm's reach.

I didn't dare miss a kick or a blink because I wanted to describe her every move to Lee in my letters. I took Polaroid shots of Reveilee from every angle to enclose in my letters, but they just couldn't capture the essence of her to my satisfaction.

The only way Lee could understand the first weeks of his daughter's life was to see them—if not in person, then on film. So I purchased a movie camera and projector. As I panned and zoomed, even I knew that I was producing the worst of home movies that only a father, maybe, could appreciate.

Despite my efforts to control my reactions to Lee's letters, my spirits soared and plunged. Lee's early January letter, which I received midmonth, said his replacement was due on the fifteenth. Perhaps by the time I was holding his note my worries were behind me and I didn't know it. I hummed and looked at the calendar.

Then, days later, I tore into the next envelope only to read that there might be a delay.

When at the end of the month I received the letter dated January 15, I held my breath. Then I read:

> Don't know how to really write this letter. I've written you that I was getting out of the field today. Well, that's been changed. Commanding General told Bn CO I was not to be replaced till a man that as qualified in the CG's eyes arrived. There are 6 captains in Bn who have never been in command. So I guess this is a very high compliment.
>
> Honey, I know you wanted me out of the field. I am ready to get out. I've told BN CO this. It is beyond my control. I guess that's the army.
>
> Guess I will be out for a while yet—depends on replacement. I don't really mind the field—just feel as though I've done my part. Still, as glad as I am, I hate to leave Bravo.

I felt ill. High compliments from commanding generals were no excelsior for me. Those bastards were going to screw around until Lee went bonkers or got killed—or both.

I awoke, startled, sensing something terribly wrong. Early morning sunlight was streaming through the blinds, yet an overwhelming dread paralyzed me. Lee. Had something happened to Lee? I turned from the window and was shocked to discover that Reveilee was still in her crib beside my bed. Oh god! It was crib death. The baby had not fussed for her two o'clock feeding. Because she was dead. I could not move. I could not breathe.

In my panic, I failed to note the rhythmic rise of her blanket. When I did finally become conscious of the soft breathing, I collapsed back onto the bed. I was in no position to judge Lee as crazy. I was the one who was going nuts. Reveilee had finally slept through the night.

Would there ever be any deliverance from this war? I wondered. Certainly it did not come in January. The last letter I received from Lee that month started with "Still in the jungle."

The only happy mail I received was from Susan and Tom on R&R in Hawaii. She described their sightseeing and ended her note, "Now I know what you meant about R&R." Her reference could have been to how wonderful the week was, but more likely it was to how hard it was to face the next six months all over again.

{Chapter 36}

> Well, this is at last the letter we have been waiting for—as of 1200 yesterday I am finished in the field.

For me, the war was over. When I received Lee's letter at the end of the first week of February, I knew we had survived. The nine and a half months of combat and worry were behind us. Now all we faced was a simple separation—which, in my view, was nothing compared to what we had been through.

I was numb, afraid to believe. I carried Lee's letter everywhere I went that day, to reassure myself that I had not misread, misinterpreted, or misconstrued what he had written.

The remaining contents of the letter helped. In one fell swoop, he had gone from combat infantryman to consummate consumer. Having procured a PX catalog, he ordered a radio/stereo. He sent me copies of the catalog pages advertising bronzeware from Thailand, knowing that the flatware was one of the things I wanted. I laughed when I read Lee's assessment: "On the bronzeware—I can't see the 12 place settings for $80. Hell, who can afford to feed 12 people?"

That was the Lee I remembered and loved. I was all but delirious with relief. How wonderful to contend with such decisions, I thought, and immediately wrote him all the rationalizations on why we should, indeed, have the 144-piece set for twelve. The idea that we would again have a home and invite people to dinner was almost beyond grasp.

The second week of February, the possibility became more real. Lee included a postscript to a letter:

> Just got my stateside orders—Fort Benning, GA, US Army Infantry School. This could mean instructor—classroom or field—jump school, Ranger, OCS, etc.
>
> Am not really surprised. Understand housing on post is unlikely with my rank. Most of my VN friends are going to Benning. Am not at all displeased—sounds good in fact.

Fort Benning. I could handle that. Jim and Judy might still be there when we arrived. In truth, I did not care if we were going to Georgia or Alaska, as long as we were going together.

A few days later, I received a copy of the official orders. I was ecstatic.

Happily, the exchange of letters between Lee and me focused on what furniture we would need to set up housekeeping again, how much money would be available, and how we would spend his leave. They were wonderfully ordinary topics, and I was intrigued with, and amused by, how many issues we disagreed about. What a relief to have to worry only about coming to consensus.

By the middle of February, we were at sixty days and counting.

On Lee's instructions, I took the orders and went to Dyess Air Force Base near Abilene to make arrangements to have our household goods, both those in storage in North Carolina and the belongings I had acquired in Roby, shipped to Fort Benning in March. Lee's homecoming was almost tangible.

I received a happy surprise in the mail: a wedding invitation from Bernie Petrocelli. He and Jeannie were finally getting married, and I hoped that the invitation was also an announcement that Bernie had been permanently dismissed from the hospital.

Lee was by now working at a rear fire base, planning and overseeing training for the troops in his battalion. It struck me as odd that the military trained during war, but then everything about war struck me as odd. I didn't care what his job was, so long as Lee was out of the field and imminent danger.

Letters were now longer and written in a more relaxed handwriting. Yet there was an underlying sense of restlessness and boredom laced into all of them. It was obvious that Lee was only marking time, as were we all.

The only cloud on the horizon was a concern I felt about Lee's lack of mention of Reveilee. He said only that it was obvious from the pictures that she was growing. He never commented on her personality or behavior, which I described in elaborate detail. Something was missing.

I spent several days mulling over the situation, finding it entirely understandable that Lee would have a difficult time imagining what Reveilee was like. Yet that wouldn't account for his all but ignoring her in his letters. So in my next letter, I asked him if he was aware of his omissions or if my imagination was just working overtime. At the end of the month, I received a long letter from Lee in which he said:

> Honey, I don't think you will find much difference in me when I get home. At least not that will be noticed. I have grown a little more fanatic in my ideas and I've aged quite a bit. I never told you but I believe if I had stayed out much longer I would have gone a little over the hill. The 3½ months after R&R were about double the first 6 months. Still I haven't changed—except maybe I've learned to love life quite a bit more.
>
> You have asked why I've not mentioned Reveilee more. You are right in that she is hard to realize. I look forward to seeing you both, as one. I don't think of you individually. While in the field I did my best not to even acknowledge she existed. I don't mean this wrong in any way. I told you before I came over here, "I will be the most surprised person there if anything happens to me." By the time I got out—especially in December—I was the most surprised person there that it didn't happen.

So it had not been my imagination—either that he was on the brink or that he had had difficulty coping with the fact that he had a baby. How naïve he was to think of Reveilee and me as one. As sweet and agreeable as she was, she was very much her own person, as he would find out when he met her.

The logistics of Lee's return provided discussion for several of our letters. Happily, this was one topic upon which we both fully agreed: We wanted time alone when he came home—just the three of us. The solution seemed to be for Reveilee and me to fly to San Francisco to meet him.

The plan was complicated by the fact that he did not know exactly when he would leave Vietnam, and wouldn't know until almost takeoff time.

President Nixon agreed to reduce the number of troops in-country by April 15. One of the Army's clever ways of meeting its numbers mandate was to give men who were due to go home a reduction of a few days in the length of their tour, thus making the statistics look valid. By this point, politics was a moot issue for me. I didn't care what kind of games officials played among themselves just as long as Lee got to come home on time or earlier.

I was not the only one anticipating Lee's return. "Say, Linda Ann," Jim said over the phone one night, "I've been doing some checking here at Fort Benning, trying to find out what Lee's job's going to be. Nobody wants to say anything for sure, but it looks like he's going to be an instructor at the Florida Ranger Camp."

"Really?" I asked, wishing I had paid more attention to the lay of the land when I had been there for Lee's graduation from Ranger School. "Does Lee know this?"

"I doubt it. They usually just cut everybody's orders for Benning and then parcel them out from here."

I laughed and said, "This will probably be the only time I know about Lee's orders before he does."

I immediately wrote Lee what Jim had learned, feeling sure that he would be pleased. Yes, Lee would like being a Ranger instructor, and living in Florida suited me just fine.

Lee's parents, too, were preparing for his homecoming. Mrs. Lanning announced one morning when they stopped by that they decided it was time for a new house. They were going to Lubbock, a plains city a hundred miles northwest, to look at pre-fabricated models.

Despite the progress of plans and preparation, February, instead of being the shortest month of the year, stretched into one of the longest, as my energy re-channeled itself from worry to impatience. Lee had done his job. Why couldn't he just come home?

March 1970

• • •

{Chapter 37}

Next month. Six weeks. Forty-two days—or less. The number changed with every letter from Lee. He wrote that some soldiers were returning stateside nine to twenty days ahead of schedule.

I originally planned to go to San Francisco the second week of April, but with Lee's optimistic predictions, I changed my reservations to the first of the month, which meant that suddenly, after so long, I had to hurry because I intended to be at Travis Air Force Base to meet Lee's plane.

I shopped for new clothes; I checked and rechecked Lee's uniforms, sorting out which ones I was to take with me to California, which to hold in Texas, and which to ship with the movers; I gathered my things scattered throughout the house.

Still, Reveilee occupied most of my time, as I elaborated the process of feeding her, caring for her, and, mostly, fawning over her. I became even more ridiculously overprotective with each passing day. We were so close to having completed that year with no one harmed that I could not tolerate the slightest hint of danger to her.

Lee continued to write, his letters farther apart now but longer. He seemed to struggle for anything to report except about coming home. I did not panic on those days when there were lapses in mail delivery, until the carriers threatened a national postal strike—which seemed an unnecessary burden to an already over-encumbered year.

I did note, however, another shift in the tone of Lee's letters. Not only did they contain an undercurrent of restlessness, but also they became more formal, businesslike, and overtly dictatorial. From the field, Lee's writings had been updates and shared confidences; now they were straightforward instructions and undisguised demands. I wasn't sure when the switch occurred, but I became aware of the change when I consistently found myself bristling in response to what I read.

I concluded there were two possible explanations. One was that I had a commander with no company to order about. Lee had become accustomed to telling people what to do, and with no troops on the receiving end, he turned his tactics on me.

The second explanation was that I had become so accustomed to making my own decisions that I had forgotten the process involved in reaching agreement. I felt a flush of resentment when Lee now announced a decision concerning both of us. It seemed that he intended to assert himself as the head of the family—a concept I had not accepted even before he went to Vietnam.

The irritation I felt toward Lee was nothing compared to the frustration I turned inward. What the hell was wrong with me? Lee was coming home alive. Nothing else should matter. His should be the perfect homecoming. I tried to shake my vexation. We would have adjustments to make, of course.

Lee's correspondence was not all authoritative. He also speculated on the future—some ideas amusing, some not. In one letter he talked about a second R&R in Australia, saying that if he decided to get out of the army, that country would offer opportunities, though he failed to be specific about what we would do there. A couple of letters later, he wrote that he had made friends with a captain getting out of the military to take over his father-in-law's carnival. Lee had now decided that being a carnie had great appeal. I tried to picture Lee and me in the Outback or in a carnival caravan; the images would not focus. By the time Lee wrote that perhaps when he grew up he would want to be a fireman, I was convinced that he was making the Army a career.

But the U.S. Army as a career had definite drawbacks, especially at the time. Plans for the future that included another tour in Vietnam did not amuse me at all. In fact, I noticed that Lee more and more frequently mentioned a second tour. When I queried him, he answered that he could expect to be stateside for only a year before going back.

To my way of thinking, Lee had had his adventure, and I had paid a great price for it. I would not be so generous again. With the thought of another 365 days of worrying, waiting, and not knowing, my anger boiled, and instantly Susan came to mind. I now understood how she felt all along. No wonder she was so furious with Tom. But such fury was the only self-protection we had. I would never, ever again leave myself open to the fear, the pain, the torment—not even for Lee. I now knew how excruciatingly long a year could be. The prospect was so dreadful I refused to deal with it.

With Lee's tour in the wind-down, preparations for his return continued to be on the upswing. The civilian movers contracted by Dyess arrived, and when they saw my small pile in the den asked, "We drove all this way for this?"

"Yep," I answered. "It's all I've got. I've just been staying here a while."

"Your husband overseas?"

"Vietnam," I replied.

"Oh," the driver said, nodding his head. "We get a lot of business because of Vietnam. Military folks moving in, then a year later moving out. Moving in, moving out. Craziest war I've ever seen. But it's sure good for business."

I had heard that war was good for the economy, but it hadn't occurred to me that a small moving company in Abilene, Texas would be sharing in the proceeds. As the men ambled to their small truck to get boxes and furniture pads, I wondered if there were no limits to the ripples of effect the war created.

When the men had strapped the last pad in place and loaded the final box onto the truck, I signed the inventory paperwork, checking off one more bench mark of Lee's journey home. The next time I would see those belongings would be when they were delivered to our new home—maybe in Florida, maybe in Georgia. The thought was exhilarating.

{Chapter 38}

I was jumping out of bed every morning in March, ready to tackle my list of tasks for the day. More often than not, I accomplished my objectives with some degree of success and then found myself climbing back into bed that night still too charged up to fall asleep easily. I had so much to think about: Had I forgotten anything? What was Lee going to think of Reveilee? Where did I pack that damned bow tie for Lee's dress blues? How was Reveilee going to react to Lee?

I fitfully fell into dozes. Then, a few hours later, I would awake wide-eyed and again jump up to greet the day. However, the days never felt new; each was somehow a repeat of the one before. It was as if I were reliving the same twenty-four-hour period over and over, with the calendar never advancing.

I had had a month of reprieve since Lee had given up command. I was stunned to realize how easily I had forgotten the unrelenting worry. Instead of remaining grateful, I grew impatient. Prolonging our separation seemed a punishment neither he nor I deserved. The Army had taken its pound of flesh, so why didn't they just send him home?

Of course, what Lee was now doing was the kind of support job that the majority of men who went to Vietnam did for an entire year. I had been so preoccupied all those months with combat and survival that I had not stopped to think about women whose husbands were never in danger. The war of waiting must have been a completely different experience for them, in some ways maybe worse. Lee had a purpose when he left. Now that he had fulfilled it, I struggled to find a reason for having him gone.

I was off on just such a mental meandering late one morning when Daddy threw open the door, excitement covering his face.

"I think I just met the Lannings' house," he said in one breathless exhalation.

I looked at him, uncomprehending.

"Out there on the highway," he said with a jerk of his head. "I'm pretty sure I met a truck carrying the Lannings' new house."

I jumped. "I want to see," I said. "Can we still catch it?"

"If we hurry."

I left Mother with instructions for Reveilee and grabbed my jacket. Daddy had the pickup started by the time I got outside. I jumped in. I had never chased a house down the road.

Before we reached the courthouse square, we had caught up with the truck and its cargo. The charcoal gray siding was the color Mrs. Lanning had described. The door on the end facing us matched where she had placed the side entrance.

The crisp structure with sparkling white shutters bordering its high, narrow windows looked inviting and comfortable—and, simultaneously, ridiculous as it rode in mid-air along steel beams that linked the wheels of the truck.

I laughed aloud, suddenly aware of how this house epitomized my whole year, and said, "It just stands to reason. You take anything out of its right environment and plunk it down someplace else and, of course, it looks absurd."

After the rig cleared the main intersection, it chugged eastward, picking up speed. Daddy and I pursued. "Let's follow it and be sure. I wish Lee could see this," I laughed as we sped down the road at fifty miles per hour. "Wait!" I yelled suddenly, grabbing Daddy's arm. "He can see it. The movie camera. Can we go get the camera?"

Daddy whipped a U-turn and we raced for Roby where I hurried into the house for the movie camera and the Polaroid, too. There was no reason Lee had to wait to see some parts of this event.

We again rushed eastward. We slowed for the Sylvester turnoff, and two curves later, I spotted the gray house moving in the distance above the horizon. We caught up with it a couple of miles outside of town and I rolled the camera as Daddy drove alongside. Then he dropped back to follow.

"This is great," I said happily. "I'd like to get a shot of the house going through Sylvester."

Daddy passed the truck and we pulled up at the post office so I could film the house passing under the caution light. Through the lens I watched the gray house glide past the lone flashing signal in the heart of "downtown" Sylvester against the backdrop of a dilapidated service station and a deserted highway that rolled endlessly into the distance. Its newness clashed with everything in sight—the tall blowing weeds along the railroad tracks, the boarded-up building that before the Depression had been the bank, the vacant lots that had long since lost their value. Kafka could not have created a more surrealistic scene.

The truck's passenger got out and crossed the road toward Daddy and me. "Your name Lanning? This your house?" he shouted against the wind before he reached us.

"Yes and no," I answered, walking to meet him. "My name is Lanning, but it's my in-laws' house. Do they know you're coming?"

"We told them 'sometime this week.' The note says we go eight miles south and then turn west for about three. Are there any landmarks to watch for?"

I looked at Daddy and he nodded. To the man, I said, "Follow us."

I hadn't had this much fun in months, which said a lot about how easily amused I was those days. I filmed more angles of the house through the rearview window and tried to catch full-length exposures as we rounded curves.

Daddy turned onto the dirt road and coasted until we were sure the truck had followed. Then we raced for the Lannings' current dwelling, passing the waiting foundation on the small hilltop about a mile and a half before reaching their old place. When we drove into the front yard, I leaned over and honked the horn a couple of times before I leaped out into the red fog of dust that had caught up with us. I ran to the porch.

Mr. Lanning was out the door before I hit the first steps, and Mrs. Lanning, hand clutched over her heart, was right behind him.

"Your house is here!" I shouted. "Come on. Let's go see it."

By the time the Lannings grabbed their coats and our two pickups reached the site, the men had aligned the truck to the foundation and were lowering the structure to its new home. I watched their practiced movements with fascination as the four of us walked circles around the house like stalkers.

Mrs. Lanning was critically eyeing every detail, checking her list to see if everything had been done to specification.

"I can hardly wait to see the inside," I said, impatient for the leveling process to be completed.

Within minutes, the house was settled, and the men were dragging the steel beams from underneath with chains hooked to the truck. From ground level, Mr. Lanning reached up, opened the screen door, and grabbed the door knob as the three of us lined up behind him, awaiting our first view of the inside.

"It's locked," he said with surprise.

He flagged down the crew. Finally, Mr. Lanning returned and said in disgust, "They don't have a key. Nobody told them the place was locked."

We stared at each other in disbelief. Here the Lannings finally had a new house after more than thirty years—and they couldn't get in. I thought Mrs. Lanning might cry, and Mr. Lanning must have thought so, too.

"I guess we can break in somehow," he offered.

"No," Mrs. Lanning said sharply. "I've waited this long; I can wait longer."

"Lee will think this is a wonderful house," I said, knowing that Mrs. Lanning needed bolstering. In truth, however, as glad as I was that his parents had a better place to live, I could not help but wish they had waited until Lee had gotten to come home to the house where he grew up. As nice as this edifice was, I knew it would never have sentimental value to him.

Still, the arrival of the house had provided an afternoon of diversion and occupied several hours of my waiting. We may have been disappointed not to get inside, but the very fact that the house was there was another sign that Lee could not be far behind.

On the night of March 30, I addressed my last letter to Vietnam. It was Number 318.

April 1970

• • •

{Chapter 39}

April again. This year, going to California was to be the happiest trip of my life instead of the most difficult.

I had scheduled the flight to the West Coast on a Saturday so I could spend the weekend with Susan. I could hardly wait to talk to her, to delve into discussions as we had for so many months.

As Mother and Daddy drove Reveilee and me to the Midland-Odessa airport, I was beside myself with excitement, talking incessantly and mentally rechecking my lists—tickets, money, bottles—as I rechecked the security of the port-a-crib that once more held the baby during the ride. Where Reveilee had occupied but a tiny space on the little mattress on the trip from San Francisco, she now stretched almost the length of the bed. I felt a tug of guilt when I thought about all the things I'd read about babies needing a sense of security and consistency. Once again her schedule was being disrupted, her environment changing. Well, if she was going to be an army brat, she would have to learn to adjust, though perhaps she was getting too early a start on the vagabond lifestyle. But she was going to meet her daddy, and that should be worth any disruption.

Finally settling back, I thought back over the twelve months since Lee left for Vietnam. I could vividly recapture the departure scene and feel the devastation of waiting—waiting for letters, waiting for R&R, waiting for the baby, waiting for Lee. Now we were almost to the end. I was shocked to realize that it felt odd for the waiting itself to be over, too. Tears stung my eyes for no reason I could explain except for a terrible sadness that washed over me—a sadness for things I could not name. Had I really been that young such a short time ago?

Susan met us at the airport and I was soon back on Collins Street, climbing the familiar garage stairs as if I'd never left. A sense of déjà vu hung in the air as I watched Susan top the steps with the diaper bag just as she had done the night Gayle arrived, only this time I was responsible for all the baby paraphernalia.

Miles had made arrangements to stay with friends while I was in town, so Reveilee and I were to share my old room. When I opened the door, I found the two twin beds not as I had left them, but in a king-size arrangement of mattresses under one spread.

Before I could say anything, Susan offered, "I didn't think you and Lee would want to sleep in separate beds, so we converted them."

I was sure I blushed, but I didn't care. I was grateful for Susan's thoughtfulness, and I knew Lee would be, too.

As I readied Reveilee for bed that night, Susan came in.

"You're pretty good at this baby stuff now, uh?" she asked.

"I get a lot of practice," I answered, "but then I've also had a lot of assistance. I've never done this alone."

"I hope you're not expecting any help from me," Susan said, leaning away. "I only play with babies. Then I give them back."

With Reveilee asleep, the two of us settled in the living room, where we talked non-stop until after two o'clock. All day Sunday I paid the price for my late night, experiencing for the first time what it meant that the buck, and the bottle, stopped here. In Roby, if I had been too tired, Mother or Daddy would have taken the baby. I was becoming aware that yet another adjustment in my life was imminent—real motherhood.

"So tell me again when Lee will be in," Susan said through a yawn when she got up around noon.

"Maybe this week, but more likely next week," I answered, returning her yawn. Suddenly, hearing myself say "this week," I stopped. "My God, can you believe it, Susan? I'm afraid I'll come to my senses any minute and find that I'm here because of some fantasy. It's really frightening."

"Yeah, but not as frightening as another two months of this crap," she said, pouring herself a cup of coffee. "I know Lee went before Tom, but it doesn't seem fair for him to come home earlier. I mean, it feels like we started this wait together and we should finish it together."

I felt somewhat guilty for being the first one through, though I wasn't out of the tunnel yet myself. I knew I still had days to wait; I just didn't know how many.

With amazing ease, we settled into a routine, Reveilee taking the change in residences without complaint. Susan and I learned we could no longer stay up late talking, and Adrienne came home from work with Susan at least every other day to see the baby.

My hopes for Lee's early release began to wane as the week wore on. Going through the motions of getting ready for his phone call accentuated my sense of absurdity. Even as I pressed away the suitcase wrinkles from Reveilee's and my dresses, I doubted that would ever happen.

The feeling shadowed me when I called a limousine company about transportation to Travis Air Force Base. I was told I needed reservations at least twenty-four hours in advance, which was impossible, of course, because I didn't know when I would need the ride. The fare of $60 shocked me but made no difference. I left the matter unresolved.

My doubts and disbeliefs did not depress me. Rather, they created a sense of unfamiliar calm. Perhaps I had finally crossed into the Twilight Zone. Nothing affected me, nothing penetrated.

"I don't understand you," Susan said, eyeing me on my second Saturday in her apartment. "I expected to be peeling you off the walls by now. What's the matter?"

I looked at her and answered her from somewhere outside myself, "I don't know. I just feel nothing. Lee's coming home soon, but those just seem like words to me. I'm not happy, I'm not upset, I'm not excited, I'm not disappointed. I'm just—what? Here."

Susan bounced Reveilee in her arms but gave me a troubled look. "I feel like I'm sitting in the eye of a hurricane. It's eerie and unnatural. Are you going to crack?"

I laughed, "No, I don't think so. If there's pressure, I don't feel that, either."

To Reveilee, she said, "I think your daddy needs to come home quick."

{Chapter 40}

On Monday night, the phone rang. Susan answered and handed me the receiver, shaking her head. "Some man," she whispered.

"Hello," I said cautiously.

"Is this Linda?"

"Yes," I answered hesitantly, not recognizing the voice.

"Well, you don't know me," the man stammered and then laughed. "My God, this is weird. My first phone call back in the World and I'm talking to somebody I don't know."

My heart stopped. "Back in the World." Only those from Vietnam used that term. "Yes?" I prompted.

"As I said, you don't know me, but I'm supposed to tell you that Lee bought me a beer in Long Binh yesterday—or was it today? Well, whatever day I got my Freedom Bird out. Anyway, Lee said to tell you that he's at the outprocessing center and should be on a manifest in a couple of days."

I felt a jolt. I was actually talking to someone who had been in Vietnam with Lee less than twenty-four hours before. This man was now in the United States.

"Thank you for calling," I said. "I know you didn't have to, but I really appreciate it."

"Well, he said you'd come all the way to California to meet him. It seemed the least I could do. I hope he gets home soon."

"I do, too," I said, hanging up.

I sat down. So Lee was now at his last stop in Vietnam. I held my breath. Throughout Tuesday morning, I waited, always within reach of the phone, bouncing Reveilee and explaining to her that her daddy just might call any minute. Her saucer eyes watched me suspiciously.

I was still irrationally composed on the outside, emotionally paralyzed on the inside when the phone rang mid-afternoon. I jumped. Reveilee, startled by my reaction, screamed.

I tried to quiet her as my trembling hand reached for the receiver.

"Linda?"

The man's voice was familiar but not Lee's. My heart dropped and then rebounded as I recognized the caller.

"Ron? Ron Piper?" It was Lee's lieutenant buddy from Fort Bragg who had left for Vietnam the same day Lee did.

"Hello, Linda. It's been a long time," he said, sounding tired and somehow older.

"When did you get back?"

"Just got into Oakland a few minutes ago. Before that I was drinking beer with Lee in Long Binh."

"What is he doing over there?" I asked, "Acting like a one-man send-off committee? When is he coming home?"

Ron laughed. "Well, it shouldn't be long now. In fact, he should have been on the next manifest after mine."

"What does that mean, in real language?"

"It means he should be on the next bird out."

I swallowed hard, caution holding my excitement in check as I slowly asked, "Ron, how often do the planes leave?"

"Military schedule, you know, so you never can be sure. He should be in sometime today, though. Is that the baby I hear?"

"Yes, and she's getting pretty tired of waiting for her daddy to show up."

"Well, tell her she won't have to wait much longer. I've got to run. I just wanted to let you know."

I thanked Ron and hung up, still emotionally suspended. If he was right, Lee was at this minute already airborne.

I didn't dare believe it. Yet I felt propelled by some force outside myself to move as if I did. I put Reveilee down for her nap and washed my hair, switching off the dryer every few seconds to make sure I didn't miss the ringing of the phone. I checked my clothes again and thought about calling the limo service, but I didn't dare tie up the line.

By the time Susan came home, I had convinced myself that I still had another day or two to wait, so I was pleased that Adrienne had accompanied her. We were still sitting in the living room when Miles and one of his friends arrived. With so many people suddenly around, the apartment took on a party atmosphere.

Miles asked if I was frying steak for dinner. I laughed and told him he was out of luck.

"Well," he mumbled with mock disappointment, "I need to get some clean clothes, but I really hoped I could talk you into cooking."

"Just a minute," I said. "Let me get some of the clutter out of your way."

I headed for the bedroom and had just reached the foyer when the phone rang. Without missing a step or being conscious of what I was doing, I picked up the receiver and said, "Hello."

First I heard static, and then Lee's voice saying, "Linda?"

"Lee! Lee, is that you?"

"It's me," he said with a laugh and then paused before adding in a quieter tone. "It's over, Honey. It's over. I'll be home in about six hours."

"Where are you? Hawaii?"

"Anchorage, and I'm freezing my ass off. Alaska is cold, especially after the jungle."

My memory was registering what he was telling me but my mind was scrambling the words. I was responding but I didn't know what I was saying. I was writing down numbers but I did not know why Lee was dictating them and having me repeat them. Finally, I heard myself say, "I'll be at Travis when you get there. Hurry."

Lee laughed and said, "It's okay, Honey, it's over. See you around midnight."

I replaced the receiver, dimly aware of Susan and Adrienne. "Was that Lee? Where is he? When will he be here?" they asked in chorus.

I turned, wanting to shout, "It's over! It's over!"

But when I opened my mouth, all I heard was my own deep gasp. Slammed by a wavecrest of emotions, I could not speak. Blindly I wheeled around and ran toward the back of the apartment, stumbling into Susan's room and crumbling to the floor in hysterical sobs. Lee was coming home alive. It was over, really over. How or why he had been allowed to survive when so many hadn't, I did not know. I knew only that I had never expected this moment to arrive. Memories of terror raced through my mind as relief poured through me and I cried, unabashed, unchecked tears. Dear god, it was over.

It was a self-absorbed, grieving cry that absolutely overtook me and made me oblivious to everyone else in the house. In fact, I had no idea how long I'd been on the floor on my knees when I slowly became aware of Susan's arm around me and Adrienne's gentle stroking on my head.

Still jerking for breaths, I suddenly felt released, free—alive!

"My goodness," I gasped, "I didn't see that one coming."

"It's okay," Adrienne said soothingly. "You've had it bottled up for a long time."

"Wow," I sniffed, wiping my eyes with a tissue that had come from I knew not where, "I'm think I'm through now."

"Thank goodness," Susan said, hoisting herself up and offering me a hand. "You scared poor little Reveilee to death. I don't know which of you was crying louder."

A look of panic crossed my face and Susan said, "She's fine. Miles is entertaining her now. So tell us what is going on."

"Lee's in Alaska and will be at Travis in six hours," I beamed. Then I remembered that I had lost all track of time. "What time is it now? How long ago did he call?"

"It's about ten after six and he only called minutes ago. You've got plenty of time," Adrienne said. "Is there anything I can do to help?"

"Oh, no," I moaned. "I don't know how I'm getting to Travis."

"I'll take care of that," Susan said. I didn't ask how because suddenly I was now in a frenzy, calculating all I had to do and how much time I had. The air force base was at least a two-hour ride away, so I decided I should leave no later than nine o'clock, which meant less than three hours from that moment.

I could have been ready within minutes had I not changed clothes twelve times and fumbled everything I touched. I repeatedly asked Susan if she minded keeping Reveilee. I wanted the baby on her best behavior when Lee saw her and disrupting her night's sleep did not seem the way to succeed at that.

"Of course, she should stay here," Susan said.

"You should plan for us to be back around two," I speculated. "That means that you should wake her up and dress her around one or so. And don't forget the white bow for her hair."

"Anything else?" Susan asked, rolling her eyes and then saying to Reveilee, "We'll do whatever we like, won't we?"

"So how am I getting to Travis?" I asked.

"I called you a taxi. When you get in the cab, you see if you can negotiate a deal for a round trip."

I accepted Susan's suggestion because I had no better ideas. In my euphoria, I did not doubt I would get where I was going. I was still giving her instructions about Reveilee when I heard a horn honk.

"Okay, you're out of here," Susan said with a slight push toward the door. "You look beautiful and Reveilee will be fine. Kiss Lee hello for me."

With that I was running down the steps. I opened the back door and climbed in as the driver pulled the meter handle. "Where to?"

"Well," I said, conspiratorially, "I need to go to Travis Air Force Base."

"Where?" he exclaimed although I knew he had understood me.

"Let's make a deal. How much will you charge to take me there, wait for my husband's plane, and bring us back here?"

The driver turned slowly around in the seat, deliberating. He was a young man about my age, lean and reserved. "Vietnam?"

I nodded.

"Well," the driver said slowly, "you were to be my last fare for the night. How much are you willing to pay?"

I wasn't stupid enough to tell him because I would have given everything I owned to meet that plane. "How much will it take?"

"How about forty bucks?" he suggested tentatively as though he expected me to haggle. "I'm supposed to have the cab back at the garage, you know, and, well, I'll have some explaining to do."

"Done," I said before he could change his mind.

• • •

The drive to Travis was a blur as the lights and darkness slid past. The driver talked nonstop but I paid little attention except to mumble some periodic responses.

As we approached the base, my heart was in my throat. I was less than an hour from touchdown and my pulse was racing. The guard at the gate gave the driver directions to the terminal and waved us through.

There was a stillness to the base and an eerie contrast between the black night and the brilliant lights that glowed in front of us as we neared the airstrip. I gripped the door handle in anticipation, finding myself surprised when we pulled up in front of a building that looked just like any other air force terminal, larger perhaps but no more distinctive. I didn't know what I had expected, but Travis had become the gateway to Vietnam, and somehow the site should have been more special. It was after all, the last piece of America thousands of young men ever saw.

"Just wait here and I'll check on the arrival time," I instructed the driver.

Inside the terminal, I found dozens of men in uniforms of every description—khakis, flight suits, dress greens, sailor suits—sprawled asleep in chairs and on the floor.

Finally I spotted a sign that looked promising and approached the airman at the counter beneath it.

"I'd like to check on the arrival time of this flight," I said, handing him the numbers I had scribbled when talking with Lee. I hoped the alphanumeric sequence made sense to him because, to me, it appeared an impossible code.

Without much interest, the airman took the paper and looked at the board above his head, out of my line of sight.

"Not due in for another four or five hours," he said with a yawn. "Could be six or more."

"Are you sure?" I cried, disbelieving. Lee had sounded so definite.

"No, ma'am," he said, shaking his head. "I'm never sure about anything. I'm just telling you what the board says."

I cursed under my breath but thanked him. The military was sure as hell punctual enough in hauling troops off to war; bringing them home should merit the same promptness. Well, that wasn't true, either, I corrected myself as I returned to the taxi. The Army had delayed Lee's flight to Vietnam by a day; I could only hope *that* pattern would not be repeated.

I reluctantly relayed the message about the flight's delay to the driver, afraid that he would either leave or demand more money. Instead, he shrugged. "I'll just pull over here and get some shut-eye," he said, pointing toward the parking lot.

I watched to see where the taxi stopped and then strolled back inside, now in no hurry. I located a set of vacant orange plastic chairs and had just sat down when the PA system blasted through the quiet. I watched, amazed, as the troops slept right through the broadcast, most never flinching.

Only by chance did I catch the last of the announcement—a flight number that sounded familiar. I ran for the counter while pulling the paper from my purse again.

"Did you just announce this flight?" I asked, breathless.

The same airman once more checked his board. "Yes, ma'am. It just touched down. Be deplaning at gate six."

"But you just told me it would be hours. Are you sure this is right?"

"I don't make the flights, ma'am. I just read them as I see them. This one is taxiing in right now. Gate six is out the door and to your left. Big sign. You can't miss it."

My god! Lee was here. On the ground! A chill ran up my spine as I tore out the door. I found the sign that read "GATE 6." But I was surely in the wrong place. I had misunderstood the airman, I thought frantically. I was at the wrong gate 6. I looked around desperately. This had to be a mistake. I was the only person there.

I was in a panic. But before I could decide how to correct my error, I heard engines growing louder. I turned to see a battered 707 jet rolling toward me across the tarmac. The plane's paint was so badly chipped that the name Saturn Airways was barely legible on its tail.

This can't be Lee's flight, I told myself over and over. I'd never heard of Saturn Airways and besides, as I looked up and down the chain link fence separating me from the plane, I could still see no other wives or parents or girlfriends.

With amazing efficiency, a stairway rolled into place beside the plane and the door opened. I clung to the fence, my fingers laced in the wires, as I tried to make to make out the dim figures now descending. The men walked slowly in my direction, shouldering duffle bags and rotating sore muscles.

Just before the first passengers reached the fence, MPs appeared out of the darkness to point them toward a shed that read "Customs." Now I understood. After they passed through Customs, the men would be directed to all the people waiting to meet them. All I had to do was follow. Yet I heard no crowd. In fact, I heard no voices at all as the men, in an unbroken file, continued to pour from the plane into the silent night.

I tore my eyes away from their single file only long enough to note the arrival of olive drab buses that halted a few feet behind me. At the same time that the first man stepped from behind the Customs shed, the door to the first bus opened. Military-precision at its finest, I thought.

But something was terribly wrong. If this was the plane from Vietnam and these men were the men returning from the war zone after a year, why was I the only one at the gate?

I turned back to the line. Lee! Lee was there, throwing me a casual wave and that half-cocked grin of his. Oh, god! He was really there, right in front of me, just twenty yards away. I leaned into the fence and returned his wave. He pointed to the shed. I nodded, signaling that I understood. I didn't take my eyes off him until he disappeared behind the wall.

While waiting for Lee to reappear, I inched toward the opening in the wire and watched troop after troop, weary and unsmiling, throw his gear into the luggage compartment and board the bus. I was overcome with the tragedy and the outrage of it all. America sent men to war and then brought the survivors home in the dark of the night with no fanfare. I hadn't expected bands and flags, but neither had I expected *nothing*. There were over three hundred men on that plane. So what if it was midnight? Somebody should have been here to welcome them, somebody besides just me.

I wanted to weep at the travesty. Instead, I stood dry-eyed, witnessing a scene I would never forget and never forgive.

Suddenly Lee stepped from behind the shed. I ran to him. I felt his arms around me. He was real. He was home.

{Chapter 41}

"Oh, it really is over!" I cried as Lee held me.

"We made it, didn't we?" he laughed in a mirthless way. He kissed me and then said, "Let's get the hell out of here."

I turned to walk beside him and then stopped. "Can you just leave? I mean, what are all these guys doing?"

"Going to Oakland, most for outprocessing from the Army."

"Lee," I said, still disbelieving, "nobody was here for them. I mean, I'm the only person to meet the whole planeload."

"People don't come out in the middle of the night to welcome back Vietnam veterans," he said sardonically. "Come on. How are we getting out of here?"

I refocused my attention on Lee and led him to the taxi. "Let's hurry. I can't wait for you to see Reveilee."

Lee grinned. "Wow, I'd almost forgotten." He must have seen my face fall because he quickly added, "I'm ready to see her, too."

I woke the driver, who stretched, blinked, and let us in.

"Let's get the hell out of here," Lee said, stripping off his envelope cap and throwing it on the seat on the other side of me.

The driver tried to talk to Lee as he had to me for the first part of the journey. I was content to hold Lee's hands and try to comprehend that he was really beside me.

"I'm so glad to see you!" I said again and again, hugging him.

Lee laughed and put his arm around me. "I'm glad to be here."

"Just wait until you see the baby. She's so beautiful."

"Won't she be asleep at this hour?" Lee frowned.

"Well, it's not every night that a girl gets to meet her daddy."

We rode in silence for a few minutes. I watched Lee under the passing street lights, measuring his mood. I was so excited that I was giddy. He was quiet, withdrawn.

"Is anything wrong?" I asked lightly.

"No, no, Honey, I'm just tired. Don't forget, I've been travelling for damn near twenty-four hours."

I laughed with relief. "Of course. I'm just so happy to have you back that I didn't think about what it took to get here."

We talked, but our topics jumped from the freezing weather in Alaska to his parents' new house and from his orders to be a Ranger instructor to the ribbon that would be in Reveilee's hair. It was a disjointed conversation, but at least it was in person.

When we finally reached Collins Street, I paid the driver and hopped out of the cab, pulling Lee up the stairs. "So this is where you lived," he said, taking in the building and the street. My year was as strange to him as his was to me.

"You can get a good look tomorrow. Right now I want you to see the baby," I whispered as I turned the key.

Susan was sitting on the couch reading when we entered. She jumped up to give Lee a hug. "Welcome home," she said with more emotion than she usually allowed herself to show.

"Hi, Susan," Lee said. "How's Tom?"

"You probably know more about that than I do," she said to him and then turned to me, "I did everything just like you said. She's in her crib in my room."

"Come on," I tugged at Lee and then led him into the lamplit bedroom.

Reveilee, all dressed in her frilly dress, stared straight up at me as though she were afraid to move in her unfamiliar garb. I chuckled at her expression and swooped her into my arms.

Holding the baby on my hip, I made the introductions. "Lee," I said, "meet your daughter Reveilee."

Lee stared down at his four-and-a-half-month-old baby, a look of awe spreading over his face. Tentatively, he reached out and took her hand. She instantly wrapped her tiny fingers tightly around his without taking her eyes off him.

"Would you like to hold her?" I asked, uncertain if Lee was ready for this step.

"Of course, I would," Lee said, taking her into his huge hands and sitting her on his right arm. I stepped back to study the sight I'd waited so long to see. Lee and Reveilee were adorable together, he so big, she so small.

Reveilee looked at me and then back at Lee, curious, perhaps, but otherwise unperturbed. Then she spotted the bright rows of ribbons on Lee's chest and her hand shot straight for them.

"Whoa!" Lee said, trying to disentangle the little fingers from his uniform. But by that time, Reveilee was already pulling the whole meritorious display into her mouth.

"Can you help me out here?" Lee asked pitifully. "I'm being attacked."

"Welcome home," I laughed, "to the real world."

{Chapter 42}

In the movies, that's where the story would have ended and the credits would begin to roll. But our story, from Lee's send-off at San Francisco International Airport until his return at Travis Air Force Base, had never been like the movies, and its ending with a "they lived happily ever after" homecoming didn't follow the scenario, either.

I had Lee home and he obviously thought his baby was wonderful. What else could I have wanted? I asked myself the question over and over, trying to deny an emptiness that would not be ignored. A hollow feeling filled the pit of my stomach.

I had simply expected too much of Lee's return, I told myself. Lee was saying all the right things, but there were no feelings behind the words. Everything about him—his voice, his movements—seemed flat. In Hawaii, I had sensed his feelings then even before he expressed them. The night he returned from Vietnam I could not get a read on his reactions.

"Something's not right," I confronted Lee that night. "You don't seem glad to be here. Do you not love me anymore?"

"Don't be ridiculous," Lee said with a disgusted sigh. "Of course, I love you. You know that." There were the words again with no feeling.

"Then what is it?" I pushed.

"Hell, Honey, I'm just tired."

"And?"

Lee could not conceal the sheepish look that stole across his face. "And," he confessed, "I've got a hell of a hangover. I feel terrible."

I stared at him and then erupted, "Goddammit! I've been waiting for this night for a year and you show up with a hangover!"

Lee tried to laugh. "I've been sitting in Long Binh for three days waiting for a plane. There wasn't anything to do but drink."

"I knew you were having a few beers because everybody who called said you were buying," I exaggerated. "Didn't you think about how you'd feel when you got here?" Lee's face sobered and he said quietly, "Yeah. That's exactly why I drank so much. Thinking about what it would be like when I got home."

I was so taken aback by his words that I could say nothing.

"Not about being with you and seeing the baby," Lee added quickly. "But about everything else."

"I don't understand."

"A year's a long time," he reflected, his eyes fixed on the wall across the room. "I mean, I was used to Vietnam, you know? I knew what to expect there. Coming home today seemed as strange as going there did a year ago. I don't know what to expect here anymore. I don't know what I'm supposed to do here. You just can't imagine how strange it is to be in a house, to ride in a regular car, to think about living like this again. For a year I dreamed of being here, promised God I'd do anything if He'd just let me live to come home again. But then the closer today got, the scarier it got. I was more terrified of leaving than of staying. So I just got drunk and stayed that way. I'm sorry if you're disappointed."

His words hung in the air. I suddenly realized how little I knew about what he had been through, how strongly the experiences had affected him. "I don't know what to say or do," I said quietly. "It hadn't even occurred to me that you would dread coming home. I was too busy thinking about how happy I was. Right now, I'm trying really hard to understand and to not let my feelings be hurt."

Lee took me in his arms and kissed the top of my head as I buried my face in his chest. "Honey, it's not you. Or the baby. It's just everything else, okay? There's nothing specific you can say, but there is one thing you could do."

I pushed myself up and looked at him, blinking back tears that were threatening.

He looked chagrined as he said, "Do you think you could find me a couple of aspirin? I've got a hell of a headache."

Epilogue

Thus we began our post-Vietnam lives together, each with our own perspectives, needs, goals, and expectations that we melded into a four-decade marriage. In December, 2007, Lee and I celebrated our fortieth wedding anniversary—a benchmark of life that the Linda of this book would hardly have believed possible at any point during the year's vigil. Amazingly, there was a life after Vietnam, and we have lived it to the fullest. Our second daughter, Meridith, was born in 1972 when Reveilee was three. Together we took on the world.

To no one's surprise, Lee made the Army his career, attaining the rank of lieutenant colonel before retiring in 1988. While he again commanded troops—the next time in Germany—and served in various field and rear positions throughout his time in uniform, no experience ever came close to challenging the impact his time in Vietnam had on him and his life. He chronicled his Vietnam experiences in the first two books he published, *The Only War We Had: A Platoon Leader's Journal* and *Vietnam 1969–1970: A Company Commander's Journal*. These personal narratives have recently been re-released by Texas A&M University Press.

I made a career of having careers. First, I threw myself into the role of officer's wife where, mimicking Mrs. Sheldon, I learned the art of entertaining, polishing silver, and whipping out checkerboard cheese sandwiches at a moment's notice. I hosted teas, served as the president of the officers' wives club, and volunteered where needed. I did all this with good cheer for the first several years until Uncle Sam sent us to Germany in the mid-1970s, where I chafed under the complete control the Army had over my life, including where I lived, what goods I purchased, what I ate. My attitude toward the military at that point made Susan's displeasure with it during Vietnam appear as child's play. My experiences there led me to reconsider what I was doing with my life; Lee's experiences during this time led him to write *Battles of Peace.*

Finally coming to grips with the fact that the Army was not the villain so much as it was my need to follow my personal ambitions that was causing the friction, I reprioritized so that I accommodated the army wife's requirements while focusing my real energies on my own goals. I earned my Master's Degree and taught college English, speech, and communications. I wrote several textbooks, and then I released *Breaking the Myth: The Truth About Texas Women.* I kept my career goals flexible and mobile enough to move nine times in the fifteen remaining years of Lee's army life. When Lee retired, I took a position at the University of Phoenix, where I became one of the institution's first woman vice presidents. Following that, I flew all over the country as a business consultant before buying my own business in Phoenix, which I have now owned for eight years.

Throughout my changing of hats in the workforce, Susan monitored my progress. We saw each other every few years when she and Tom came back to the States for home leave from the Philippines where they lived for almost two decades. She, who was not allowed to work in foreign countries, said she never had to have her own career—she could simply experience lots of different ones vicariously as she watched me rotate from being the officer's wife to the professor and then to the author. She continued to follow my progress as I evolved into the university administrator and then the business woman.

In 1994, while the Hargroves were living in Colombia, Tom was kidnapped and held captive in the mountains of South America by guerillas forces for a year. Susan had her "second Vietnam" with this ordeal while she worked unrelentingly to get him freed. Their saga became the "based on a true story" scenario for the movie *Proof of Life.* Had I only known I was living with the inspiration for the Meg Ryan role all those months in San Francisco!

If I was amazed that there was life after Vietnam, I was astonished to learn that there would be another whole set of experiences in the civilian world. Lee and I settled in Phoenix in 1988, where we enjoyed the desert climate for nineteen years while he wrote another fifteen books and I tried out yet another couple of career options.

No better now than I ever was at anticipating the future, I was stunned last year to learn that Lee is embroiled in yet another fight for his life. This time the enemy is within. When he had a malignant kidney removed in 2003, we embraced the prognosis that the doctors had removed all the cancer, and we charged forward with life as we knew it. But in June 2006, the radiologists detected menacing shadows in his routine followup tests, revealing that the disease had returned and metastasized to Stage IV.

As I write this, Lee is thriving as he proves his prowess once more. To combat the cancer, he has adopted a raw vegan vegetarian lifestyle—a radical change for a meat-and-potatoes man. We moved to the Bolivar Peninsula in Texas to be near the water and to enjoy our days of quasi-retirement in which Lee continued to write and I managed the store from afar.

We had mistakenly supposed, yet again, that our beachfront house in Crystal Beach would be our geographical destination for the foreseeable future. However, in September 2008, Hurricane Ike struck the Peninsula with a fury and a twenty-foot surge that all but cleaned the sand barrier on which we lived. Ours was one of the 1,200 houses in the town that completely disappeared on the night of September 12–13. So we are back in Phoenix, Arizona once again, adjusting to the demands of starting all over again—not completely unlike we did in April 1970.

Despite all that we have done, seen, and experienced, the Vietnam era remains a truly significant time for each of us. Lee was one of the first writers to stand against the tide of anti-Vietnam veterans and their apologist war stories, to say that he was—and remains—proud of his role in leading the best troops America has ever fielded. He followed the publication of his two journal books with six more works about Vietnam. As I edited them all, I thought I'd lose my mind if I ever had to read anything else about that war, wondering if we would ever leave it behind. I suppose this book means, "Not yet."

Afterword

and whatever happened to. . . .

Reveilee, who did learn to say and spell her name much more quickly than I had feared and who then came to love it because no one else shared it, graduated from Texas Tech University and then several years later earned her MBA at The American School of International Management (Thunderbird). Now living in Phoenix, she is the mother of our three fantastic grandchildren. Allyanna, David, and Michael are the lights of our lives.

Meridith, an extraordinarily independent soul who began her career in the music industry even before she graduated from college, was struck with multiple sclerosis at the age of 24. She has made her home in Hollywood, California.

Susan and Tom made Galveston, Texas their home after Tom's release from being held captive for a year by FARC in Colombia, an ordeal that he chronicled in *Long March to Freedom*. On Galveston Island, Susan and her mother completely renovated one of the city's major historic sites. The Hargroves are currently in transition to retirement, and Tom's book on his Vietnam experiences, *A Dragon Lives Forever*, has just been re-released by Texas A&M University Press.

Marjorie Sheldon moved to Galveston after her husband died, and she lived on one of the floors of the renovated building with Susan and Tom until her own death a few years ago. She always remained my "social" mother, and I remember her fondly.

Miles Sheldon became an extraordinarily successful businessman and headed American companies based in Kuwait. He died tragically young of complications from cancer.

Connie established herself in the banking industry and shattered many glass ceilings in her rise to the top before she experimented with an early retirement. After a few months of leisure, she returned to frays of banking and continues to chart new territory for successful women.

Major General (Ret) Bernard Loeffke, that newcomer battalion commander whom I was convinced was going to get Lee killed with his experimental maneuvers, ended up saving Lee's life. Loeffke remained in contact with Lee periodically through the years as he obtained his two general's stars and then retired. He became a Physician's Assistant so that he could focus the remainder of his life on healing. He is the one who convinced Lee to adopt the raw vegan lifestyle.

Jim and Judy Lanning have three grown children—including James David—and four grandchildren. Jim retired from the Army, after twenty-two years of service, to become a minister. Judy remains a supporter in his endeavors and a loyal sister-in-law.

The Lannings lived in their new house until Mr. Lanning (James Maurice Lanning) died less than a year after Lee retired. Mrs. Lanning (Alice Coskey Lanning) lived three more years, and—amazingly—she was one of my biggest fans in the last years of her life. I guess I finally proved that I was worthy enough to be her son's wife.

My grandmother (Anna Tomlinson Knox) inspired me by the way she lived her life until she died at home and still living independently at the age of ninety-eight.

My mother (Glenna Gene Knox Moore) lived to be seventy-nine and died peacefully in her home in Roby.

My father (James Garland Moore) remained active in farming and engaged in projects for the rest of his life, including installing drip irrigation systems on two of his farms when he was eighty-two. He died at age eighty-five this year. We placed a flag on his coffin to honor the role he played in World War II as a part of the Greatest Generation.

The Waiting Wives of the Vietnam war. . . . Well, I can't say for certain or in specifics. During the remaining twenty years around military wives I never participated in or overheard a conversation centered on the topic of being a waiting wife during this era. There were aside references to it, such as "when John was in Vietnam" and "while I was waiting for Jim to come home." But never did a group of us discuss how we felt or how we coped with the ordeal of having a man at war. Thus, I do not know if my story is summarily typical or singularly unique. It is simply one wife's year of the Vietnam War.